Cases in Marketing Management

Cases in Marketing Management

Edited by
Ross Brennan
Senior Lecturer in Marketing
Middlesex University Business School

PITMAN
PUBLISHING

PITMAN PUBLISHING
128 Long Acre, London WC2E 9AN

A Division of Pearson Professional Limited

First Published in Great Britain in 1995

The right of Ross Brennan to be identified as Editor
of this Work has been asserted by him in accordance
with the Copyright, Designs and Patents Act 1988.

The right of Bal Chansarkar, Ghalib Fahad, Stephen Hearnden,
Annabelle Mark, Karin Newman, James Patterson,
Simon Speller, Derek Thurley and Frederick E Webster Jr
to be identified as Contributors of this Work has been
asserted by them in accordance with the Copyright,
Designs and Patents Act 1988.

ISBN 0 273 61694 3

British Library Cataloguing in Publication Data
A CIP catalogue record for this book can be obtained from the British Library

10 9 8 7 6 5 4 3 2 1

Typeset by 🖌 Tek-Art, Croydon Surrey
Printed and bound in Great Britain by Bell and Bain, Glasgow.

The Publishers' policy is to use paper manufactured from sustainable forests.

CONTENTS

Section 3
CASES IN CONSUMER SERVICES MARKETING

LIST OF CONTRIBUTORS

Ms Paola Bradley, Research Fellow in Management, Middlesex University Business School.

Mr Ross Brennan, Senior Lecturer in Marketing, Middlesex University Business School.

Dr Bal Chansarkar, Principal Lecturer in Statistics, Middlesex University Business School.

Dr Ghalib Fahad, Senior Lecturer in Marketing, Middlesex University Business School.

Mr Stephen Hearnden, Principal Lecturer in Marketing, Middlesex University Business School.

Ms Annabelle Mark, Associate Senior Lecturer in Management, Middlesex University Business School.

Dr Karin Newman, Reader in Marketing, Middlesex University Business School.

Mr James Patterson, Senior Lecturer in Marketing, Middlesex University Business School.

Mr Simon Speller, Senior Lecturer in Operations Management, Middlesex University Business School.

Mr Derek Thurley, Senior Lecturer in Marketing, Middlesex University Business School.

Professor Frederick E. Webster Jr, Charles Henry Jones Third Century Professor of Management, The Amos Tuck School, Dartmouth College, USA.

PREFACE

The use of the case study method is well established in marketing education. In a sense, therefore, this book is simply an addition to the substantial and, often very good, body of case material available to marketing educators and their students. However, we flatter ourselves that our book does a little more than this. While you will certainly find, within these pages, examples of the 'traditional' marketing case study, the diversity of the cases may well surprise you. Marketing itself is evolving, and extending its reach far beyond the consumer goods environment in which much existing theory was originally developed. Marketing education is also evolving, partly in response to the evolution of marketing itself and partly as innovative – and increasingly flexible – methods of designing and delivering courses are introduced into the vocational, further and higher education systems.

This book is designed to help marketing educators, and their students, in adapting to these changes. The case studies are drawn from a wide range of organisations, from some of the biggest in Europe, to very small, start-up businesses. Consumer goods companies are certainly not neglected in the case studies, but constitute only eight out of the 22 cases in the book. Case studies in the marketing of consumer services and the marketing of goods and services to business customers are also presented. In two of the cases (Famagusta Bakery and The Niger Restaurant), the particular problems facing entrepreneurs from ethnic minorities are explored. Issues associated with the marketing of public sector organisations, or recently privatised organisations, are addressed in cases 1, 5, 10, 14, 20 and 22, which look at such organisations as London Electricity plc, the National Health Service, London Underground Ltd and British Telecommunications plc.

The book is designed to be a flexible resource for the student and educator. Chapter 1 provides a substantial introduction to the subject of marketing management which can either be used as a mini-textbook in its own right or used to supplement the more extended treatment which will be found in any major marketing textbook. In Chapter 2 guidelines are provided on how to approach the analysis of case studies. The cases themselves vary substantially in length. The short case studies are designed to illustrate a few key points about marketing management, while the longer cases incorporate a wide range of marketing issues which the reader is required to disentangle for him or herself. The shorter cases provide useful illustrations of marketing in action. The longer cases provide greater insight into the real complexity underlying practical marketing management decisions and a better understanding of the demanding nature of marketing as a profession.

Ross Brennan
Senior Lecturer in Marketing,
Middlesex University Business School

INTRODUCTION

THE STRUCTURE AND PURPOSE OF THE BOOK

The practice of marketing has been around for a very long time. Ever since human beings, millennia ago, first entered into voluntary exchanges with one another, marketing has been going on. However, as a professional activity and, as a subject for formal study, marketing is younger than most of the other functions which contribute to value creation within organisations. Throughout its comparatively short life, those introduced to the subject of marketing have usually found themselves facing marketing case studies at an early stage. As they progress through a hierarchy of qualifications, they find that the case studies get longer and more complex, but the essence of the case method of learning remains with them.

The team responsible for putting together this book, like the majority of those involved in marketing education, believes that the case method has a major contribution to make to the illumination of marketing concepts, tools and techniques for aspirant marketers. However, the simple process of reading a case history on its own yields little reward. Marketing practitioners and marketing academics have put together a powerful portfolio of analytical tools which can be brought to bear on practical marketing problems. Through the process of applying these tools to case material, the aspirant marketer can gain an understanding of the realities of marketing management. That, very simply, is the reasoning behind the structure and content of this book. In a single volume, we have brought together a set of case studies and a summary of the marketing tools which you will need to make sense of them. Chapter 1 can be read as a 'Mini-textbook' in marketing or it can be used as a reference source when you are tackling a particular case. References are provided from the case material back to the theoretical ideas in Chapter 1, to help in this process. Chapter 1 includes five 'micro-cases' with questions, which you can use to test your understanding as you read the material. In Chapter 2 the process of case study analysis is discussed. The objective is to give you confidence when you tackle a case study, since you will have a framework with which to work. Chapter 2 is also designed to give you greater confidence when it comes to the process of presenting the results of your analysis, by offering some practical guidance on effective communication.

The major part of the book is devoted to 22 case studies. Our aim was to provide a diverse set of cases and you will probably judge that we succeeded! The organisations featured in the book range from companies with multibillion pound turnover and hundreds of thousands of employees, to a sole trader company turning over less than £100 000 per year. The remainder of the Introduction is devoted to explaining the diversity of the cases and how it can be exploited to help you to learn more about marketing.

AN OVERVIEW OF THE CASES

Industry sector

The professional application of marketing evolved most quickly in the field of consumer goods marketing. As marketing has developed, so the benefits of professional marketing have been felt in the consumer services sector, and in the marketing of goods and services to business customers. We have provided case material from each of these areas of marketing, in an attempt to strike a balance:

- between cases concerned with the marketing of goods and those concerned with services
- between cases concerned with consumer markets and those concerned with business markets.

Of the 22 cases in the book, 11 focus primarily on the marketing of goods, and 11 primarily on services marketing; 14 of the cases look at consumer markets, while eight look at business markets. The structure of the book is designed to emphasise this point, with the following sections:

- Section 2: eight cases in consumer goods marketing
- Section 3: six cases in consumer services marketing
- Section 4: three cases in business goods marketing
- Section 5: five cases in business services marketing.

Naturally, some of the cases do not fit neatly into any one of these categories. Examples are Case 11 (The Beaufort Hotel) and Case 22 (British Telecommunications plc). Both of these organisations serve consumer and business markets simultaneously with indistinguishable services (hotel rooms and telephone calls). The somewhat arbitrary decision was taken to allocate the Beaufort Hotel to the 'consumer services' category, and British Telecommunications plc to the 'business services' category.

Themes

Business problems in general, and marketing problems particularly, do not come neatly labelled. However, in teaching about marketing, it is necessary to categorise the tools and techniques available in order to structure the learning process; the 'marketing mix' is one example of a system of categories. While the 'micro-cases' in Chapter 1 have been designed to have only a single theme, all of the cases in the main body of the book contain multiple themes. Rather than simply leave it up to you to identify the themes in the cases, we have summarised the main themes of each case in Fig 0.1, using a set of standard topics – which might be used to structure practically any marketing course – for our 'themes'. This will assist the tutor, in selecting cases to use at different stages of a course, and will assist independent learners to identify cases illuminating particular topics mentioned in standard marketing textbooks. For each case a **principal theme** is identified, plus one or more **secondary themes**.

Fig. 0.1 Principal marketing themes covered in the cases

Cases \ Themes	Marketing environment	Marketing research	Market segmentation	Target marketing	Product management	Advertising and communications	Marketing channels	Pricing	Marketing strategy	International and overseas	Small and medium-sized enterprise
1. Market research brief – London Electricity plc: Appliance Retailing		▲	◁				◁		◁		
2. Advertising the Autostore			◁	◁		▲					
3. Castlemaine XXXX			◁	◁	▲						
4. Ice-cream wars: the UK ice-cream market in 1990			◁	◁	◁	◁			▲		
5. A case of too many cooks? The UK electrical goods retail sector	◁						◁		▲		
6. The 'quality' newspaper price war of 1994			◁				◁	▲			
7. Taiwai SA			◁	◁			◁			▲	
8. Famagusta Bakery Ltd							◁	◁	◁		▲
9. Sketchley and Supasnaps: under the same roof!	◁				▲		◁				

	1	2	3	4	5	6	7	8	9	10	11
10. Rationing or demarketing? That is the question	▲								△	△	
11. The Beaufort Hotel	▲	△								△	
12. The Niger Restaurant	△	△	△		△						▲
13. Freddy Slinger's bed & breakfast		△	△		△						▲
14. London Underground Ltd Customer Charter	▲	△							△		
15. Ethical issues in marketing research	▲	△									
16. Distribution in Hungary		△	△	△						△	
17. Svenska Ackumulator AB Jungner		△	△			△			▲		△
18. Innovative Cleaning Solutions – the industrial cleaning winning formula		△					▲				
19. The 19th Hole Conference Rooms		▲	△								
20. The price of keeping in touch – BT's international phone service								△		▲	
21. Elite Technology Services								△			▲
22. British Telecommunications plc: facing up to the 1990s	△								△		▲

△ Secondary theme   ▲ Principal theme

Case length

The cases in the main part of the book vary in length; the longer cases can be assigned for analysis, with formal reporting back of results and conclusions. The shorter cases are less suitable for this purpose (unless the gathering of additional information is made part of the task) but can be used as the basis for lively group discussion sessions. Ideally, any case which is to be discussed should be prepared by all members of the group in advance but the short cases do make it possible to read and discuss a case within a single session, should this be desired. The classification of cases by length is as follows:

	Shorter cases	*Longer cases*
Consumer Goods	Case 1	Case 4
	Case 2	Case 5
	Case 3	Case 6
		Case 7
		Case 8
Consumer Services	Case 9	Case 11
	Case 10	Case 12
	Case 13	Case 14
Business Goods	Case 15	Case 17
	Case 16	
Business Services	Case 18	Case 19
	Case 20	Case 22
	Case 21	

Other aspects of the cases

The majority of the cases are descriptions of real marketing situations. For this reason several of the cases have been disguised, so that the company – and the employees – upon which the case is based cannot be identified. In other cases the organisations discussed are household names, like British Telecommunications plc and Wall's Ice Cream Ltd. Four of the 22 cases are 'hypothetical' case histories – Cases 2, 13, 15 and 19 fall into this category.

Suggested questions are provided on each of the cases in Section 6. These are by no means the only questions which one could ask but they do point to what the author considers to be the key decisions associated with the case.

Finally, you will find that a number of the cases are linked: For example, Case 1 on London Electricity plc can be linked with Case 5 on electrical goods retail in the UK; Cases 9 and 5 both include references to Supasnaps; Case 20 deals with a particular sector of the telecommunications market while Case 22 discusses the strategy of British Telecommunications plc. By tackling linked cases together, or one after the other, you will obtain a deeper and broader grasp of the issues which confronted the marketing managers facing the situations described.

SECTION 1

The marketing management process and marketing case analysis

CHAPTER 1

Introduction to marketing management

Ross Brennan

THE DEVELOPMENT OF MARKETING

KEY CONCEPTS

- marketing as a management process
- marketing as a philosophy of business
- making what you can sell or selling what you can make?
- marketing, advertising and selling
- the marketing mix and the 4Ps
- the marketing environment and PEST analysis
- the competitive environment and five-forces analysis
- relationship marketing
- marketing in for-profit and non-profit organisations
- marketing in private and public sector organisations
- the consumerist movement
- the environmentalist movement
- demarketing

Definitions of marketing

In 1994 both Procter & Gamble and Unilever spent well over £100 million in the UK advertising brands like Ariel, Radion, Crest and Domestos. Some of their brands, such as Pampers nappies (Procter & Gamble) have become virtually synonymous with the product category to which they belong. It is hardly surprising, given the high profile that television advertising (in particular) has in our everyday lives, that 'marketing' tends to be very strongly associated with 'advertising' in the minds of the public. Many marketers may feel disinclined to alter this public perception, since there is a certain glamour by association to be enjoyed! However, most marketing managers on most of their working days spend none of their time thinking about how to advertise their products. The question of how to communicate a message to a target group of consumers only arises once the product (or service) has been decided upon, the appropriate message developed, a target group selected and the most effective communications media identified. Underlying these decisions is a process of gathering, interpreting and analysing data about customers, competitors and the business environment which is, arguably, the most important part of the marketing manager's job.

Discussing marketing in this way suggests that marketing can be thought of as a management process. Indeed the Chartered Institute of Marketing defines marketing as:

> *the management process which identifies, anticipates and supplies customer requirements effectively and at a profit*

Although the Chartered Institute of Marketing is the professional institute for marketing managers in the UK, one might object to its definition on the grounds that it appears to exclude 'marketing' carried out by non-profit organisations. Do Greenpeace, Amnesty International and the Royal Society for the Prevention of Cruelty to Animals (RSPCA) not do marketing? Of course they do. An altogether simpler definition – which has the great merit of memorability – is suggested by Michael Baker (1991):

> *Marketing is selling goods that don't come back to people who do.*

If we are to accept this as a workable definition of marketing, then we must interpret some of the terms fairly generously – 'goods' must mean goods, services and even ideas; 'selling' might mean exchanging something for money, but it could also mean convincing someone to give money to charity or even persuading them to give up smoking.

In truth, to search for the perfect definition of marketing is as futile as searching for the meaning of life and some people find it equally fascinating! It is pretty clear, however, that marketing:

- is about much more than advertising
- is about much more than selling
- is applied to products, services and ideas
- is applied in the private and public sectors of the economy, by both profit-seeking and non-profit organisations.

The marketing concept

There is an alternative to defining marketing as a management process and that is to define marketing as a concept, or a philosophy of business. The marketing concept is no more or less, in essence, than the idea that the organisation should be customer centred. One way of encapsulating that idea is to 'invert' the traditional organisational pyramid, as British Telecommunications (BT) plc did (*see* Fig 1.1).

Rather than placing the chief executive at the apex, with middle and junior managers arrayed underneath, BT redesigned their organisation chart with the customer at the top and the rest of the organisation shown below in order of their 'closeness to the customer'. Redesigning an organisation chart is easy; the difficult part is to make the organisation behave as though the customer really was at its centre. This, as BT itself has found, is a process of

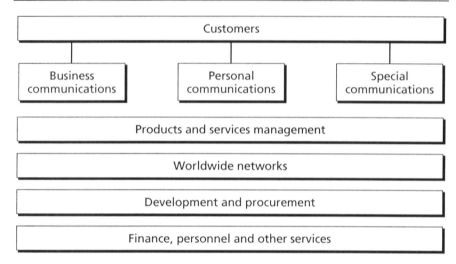

Source: *BT Annual Review,* 1991.

Fig. 1.1 Putting customers first: BT organisation from April 1991

transformation which can take a decade or more.

Peter Drucker (1954) provided a very clear definition of marketing as a philosophy of business when he wrote:

> *Marketing is not only much broader than selling, it is not a specialised activity at all. It encompasses the entire business. It is the whole business seen from the point of view of its final result, that is, from the customer's point of view. Concern and responsibility for marketing must therefore permeate all areas of the enterprise.*

Even such an apparently clear statement as this, however, may pose problems to those marketing managers who cannot readily identify exactly which group of people constitutes their 'customers'. Commercial firms in competitive markets rely on customers, without whom they could not continue in business. Monopolistic firms, whether state-owned or private, have less incentive to satisfy the desires of customers since the customers have no one else to turn to. Many non-profit organisations in the private and public sectors of the economy have difficulty in defining their 'customers' in the first place. It may seem obvious that the 'customers' of a charity are the beneficiaries of its charitable acts. But since the beneficiaries are not the people who resource the charity, it is perfectly possible for a charity to fail to satisfy them and yet 'succeed' in the sense of raising money and continuing to exist. The people who resource the charity are its donors and, while the charity must satisfy this group in order to exist, it would be difficult to argue that they are its 'customers'. In this way the two key characteristics of a customer of a commercial firm – receiving benefits and generating resources – are divided for charities and many public sector organisations.

The development of the marketing concept is often described as an evolutionary process. Marketing orientation, simply defined as 'making what you can sell', supplanting production orientation where the company strove to 'sell what it could make'. An influential article by Robert Keith (1960) contributed to the popularity of this idea. The idea is beguilingly simple and has the added attraction of implying that what marketers do today is superior to what was done in the past – that there has been continuous improvement in the marketing profession. However, the development of modern marketing thought has been far more complex and less systematic than Keith's description would suggest. Nico Vink (1992) described the evolution of marketing as:

> a complicated and fluid process that involves simultaneous dramatic change, incremental change and continuity.

The marketing mix and the marketing environment

Marketers have adopted the word 'mix' and stand ready to use it at every available opportunity. There is a product mix, a promotional mix and a media mix to name but three. The greatest of the mixes, however, is the marketing mix itself. Often referred to as the **4Ps** of marketing (standing for product, price, promotion and place), the marketing mix includes all those things which are under the control of the marketing manager and which can be used to pursue marketing objectives. A very common marketing objective is to persuade customers to buy (or buy *more* of) something that we wish to sell, and the marketing mix is often thought of, therefore, as the means at the disposal of the marketing manager to convince the consumer to buy a product or service. The marketing mix concept was developed by Neil Borden (1964) who conceived of the marketing manager as a 'mixer of ingredients', sometimes following a well-tried recipe and sometimes trying something new. While the 4Ps represent a useful set of headings under which to develop a marketing mix checklist, they are only headings. The marketing mix, in a typical consumer goods marketing context, will comprise many tens, possibly hundreds of elements including, for example:

- product design and redesign
- product launch and withdrawal decisions
- product name decisions
- packaging design and redesign
- sales promotion activities (such as competitions or money-off vouchers)
- personal selling
- merchandising
- choice of media for an advertising campaign
- appropriate messages for different target markets in an advertising or other communications campaign
- effective scheduling of the communication campaign
- recommended selling price
- discounts offered to wholesalers or retailers.

It is important to distinguish between the marketing mix and the marketing environment. The marketing environment is a catch-all expression for anything outside the control of the firm which will affect its ability to achieve its marketing objectives. Such factors include trends in consumers' disposable income, legislative changes (for example, if a ban on all advertising of tobacco products were to be introduced) and technological innovations (the development of the personal computer posed a marketing challenge to manufacturers of traditional typewriters). In the same way that the 4Ps can be used as a mnemonic for the marketing mix, so **PEST** can be used as a mnemonic for the marketing environment. PEST stands for political, economic, social and technological factors. Just as the 4Ps should be used as a helpful checklist, rather than a definition of the marketing mix, so PEST is merely a useful tool for helping us to decide what the key factors in the marketing environment are. It is not enough to say that there are political, economic, social and technological factors affecting an organisation, one must understand:

• exactly which factors are important under each heading
  – for a particular organisation
  – at a particular time, and
  whether their potential impact is favourable (an 'opportunity') or unfavourable (a 'threat').

A factor which is important to one organisation may be irrelevant to another (the popularity of the institution of marriage is of great concern to Pronuptia, who supply wedding trousseaux, but of limited interest to JCB, who manufacture earth moving equipment). A factor which is critical at one moment can, overnight, cease to be a matter of concern (uncertainty over the future of certain tax-free savings products, such as tax-exempt savings schemes and personal equity plans increases prior to a general election and abruptly vanishes if the Conservative party wins).

It is helpful to distinguish between the broad **macro-environment**, within which political, economic, social and technological changes may take place which affect the ability of the organisation to achieve its objectives, and the **competitive environment**. While it is quite obvious that direct competitive rivals are an important factor affecting the development of marketing plans – perhaps the single most important factor – Michael Porter has argued that the competitive environment is wider than straightforward competitive rivalry. Porter summarised the competitive environment in his **Five Forces**:

• the intensity of direct competitive rivalry
• the threat from substitutes
• the threat from new entrants to the market
• the bargaining power of buyers
• the bargaining power of suppliers.

Doubts about the notion of the marketing mix

The marketing mix, and the 4Ps as a mnemonic for the marketing mix, are certainly the best-known concepts in marketing. Various attempts have been

The Five Forces of the competitive environment

Direct competitive rivalry between firms is the stuff of daily news bulletins in the papers and on television.

- British Airways and Virgin play out a sort of competitive soap opera, competing with each other to offer low prices and good quality service, while allegations of 'dirty tricks' and even legal actions are also part of the competitive battle.

- Procter & Gamble and Unilever compete head-on in the domestic detergent market, frequently offering new products, new advertisements and new promotional offers.

It is also obvious, after only a moment's thought, that in addition to competing head-on, like British Airways and Virgin, Procter & Gamble and Unilever, firms compete with other companies offering good **substitutes** for what they sell.

- The Littlewoods and Vernons football pool organisations (which take millions of pounds each week in a form of betting on professional football results) were appalled at the prospect of the National Lottery in the UK. Following the launch of the Lottery, both Littlewoods and Vernons reported substantial declines in their revenue.

Furthermore, companies must always be on the look-out for prospective **new entrants** to their market.

- Until comparatively recently, the market for good quality 'celebration' wine in Britain meant only one thing – Champagne! However, the Champagne producers of France are increasingly concerned that good quality sparkling wines from Australia and the USA, produced using the *methode champenoise* (Champagne method) taste as good as their own products, but are considerably cheaper.

These three forces direct competitive rivalry, substitutes, the threat of new entry, are the key to understanding competition within a market. To these forces, the renowned business guru Professor Michael Porter added the **bargaining power of buyers** and the **bargaining power of suppliers** to make a total of five competitive forces.

- In order to compete successfully in fast-moving consumer goods markets, it is indispensable to have good access to mass distribution outlets. The major supermarket buyers, at firms such as Sainsbury, Tesco and Safeway critically affect the ability of fast-moving consumer goods (FMCG) companies to achieve their marketing objectives.

- Personal computers based around microprocessors developed by the Intel organisation have become established as a worldwide standard. Intel jealously guards the intellectual property contained in its chips (286, 386, 486 and Pentium). To be successful, computer manufacturers must rely on supplies of Intel chips.

made to extend the 4Ps, almost always by adding some more Ps to the list – for example, the fifth P for 'people' in the marketing of services (and even a sixth P for 'physical evidence'!). However, it has also been suggested that the whole concept of the marketing mix and the 4Ps has been a blind alley for marketing theory, and even, according to Gronroos (1994) that:

> *the marketing mix and its 4Ps constitute a production-oriented definition of marketing, and not a market-oriented or customer-oriented one.*

Increasingly, in the field of organisational marketing (where the customer is an organisation, such as a manufacturing firm or a government department, rather than a private individual) marketers are thinking about how to initiate, develop and maintain long-term business relationships, rather than how to devise a marketing mix with which to attract customers. As we enter the next century, the emphasis in marketing – particularly organisational marketing – can be expected to switch from the management of a marketing mix, to a focus on relationships. The term 'relationship marketing' has been coined to express this approach.

Consumerism, environmentalism and the marketing concept

According to the *New Webster's Dictionary of the English Language*, consumerism is a 'programme to promote consumer interests including protection of the environment, restraint on abuse by business etc.', while an environmentalist is 'one devoted to protecting the ecological balance of the earth'. Both consumerism and environmentalism are movements which cannot be ignored by marketers as we near the 21st century.

Consumerism is epitomised in the UK by the Consumer's Association and its magazine *Which?*, launched in 1957 as a medium through which consumers could obtain objective and impartial advice on goods and services. The consumerist movement is easily perceived by business people and marketing managers as a threat. A poor review in *Which?*, for example, can cost sales and, in the extreme, necessitate design changes to an established product. The consumer movement has had at least a part to play in the substantial increase in labelling requirements on packaged groceries, which means that consumers now know what ingredients were used in the manufacturing process and have access to considerable nutritional information. Some of the changes brought about by the consumer movement have probably increased business costs.

However, the objectives of the consumer movement do not seem so far removed from the marketing concept. Ultimately, the aim of consumerism is to create a satisfied customer. It is only if one reverts to a production or sales-orientated view of marketing that this can be regarded as threatening. Indeed, on the positive side, the consumer movement provides a great deal of potentially valuable market research information on one's own and on competitors' products. Marketers pay out millions of pounds each year to hear what consumers have to say, yet here are consumers coming forward for nothing and asking to be heard!

Whatever the value marketers attach to the views put forward by the consumer movement, no organisation can ignore the ultimate expression of consumerism, the consumer boycott. In the 1970s and 1980s, Barclays Bank was perceived to have substantial business interests in South Africa, a country in which racial segregation ('apartheid') was practised, and in which the black majority was denied access to political power. Barclays became a target for anti-apartheid groups and was subject to a boycott campaign by students. After resisting any changes for several years, Barclays reduced its involvement in South Africa in the late 1980s. At least part of this change can be attributed to the direct action of consumers, which may have directly affected business on only a fairly small scale, but which resulted in a constant stream of undesirable public relations stories.

Just as consumerism can be seen as both a threat and opportunity, so too can environmentalism. Issues such as global warming, the depletion of the ozone layer, the destruction of the rain forests and environmental pollution became matters of general knowledge in the 1980s. Concerned consumers could buy such books as *The Green Consumer Guide*, and learn what were the key issues for the 'green consumer'.

Some of the changes in business and marketing practice which have been seen in recent years can, in part, be attributed to the environmentalist movement. Consumers who once gave no thought to such issues are now aware of

---

Key issues for the green consumer

In general, the green consumer avoids products which are likely to:
- endanger the health of the consumer or of others
- cause significant damage to the environment during manufacture, use or disposal
- consume a disproportionate amount of energy during manufacture, use or disposal
- cause unnecessary waste, either because of over-packaging or because of an unduly short useful life
- use materials derived from threatened species or from threatened environments
- involve the unnecessary use – or cruelty to – animals, whether this be for toxicity testing or for other purposes
- adversely affect other countries, particularly in the Third World.

(Source: *The Green Consumer Guide*, J. Elkington & J. Hailes, Guild, 1989).

---

the energy efficiency score of their fridge, of the volume of water consumed by their washing machine, and of the proportion of recycled paper in their roll of kitchen towel. What was once perceived by the business community to be a threat appears to have been transformed into an opportunity to design, launch and promote a wide range of new 'environment-friendly' products.

It is by no means clear what these tales of consumerism and environmentalism say about the marketing concept, but they appear to present something of a challenge. The job of marketing is to stay in touch with the needs and wants of consumers and to constantly review the products and services on offer in order to satisfy those changing needs and wants. The consumerist and environmentalist movements appear to have identified genuine needs and wants: for objective, impartial advice; and for products which cause less environmental harm, which marketing organisations had neglected. Arguably, these needs and wants are felt by only one market segment. Nevertheless, it is a substantial segment, and one which had hitherto been ignored.

Marketing in the public sector

Consumerism and environmentalism are not the only challenges which have faced the marketing profession in the latter part of the 20th century. One of the major growth areas for marketing in the 1980s was the public sector of the economy. In part, this can be attributed to the expansionist tendencies of the profession itself, seeing a large number of substantial organisations operating without any professional marketing guidance. A major contribution to the penetration of the UK public sector by the marketing profession, however, must be attributed to government policy. The British government throughout the 1980s was concerned to restrict the rate of growth of public spending, and insisted on careful scrutiny of the budgets of public bodies such as health authorities and local authorities. The result has been that many public bodies, in central and local government, have seen their income from the public purse grow more slowly than the demands for service placed upon them. Marketing seemed to be a natural place to turn to find new ways of generating income.

Although many public bodies have appointed marketing managers, and profess a commitment to marketing, the difficulties encountered in introducing professional marketing to the public sector should not be underestimated for the following reasons:

1 The modern conception of marketing as a process of identifying consumer needs, developing products and services to satisfy them, and then communicating with the customer, is not widely understood by public sector managers. Marketing is an unknown quantity, often associated with television advertising and high-pressure salesmanship. There can be considerable suspicion that marketing will simply be used to sell social services, or educational psychology services, like soap powder. Even worse, there is a suspicion that scarce resources will be diverted from critical service areas, such as spending on new medical equipment or on computers for schools, only to be wasted on costly advertising campaigns.

2 The marketing concept places the customer at the focal point of the organisation. In public sector organisations it is often not clear exactly who the customer is, and the demands of different potential customers may conflict. For example, the beneficiaries of child protection services are children at

risk. To call the children the customers of the service would be nonsensical, however. They probably never knew that such a service existed, certainly do not pay for it and, in some cases, might not even agree that they wish to receive it!

3 Because of the hostility which can be encountered in the public sector, and because it is often difficult to apply the tried and trusted textbook methods to public sector problems, marketing can become an isolated and marginal activity in the public sector. Rather than answering the very challenging question, 'How can we adapt marketing to fit this organisation?', there is tendency to ask 'Where *can* the tried and tested methods be applied?' Answers to the latter question are not difficult to find. There is a long history of using public relations in the public sector. Public sector organisations need to advertise and promote their services like any other. The problem is, however, that by simply taking over these roles within public bodies marketing professionals may reinforce the stereotype of marketing as essentially a communications activity.

For these reasons it is necessary to proceed with care when introducing marketing into public sector organisations. This involves:

- avoiding the marginalisation of marketing as a function – marketing is everybody's responsibility
- the 'marketing of marketing' within the organisation, explaining what contribution marketing can make, and allaying fears that scarce resources will be diverted to unnecessary tasks
- accepting that there may be no clear parallel to the private sector 'customer', and that the interests of several different stakeholders may need to be considered in making marketing decisions.

One specific, and comparatively little known, branch of marketing which can be relevant to the public sector is *demarketing*. Marketing, in most cases, is about increasing the level of demand for something. Demarketing is the systematic application of the marketing mix to reduce the level of demand. In the public sector many services (state education, domestic waste disposal, consultations with general medical practitioners, to name but a few) are provided free to users at the point of use. Under such circumstances there is a risk that *wasteful* use might be made of the service – for example, patients attending the accident and emergency unit at the local hospital for a simple cut which could have been treated at home. One answer would be to charge for such services, but this may be judged politically unacceptable, since it could be seen as a 'tax on misfortune'. By deploying the other elements of the marketing mix, particularly marketing communications, it may be possible to achieve the goal of lower demand without the political penalty of imposing charges.

ANALYSIS FOR MARKETING DECISIONS

KEY CONCEPTS

- bringing about behavioural change through marketing
- market segments – groups of consumers which exhibit similar consumption behaviour
- psychological profiling (psychographics) as a basis for market segmentation
- population characteristics (demographics) as a basis for segmentation
- segmenting organisational markets: emporographics, macro- and micro-segmentation
- socioeconomic classification of consumers
- identifying and analysing market opportunities using marketing research
- exploratory, descriptive and causal marketing research
- primary and secondary marketing research
- retail trade audits, consumer panel research and omnibus surveys

Buyer behaviour and market segmentation

Underlying the concept of the marketing mix is the idea that by developing the right mix the marketing manager will achieve the desired objectives – consumers will buy the product, donors will give more to the charity, citizens will adopt a healthier diet, for example. The ultimate aim of marketing is to affect the behaviour of a group of people. The marketing concept says that these behavioural changes will be achieved by understanding what people want, and then developing products or services to satisfy those wants. Where marketing is employed for purposes of improving public health, the marketing concept is extended to include things which people may not even know themselves that they need, such as a reduced intake of fatty foods or of alcohol.

Since affecting the behaviour of consumers (or others) is central to marketing, it is not surprising that the study of buyer behaviour is regarded as the first step in the development of successful marketing plans. The behaviour of each individual consumer is unique. However, research into almost any market will show that consumers can be grouped together so that the behaviour of group members is similar to each other, and noticeably different from the behaviour of other groups. Groups of this nature – groups of consumers showing common patterns of consumption behaviour – are called market segments, and the process of dividing the market up into groups is called segmentation.

If segmentation is carried out effectively then each segment will respond uniquely to a given marketing mix. In order to achieve the best possible response from the market, a different marketing mix will have to be developed for each segment. Typically, some segments will be found to be more sensitive to the price of a product than others, some will be more concerned about quality, some about after-sales support, and so on.

Since segmentation is essentially about dividing consumers up on the basis of their behaviour, a logical basis for segmentation would be the 'psychological profiles' of consumers. We can reasonably assume that people who think about the world in a similar way will respond similarly to the marketing mix. This is the basis used in 'psychographic' or 'lifestyle' segmentation. The main advantage of this approach to segmentation is the attempt which is made to understand the basis for consumer behaviour in underlying psychology. The major disadvantage is that it is based on complex information – consumer psychology – which cannot readily be observed, but which must be analysed using psychometric profiling techniques. Psychographic segmentation can be contrasted with demographic segmentation in which a market is divided into subgroups (segments) on the basis of readily observable personal characteristics such as age, gender, occupation and ethnicity. Occupation is the normal method of defining 'social grade'. Demographic segmentation is much more straightforward to implement than psychographic segmentation, since demographic data on most populations are readily available in published form. For example, the division of the UK adult population on the basis of the standard social grade classifications defined by the National Readership Survey is shown in Table 1.1.

Table 1.1 UK social grade definitions

Social grade	% of adult British population	Occupational descriptions
A	3.1	Higher managerial, administrative or professional
B	15.7	Intermediate managerial, administrative or professional
C1	25.7	Supervisory, clerical, junior managerial, administrative or professional
C2	26.0	Skilled manual workers
D	17.0	Semi and unskilled manual workers
E	12.6	State pensioners or widows (no other earner), casual or lowest-grade workers

Intuitively it seems as though demographic segmentation should be a fairly good method of dividing consumers into groups with common behaviour patterns. We might expect to see differences in behaviour between, for example, men and women, young people and older people, people in manual jobs and people in managerial jobs. Consider the different readership profiles of two popular British newspapers, the *Daily Mail* and *Today* (*see* Table 1.2).

Obviously, there are significant demographic differences between the readership profiles of the two newspapers. The *Daily Mail* has greater appeal for women, for older people and for people in managerial and supervisory jobs than *Today*. The point could have been made even more strongly by comparing a 'serious' newspaper such as the *Daily Telegraph* (84 per cent of readers

Table 1.2 Newspaper readership profiles

	Daily Mail	Today
Circulation	1 775 000	538 000
Readers by gender men women	 50% 50%	 61% 39%
Readers by age 15–34 35–54 over 55	 30% 35% 35%	 41% 38% 21%
Readers by social group ABC1 C2DE	 61% 39%	 43% 56%

Source: *Marketing Pocket Book*, 1994, NTC Publications.

in social groups ABC1) with that epitome of British popular newspaper culture, the *Sun* (27 per cent ABC1).

Segmentation of organisational markets

The aim of consumer market segmentation is to identify subgroups within the overall market which will respond in a similar fashion to the marketing mix. When addressing organisational markets the aim is the same, but rather than groups of individuals or families, the marketing manager must identify coherent groups of organisations. The parallel with consumer market segmentation can be taken somewhat further. As in consumer markets, the easiest method of segmenting organisational markets is on the basis of observable and well-documented characteristics. In the case of organisational markets these characteristics are such factors as:

- **organisational size**, which might be measured in terms of annual sales turnover, or number of employees
- **industry sector**, which is usually measured using the Standard Industrial Classification, under which each business establishment is allocated a numeric code which indicates the primary activity carried out at that location
- **geographical location**.

Often such factors are referred to as 'business market demographics', but the alternative expression 'emporographics' (from emporium meaning 'a place of commerce') has been proposed in one influential textbook (Gross et al., 1993). Just as in consumer markets, the major strengths of such characteristics as a basis for segmentation are that they are easy to understand, and that extensive data can be found already analysed under these headings. The Standard Industrial Classification, for example, is the primary basis on which government information on commerce and industry is classified.

MICROCASE 1

Ford pursues the over–50s

One of the most significant factors in the marketing environment of the developed countries (such as America, Japan, Britain, France and Germany) over the next three decades will be the 'ageing population'. Improved health care means that people tend to live longer, while the fertility rate (the average number of children a woman has in her life) has declined to below 2.0 in many developed countries. It follows that, so long as there is no great natural or human engendered catastrophe, there will be progressively fewer children and more old people as a proportion of the total population in these nations. The average age of the population will increase. Ford Motor Company, well aware of this trend, has concluded that drivers aged between 50 and 75 will represent a growing potential market for private motor cars. Many of these people will be relatively affluent, either still at work but with few remaining financial commitments, or retired and benefiting from an occupational pension scheme. The needs of drivers in this age group are certainly different from those of younger drivers. For example, greater emphasis is placed on factors affecting the comfort and ease of use of the car, and rather less on acceleration or load carrying capacity. As one element in their research into this market, Ford has developed a 'mobility impairment suit' to be worn by (relatively youthful) designers as they work on car designs for older people. According to the *Daily Telegraph* (25 November 1994):

> *The elasticated suit comes with a special pair of mittens to stiffen the fingers and a range of spectacles reproducing the deterioration in vision among older drivers.*

The suit will enable designers to appreciate the problems encountered by older people in operating switch controls, adjusting seat-belts, and getting in and out of the car.

Question
What are the implications of the ageing population for (a) a major national UK housebuilding company and (b) a major British insurance company?

However, in the discussion of consumer market segmentation it became clear that the most convenient method of classifying consumers (demographics) was not necessarily the most meaningful way of dividing them up for marketing purposes. Similarly, it has been proposed that more sophisticated tools should be applied in the segmentation of organisational markets. The distinction has been drawn between *macro-segments*, which are groups of organisations classified together using 'emporographic' measures, and *micro-segments*, which are groups of organisations which have similar product or service needs. One micro-segment might be relatively insensitive to price, for example, but demand the very highest quality; while another micro-segment might demand particularly levels of after-sales service. While organisations can be easily allocated to macro-segments on the basis of published information, in order to identify micro-segments it is necessary to carry out detailed market research studies. Furthermore, some doubt has been cast on the usefulness of micro-segmentation for practical marketing purposes by Sally Dibb and Lyndon Simkin of the University of Warwick (1994). They found that highly sophisticated market segmentation techniques could not clearly be demonstrated to improve upon the elementary business practice of allocating business customers to industry sectors.

Managing marketing research

The identification of market opportunities, the division of markets into segments, the evaluation of the attractiveness of different segments, and the development of the marketing mix all demand large amounts of information. Marketing research is the process by which this information is created and analysed so that it can be used to assist in decision making. In the sections which follow, the management of marketing research is discussed. We start by looking at the research process, then examine the gap between what information we have and what we need to make a decision, before considering the various means available to fill this information gap.

The research process

Peter Chisnall (1992) summarised the marketing research process in five stages:

- research brief
- research proposal
- data collection
- data analysis and evaluation
- report.

   The research brief is a statement of what the research is intended to achieve. Often it will originate with one organisation – known as the client – to be acted upon by another – an independent market research agency, since much marketing research is carried out by specialist firms. The research proposal is a statement of how the objectives of the research will be achieved, and is often a formal document presented to the client by the research agency. The proposal represents a detailed plan for subsequent stages in the research where the data is gathered and analysed. In most cases data is analysed using specialist computer software packages which can readily provide tables of figures, graphs, descriptive statistics and more complex statistical analyses of the raw data.

   Although the marketing research process is shown above to be logical and sequential, in practice it may be necessary to repeat steps. For example, a pilot survey (often the first step in 'data collection') may well reveal deficiencies in the research brief or research proposal, necessitating a review of these elements of the process.

Establishing the information gap

The first step in any research project is to identify clearly what the information is needed for. While information cannot *make* decisions, it is frequently an indispensable aid to managers in making decisions. Some of the most important uses of information in marketing will be to assist with the following kinds of decision:

- marketing mix decisions (tactical)
  - product planning
  - price planning
  - distribution planning
  - promotion planning
- marketing planning decisions (strategic)
  - customer behaviour and segmentation
  - competitor analysis
  - marketing environment.

In all cases, research may be *exploratory*, *descriptive* or *causal* in nature. Exploratory research is often the first step in a research project – a certain amount of research may be needed to define what the fundamental nature of the marketing problem is. Probably the bulk of marketing research is *descriptive* in nature – telling the marketing manager how big the market is, how fast it is growing, how customer preferences are changing, and so on. However, descriptive information does not tell the manager why the market is the way it is. *Causal* research involves exploring relationships between marketing variables to try to establish causal links, such as the impact of advertising on sales or, at a more detailed level, the relative impact of advertising in different media on sales among different market segments.

Comparison between the (clearly defined) information requirement and the information which is readily available from secondary research will reveal the extent of the information gap. *Secondary research* involves the use of existing data, such as:

- Internal records, e.g. sales records, field sales intelligence, financial records
- External sources, e.g. government publications, trade associations, the trade press, commercial organisations.

Primary research

Secondary research is, as a rule, relatively inexpensive and fairly quick to carry out. Where new information has to be created by going into the market and asking peoples' opinions or observing their behaviour – primary research – marketing research is generally more expensive and more time consuming.

However, if secondary research is insufficient to satisfy the information requirement, and the value of the information to the organisation justifies the expense
of primary research, then a range of services may be considered:

- syndicated services
- omnibus surveys
- ad hoc research.

Primary research often involves the use of an external market research
agency. In a *syndicated service* the client organisation has the lowest level of
control over the research process, while in an *ad hoc research* project (wholly
paid for by a single client) the client has the greatest control. *Omnibus surveys*
fall between these two types of research.

Trade research

This kind of information is the 'bread and butter' of marketing decision making in consumer goods companies. Manufacturers do know what level of production is leaving their warehouses bound for wholesalers and retailers, but
they do not know what is actually being sold. Trade audits provide this information. The data are collected by researchers who visit retail premises to
inspect physical stocks and delivery invoices. This information is used to calculate actual sales over a given period using the formula:

$$sales = opening\ stock + deliveries - closing\ stock$$

The information is collected for a sample of retailers, and then 'grossed up' to
the universe of retailers using the formula:

$$estimated\ total\ sales = (universe/sample) \times sample\ sales$$

The basic information presented to subscribers to the trade audit will be as
follows:

- consumer sales (cash/volume/share)
- retailer deliveries (volume)
- retail stock (volume)
- stock cover (weeks/days)
- average sales (per shop)
- average stocks (per shop)
- average prices paid
- distribution (maximum/effective)
- showings.

In the absence of resale price maintenance (which, with some notable exceptions is illegal in the UK) manufacturers cannot know what prices their goods
are actually selling for without examining what is happening in shops.
Maximum distribution is the highest number of retailers which were in stock
of a given product line during the reporting period. *Effective distribution* is the
number of retailers in stock at the end of the period. *Showings* refers to point

of sale promotional activity – both display material and special displays of goods.

Panel Research

Several market research companies have established consumer panels. This enables regular information to be collected on the actual purchasing behaviour of known consumers, facilitating both longitudinal – time-series – studies and cross-sectional – segmentation – analyses of buyer behaviour. Results are usually reported monthly.

The panel is designed to be a representative sample of the relevant universe (e.g. housewives, motorists, mothers with babies). Panel members either record their purchases in a 'diary' or keep the packaging in a special receptacle. The diary may be returned by post or, on some panels, is collected by a researcher. Where panellists collect packaging material, a researcher will itemise purchases by inspecting the used packages – the 'home audit' method. Panels may be made up of specified individuals, or may be made up of households. Increasingly, use will be made of information technology in collecting panel data (e.g. panellists using bar code readers at home to record purchases).

A strong argument in favour of panel research (courtesy of Worcester and Downham, 1989) is that:

> It is generally accepted among researchers that if you interview a respondent asking him . . . to recall purchasing behaviour in a consumer product field, there is a strong likelihood that the frequency and quantity of purchases will tend to be exaggerated and the complexity of purchasing behaviour over-simplified.

Panel data can provide equivalent information to trade audit data about overall sales trends for a given product line, but can also provide detailed information on sales trends within market segments (demographic, socio-economic, geographic, etc.). Problems associated with panel research are that panel members drop out and may even die – affecting sample representativeness – that new members may alter their behaviour (having one's purchases scrutinised can alter behaviour in itself), and that panels almost inevitably under-represent mobile consumer groups such as students.

Omnibus surveys

These are defined by Worcester and Downham (1989) as:

> syndicated surveys where the questionnaire is a combination of smaller questionnaires each of which is unique to a particular project and where the client has control over the questions to be asked in his particular section.

In essence, several clients 'club together' to purchase research, with each buying space in a single large questionnaire which will be administered to a common sample of respondents. The clients save money by sharing the fixed costs associated with an ad hoc research project, and may well benefit from a larger sample size than they would be able to afford individually in an ad hoc project. On the other hand, clients are limited in the way in which they use their questionnaire space – questions must be kept reasonably simple, otherwise the overall questionnaire will become unwieldy, and there are usually fairly strict limitations on the use of visual stimuli (e.g. showcards).

Made-to-measure vs off-the-peg research

According to Tim Bowles (1991), most of the growth in the market research industry is in syndicated services. He argues that clients buy market research on the strength of the *people* in the agency, and that first-class market researchers are relatively scarce. There may be confidence that a syndicated service has been designed by the best researchers available to the agency, whereas clients often worry that the people carrying out the research design for an individual ad hoc project may not be the very best (particularly if the client is not considered an important account of the agency). Table 1.3 summarises the pros and cons of syndicated services.

Table 1.3 Pros and cons of syndicated services

Pro	Con
• Cost effectiveness – the fixed costs are shared among clients • Speed – results can be obtained quickly • Historical database is available • Easily integrated with the marketing information system • Satisfies many recurrent data needs	• Limited customisation • Unique problems need unique solutions • Limited confidentiality – other clients receive the same Information

THE PRODUCT

KEY CONCEPTS

• the product is whatever is being marketed
• products may be physical things, intangible services, or ideas
• any product can be thought of as a bundle of consumer benefits
• the product life-cycle: introduction, growth, maturity, decline
• product class, product form and brand
• generating ideas for new products
• evaluating new product ideas
• developing a business plan for a new product
• test marketing and full market launch
• services: intangible, inseparable, variable, perishable

The concept of product

The term 'product' is used as a generic term in marketing to mean whatever it is that is being marketed. So a physical product (e.g. training shoes) is a product, intangible services (e.g. the telephone service) are also referred to as products and so might be ideas, such as the idea of helping to protect endangered animal species. Although odd at first sight, this makes sense once it is understood that marketers are encouraged to focus not on the product itself but on the needs which it satisfies for the consumer.

It is a basic principle of marketing, most famously stated by Theodore Levitt (1960) that consumers buy *benefits* not *products*, or as Levitt put it:

> *The view that an industry is a customer-satisfying process, not a goods-producing process, is vital for all businessmen to understand.*

There are several different ways of delivering the consumer benefit of travelling from London to Edinburgh, for example, by car, train, coach and plane. Each of these alternatives combines a range of other benefits; the coach is the cheapest, the train is probably the most comfortable, and so on. Consumers make decisions about alternative means of delivering the benefits which they desire, rather than the physical manifestation of those benefits which is the product itself. Different market segments with different needs base their decisions on different criteria – students choose to travel to Edinburgh by coach because that is the cheapest alternative, business executives may choose the plane because it is the quickest, salespeople choose the car because they have samples to take with them.

In thinking about the product, then, it is necessary to go beyond the tangible product – or service – itself and to see it from the customer's point of view, in terms of the benefits which it yields. This idea is often referred to as the 'core product', while the thing itself is referred to as the 'tangible product'.

The product life-cycle

A new product is launched and, if successful, enjoys a period of sales growth which would normally be followed by a gradual decline in the rate of growth as the market saturates. This idea has been formalised as the *product life-cycle* concept, in which it is proposed that all successful products move inexorably through four phases – introduction, growth, maturity and decline. Attempts have been made to demonstrate that marketing management decisions can be guided by an understanding of the position of a product in its life-cycle. For example, John Smallwood (1973) provided a cross-table showing how elements of the marketing mix should be adapted to the life-cycle stage of the product. There is an intuitive appeal about Smallwood's recommendations. In general terms, it would make marketing management easier if there was some kind of formula which could be applied. In specific terms, much of what Smallwood proposes looks sensible – for example, as the product goes from the introduction to the growth phase it should become more sophisticated, in the maturity phase the market should be segmented and multiple product

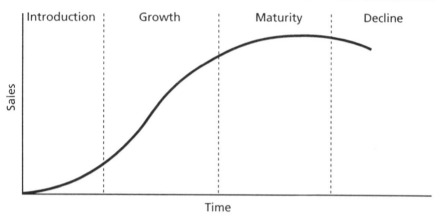

| Introduction | Growth | Maturity | Decline |

Sales

Time

Fig. 1.2 The product life-cycle

variations offered, while in the decline phase the number of product variations on offer should be reduced.

The general opinion today is that the idea of the product life-cycle is of value
as a general statement of the inevitability of product decline, as a spur to new
product development, and as protection against the complacency which rapid
sales growth can bring about (which was remarked upon by Levitt). There are
grave problems involved in using the product life-cycle as a practical marketing tool. It is difficult to tell exactly which of the stages a product is in at
any one time, and many products have gone into apparent decline only to be
revived through the application of creative marketing.

The Gillette example in Microcase 2 illustrates the most damning criticism
levelled at the product life-cycle, namely that the life-cycle is the *result* of rather
than the *precursor of* marketing actions. This point was argued strongly by
Nariman Dhalla and Sonia Yuspeh (1976), who also pointed out that it is
unclear just what is meant by the 'product' part of the product life-cycle.

Does it mean a product class (e.g. motor cars), a product form (e.g. family
saloon cars), or a brand (e.g. Ford Mondeo)? On the basis of recent evidence
from an analysis of consumer goods brands in the UK, Mercer (1993) concluded of the product life-cycle that:

> this product life-cycle theory cannot any longer be justified in terms of general
> applicability – and should be relegated to usage (albeit valuable usage) in special
> circumstances.

New product development

Whatever one's views on the product life-cycle, the ultimate inevitability of
product obsolescence can hardly be denied. Even motor cars and television
sets, which might be imagined to have infinite product life-cycles, will eventually be substituted by other products which satisfy the same consumer needs
(for example, flexible personal transportation and home entertainment)

MICROCASE 2

> # Bucking the product life-cycle at Gillette
>
> In the 1980s it seemed that the market for durable, metal razors was in termi-
> nal decline because consumers preferred plastic, disposable razors. The process
> at work in the market seemed to be one of 'commoditisation', which is where
> marketers find it increasingly difficult to differentiate products on the basis of
> such factors as features or quality, because consumers begin to choose more
> and more on the basis of price alone. In a commodity market there is a strong
> temptation to cut back on advertising and product-development spending to
> keep costs down in order to maintain competitive prices. Faced with this, Gillette
> took the bold step of developing and launching an innovative new metal razor
> (Sensor) which proved enormously popular and reversed the decline in demand
> for durable razors. According to *The Economist* (15 August 1992), Sensor was:
>
> > *that rarity in today's supermarket: a product that is demonstrably better
> > than its competitors.*
>
> Had Gillette acted naively on the basis of product life-cycle theory, on seeing
> that durable razors were in the decline phase of the life-cycle they would have
> cut back on advertising, product development and on channels of distribution
> and might also have increased prices. The inevitable result of such action would
> have been to reduce the demand for durable razors even further, providing
> further evidence that the product was in its decline phase.
>
> **Question**
> *Who buys razors (consider electric and blade razors)? How might you segment
> this market? What product benefits are most important to each of your
> segments?*

better. If this is true of a whole product class, it is still more true of individual
varieties – brands – produced by individual companies. So the development
of new products from the stage of bright idea to market launch is an important management process in which marketing has an important role to play.
The process of developing and launching new products may be considered
to involve four steps.

1 **Idea generation**. Ideas for new products and services are generated from a
  wide variety of sources. Sometimes ideas are actively sought – created during a team brainstorming session, copied from a competitor, copied from
  an idea already in use overseas, or identified from a market research project. On other occasions new product ideas 'just happen'. This could be a
  passing remark from a customer to a salesperson, or it could be the result
  of a happy accident in the product development laboratory (which, according to legend, is how the ubiquitous Post-it note was born).
2 **Idea screening**. Not all of the ideas generated could be developed to an

advanced stage. Some method of identifying those most likely to succeed is necessary. Many organisations use a form of scoring system to screen out those ideas which are least likely to succeed, and to provide a rough rank order of the remainder. The details of the screening system in use in any organisation will vary, but the fundamental characteristics remain the same, namely:

- a set of criteria against which ideas will be judged, such as estimated size of market, fit with the existing competences of the organisation, and likely competition
- a weighting of the criteria – in some companies marketing criteria may be most important, while other companies may emphasise production feasibility
- a simple scoring system, for example zero to ten, with zero indicating 'no hope' and ten signifying 'an absolute cert'
- a 'hurdle value', which is the minimum score that an idea must achieve in order not to be rejected
- a ranking system, putting all of the ideas screened which exceed the hurdle value in order from 'most likely' to 'least likely'.

3 **Development of a business plan**. For those ideas which survive the screening test, a detailed business case will be developed. Such a business case combines substantial amounts of marketing research with detailed costings of the development, production and launch of the new product. Market research will be designed to estimate as accurately as possible the likely volume of demand at different price levels and the product characteristics desired by consumers, and to suggest promotional strategies for the launch. The business case will normally be presented to senior management for authorisation.

4 **Product development and test market**. Once authorisation has been received, substantial resources will be invested in producing the final product which will normally be test-marketed before the full-scale launch. A test market involves a limited market launch, usually on a geographical basis (where TV advertising is to be used, the test market area will probably be confined to one or two commercial television regions). The test market is carefully evaluated to assess how accurate the original demand estimates were and how effectively the distribution system is working. If the evaluation proves satisfactory, the product is then ready for a full-scale market launch, and it enters the 'introduction' phase of the product life-cycle.

Marketing services

Throughout this chapter the term 'product' has been used to mean physical things, like a mountain bike, services, like a hair cut and ideas, like 'eat less fat and live longer'. The marketing of these various 'products' has a great deal in common. However, in this section the particular characteristics of services, and their implications for services marketing, are explored.

MICROCASE 3

New product options for Megafax plc (hypothetical case)

Megafax plc designs and markets personal organisers. Their marketing department is discussing the options for developing new products. There are two favoured options – a substantial new paper insert, the *Megafax Dictionary of Quotations*, or a move into the emerging market for electronic personal organisers, the *Megafax Electronic Workmate*. Pamela, the sales manager, favours the *Megafax Dictionary of Quotations*:

I know it doesn't expand our market, and the market will only grow steadily, if at all. But we know the market and the product. The chances of successful product development are high. We have the right sub-contractors ready to print it. It looks like the best option to me.

But Mark, the advertising manager, advocates the *Megafax Electronic Workmate:*

The market for electronic organisers is where the growth will be over the next five years. I know we'd face a tough research and development process, and it isn't the sort of product that we've sold before, but this market is too big to ignore.

Meanwhile, Jim the marketing manager, had begun scribbling on the flipchart.

- Market attractiveness   50%
- Product fit   20%
- Research and development   10%
- Production   20%

He explained:

I've listed the criteria which you said were important – how attractive the market is, how well the product fits our range, whether it would be easy to design, whether we have experience on the product side. Then I've given an opinion on how important each criterion is. So the market is the most important thing, rating 50 per cent. Now, if we score the two options out of ten, against each criterion we can get a quick idea of their relative attractiveness. Give the electronic organiser 8 for market attractiveness, 4 for product fit, 1 for R&D and 2 for production; that would make a score of 5.3. Give the dictionary 4 for market attractiveness, 8 for product fit, 6 for R&D and 8 for production . . .

Question
What score would the dictionary of quotations achieve? How would you use the two scores? What would you do next?

(see page 53 for solution).

Table 1.4 Characteristics of services

Intangible	Inseparable
Variable	Perishable

The four characteristics which differentiate services from physical products are identified in Table 1.4. The first of these, *intangibility*, can be used as a way of defining services. It is of the nature of services that they are intangible. What this means is that:

- services cannot be seen
- services cannot be smelled
- services cannot be tasted
- services cannot be picked up and inspected.

The service of transporting someone from London to New York by air, for example, is fundamentally less tangible than the laptop computer which the passenger uses in the aircraft, or the suitcase in which their luggage is carried. And while it was quite possible for the passenger to buy the suitcase without ever directly encountering a representative of the company which manufactured it, in order to travel from London to New York it is very necessary to meet representatives of the airline and to sit in a machine owned by the airline. This is what is meant by the *inseparability* of services – they are inseparable from the people who provide them. While travelling on the aircraft, the quality of the service that the passenger receives depends on the crew providing the service and, since different crews will behave differently (and a single crew might behave differently from one day to the next), the quality of service received is *variable*. A manufacturing firm tries to provide a consistent level of quality by controlling the manufacturing process in the factory. A service firm must rely on its representatives to control quality at the point of delivery. Finally, should the seat next to our aircraft passenger be empty, then it cannot be put into stock for the next flight – it is *perishable*. Even relatively perishable physical goods, such as dairy products, can be stored safely for several days to allow for fluctuations in the level of demand. Services cannot be stored in the same way.

There are many different types of service, and they vary in the degree to which they exhibit the characteristics of intangibility, inseparability, variability and perishability. In fact, rather than think in terms of two simple categories – product or service – it may be more realistic to think in terms of a continuum, with 'pure products' at one end, and 'pure services' at the other; this is illustrated in Figure 1.3. The two dimensions of Figure 1.3 are 'physical good emphasis' and 'service emphasis'. The former indicates things which are more tangible, with canned beans and lightbulbs coming close to this end of the continuum. The latter indicates things which are less tangible. Insurance services and legal advice are examples at this end of the scale. Many products fall between the two extremes. The enjoyment of a meal in a restaurant, for

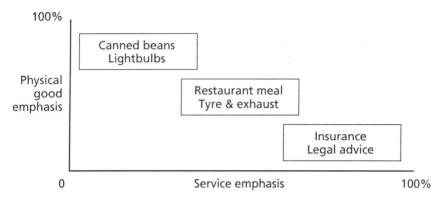

Fig. 1.3 Products and services

example, is heavily influenced both by the quality of the food (tangible) and by the 'atmosphere' of the restaurant (intangible). A customer's satisfaction with a new car exhaust installed at a quick-service garage will depend partly on the courtesy of the staff (intangible) and partly on the longevity of the new exhaust (tangible).

The characteristics which define services have certain implications for marketing activity.

Intangibility　Even more than with physical products, the marketer must convince customers of the *core benefit* of the service. Since customers cannot physically inspect the product before purchase, the reputation of the service provider and the brand strength of the product are extremely important.

Inseparability　Whereas the manufacturer of products can use stock levels to iron out fluctuations in demand, the provider of a service cannot. This makes the accurate forecasting of demand, and the effecive planning of service provision to meet demand, imperative. Wall's Ice Cream can stockpile ice-cream for the summer peak in demand. British Airways must supply just sufficient seats to meet demand at any point in time, or lose sales (and disappoint customers), or fly planes with empty seats.

Variability　In many service industries the variability of the service results from variations in the way in which staff deliver the service. The recruitment, training and motivation of staff becomes a matter of critical concern to the effective marketing of the service. For example, the McDonald's fast-food organisation is legendary in its attention to detail in providing instructions and training to staff in the conduct of their jobs. The objective is for customers to be served in a virtually identical manner regardless of which McDonald's restaurant they use. The British pest control firm Rentokil applies similar principles to its business. Employees are positively discouraged from using their initiative. According to chief executive, Clive Thompson (*The Economist*, 6 March 1993):

Implementation is more important than any single good idea. By necessity we have to be rather autocratic, almost militaristic.

Perishability   Finally, the characteristic of perishability accounts for many of the pricing and promotional tactics which are characteristic of service industries.

- It is more expensive to travel by rail at periods of peak demand (rush hours) than at other times (such as mid-morning). During the peak periods the railway operator can fill all its available capacity, and uses price as a means to discourage customers who can postpone their journeys. Many forms of discount rail ticket cannot be used at peak periods – the purpose of the discount is to fill seats which would otherwise be empty at off-peak periods.
- Package holiday operators charge high prices for 'sunshine holidays' during the summer peak demand period, and lower prices during the autumn and spring (though prices rise sharply around Christmas!). During the off-peak periods they advertise specifically to a segment of the market which has the available time, the retired. Of course, the same package holiday operators charge more during January, February and March for holidays in ski resorts, when demand is highest.
- Many city centre hotel operators raise their prices midweek and bring them down at weekends, because their primary target market is business people. Other hotel operators, for example those located in seaside resorts, have entirely different pricing policies. In both cases, the objective is to maximise the hotel room occupancy rate, and to minimise the number of empty bedrooms.

MARKETING COMMUNICATIONS

KEY CONCEPTS

- communications mix
- media mix
- advertising: dedicated space or time bought for the purpose
- direct mail: targeted delivery to office or home
- geodemographic segmentation
- sales promotion: price-related and non-price incentives
- public relations: 'free' coverage in the media
- proactive and reactive public relations
- salesforce training: product knowledge, competitor knowledge, customer knowledge, selling skills
- personal selling: identify customer needs, interest the customer, overcome objections, close the sale.

Advertising

Having carefully researched the needs of a lucrative target market, and developed a product designed to satisfy those needs, it is necessary to let the market know of their good fortune. Since consumers in developed countries are subject to a constant barrage of commercial messages, it is important to devise the most potent possible message and deliver it in the most effective possible way if the chances of success are to be maximised. The broad term for this process is 'marketing communications', and the combination of channels which are used to deliver a marketing message is known as the 'communications mix'. Each of these communications channels has spawned its own industry, and represents a career opportunity for the prospective marketing manager in its own right. The communications mix comprises advertising, direct mail, sales promotion, public relations and personal selling.

The best-known form of marketing communication, advertising is distinguished by the fact that space or time in an advertising medium is bought for the dedicated purpose of conveying a specific message. The main advertising media are television, newspapers and magazines ('press'), radio, cinema, and posters. Approximately £5 900 million was spent on these forms of display advertising in the UK in 1992. The largest share of this expenditure was on press advertising, with television a close second, and much smaller amounts spent on other advertising media. Whichever medium is used, there is always a high degree of 'wastage' when mass-market advertising is employed, since a large part of the audience of the medium will not be in the advertiser's target market. It is the job of the media planner (usually working for an advertising agency) to try to maximise the overlap between the target market and the audience of the advertising medium. To help in this process, extensive data are available on the demographic profiles of the audiences of different media (for a small example, *see* the readership data on the *Daily Mail* and *Today* on page 15).

Direct mail

An increasingly popular form of marketing communications, direct mail involves the delivery of a message directly into the home of the target consumer (or office of the target manager). In 1992 over two thousand million direct mail items were delivered to UK homes, at a total cost (in terms of producing and delivering the material) of around £1000 million. Once the marketer has specified the target market which he or she wishes to reach through a direct mail campaign, it is the job of the market researcher to specify how this market can be reached. The tool which is employed to translate a target market into a direct mailing list is *geodemographic segmentation*, in which data from the population census are linked with the postal code database and the Target Group Index (a commercial report which shows consumption behaviour broken down by multiple demographic characteristics). This form of analysis enables local geographical areas (small groups of addresses) to be identified which are likely to be interested in a product or service. A number of commercial market research firms have created their own geodemographic databases. The first, and best known, was the ACORN (A Classification of Residential Neighbourhoods) system developed by CACI Limited.

Sales promotion

Everyone is familiar with the money-off coupon with which marketers try to tempt consumers to sample their products. Money-off coupons fall under the general heading of 'sales promotion', which includes both price-related tactics (like coupons) and non-price-related incentives, such as consumer competitions and 'give-aways'. Petrol retailing is an example of an industry which has made long-term extensive use of sales promotions to try to build up consumer loyalty. One risk of sales promotions, which has been observed in petrol retailing, is that – far from building loyalty – consumers may switch from retailer to retailer depending on who is offering the best promotion at any one time. It is difficult to calculate the total value of expenditure on sales promotions but estimates put the scale of sales promotion expenditure on the same scale as direct mail expenditure; at between £1 000 and £2 000 million per year in the UK.

Public relations

In addition to developing advertisements, mailshots and sales promotion devices, the marketer will also seek opportunities to obtain favourable free publicity in the news media. Ideally, public relations should be a planned activity in which a regular flow of interesting stories is fed to the media, so that a favourable impression of the company or its products is built up among the desired target groups. In contrast to any of the media discussed above, however, the company cannot maintain total control over the message it wishes to convey. Ultimately, and despite very careful preparation of a message (often in the form of a press release), it is up to the editor of the newspaper, magazine or radio/television show to decide exactly how the message will be used, if at all. To compensate for this loss of control, public relations incurs no direct media cost, and messages conveyed in this way can carry more weight since they are perceived to come from an objective commentator.

Market research, target markets and marketing communications

While market research is an essential basis for the development of all elements of the marketing mix, there is a particularly intimate relationship between market research and marketing communications. A planned approach to marketing communications is based on a profound understanding of the target markets which are to be addressed through the communications media. Market research serves three key purposes in support of marketing communications: media selection, researching the message, and evaluating the campaign.

Media selection

The media selected for the campaign will be chosen on the basis of the viewing, listening and reading habits of the target markets. The objective is to

MICROCASE 4

Reactive public relations at Perrier

In many cases, public relations cannot be a proactive communications medium, but must be used reactively. For example, in 1990 the Perrier company had to deal with a public relations emergency when small amounts of a potentially dangerous chemical, benzene, were found in some bottles of their sparkling mineral water. According to *The Economist* (3 August 1991), Perrier failed to react appropriately to the crisis and attempted to explain away the contamination as the result of a minor problem in bottle cleaning. In fact, benzene, which occurs naturally in Perrier water, has to be filtered out, and the problem was the result of a failure in the filtration process. As *The Economist* put it:

because Source Perrier in France fumbled its initial explanations so badly, the company got a rotten press worldwide

and the conclusion was that the public relations procedures to be used in the event of such a commercial emergency should be carefully planned. In the absence of such a plan, contradictory stories had emerged from different parts of the Perrier organisation.

Question
Suppose that you were marketing manager for Evian mineral water (a major rival to Perrier), what action would you have taken to exploit Perrier's embarrassment?

maximise the overlap between the audiences for the media and the target markets, while taking into account the widely different cost of advertising in different media. For example, a full page colour advertisement in the *Sun* newspaper could cost as much as £32 500 per day, but would only cost about £6 200 in *Today* newspaper – but the *Sun* delivers a circulation of around 3.5 million and a readership of nearly 10 million (each copy is read by three people, on average), whereas *Today* has a circulation of around 0.5 million and a readership of 1.7 million. In simple terms of the cost per reader, there is, therefore, very little to choose between these two newspapers. This simple quantitative comparison of media is usually summarised as the 'cost-per-thousand' (CPT), that is to say the amount spent to reach one thousand members of the target audience. The best single source of media information is the monthly directory *BRAD – British Rate and Data*.

Researching the message

Given the large number of commercial messages to which people are exposed every day, it is important to attract the attention of the potential consumer with the most potent message at your disposal. In many cases, the substance of the message – 'this powder will make your clothes cleaner', 'this car will keep you safer in an accident' – is supported by an emotional appeal, such as the use of humour in much beer advertising. Market research is used to identify the message and the emotional tone which will best achieve the objectives of the campaign.

Evaluating the campaign

A great deal of money is spent on marketing communications each year, and considerable efforts are made to evaluate the effectiveness of these efforts. The most elementary form of monitoring is to look at the trend of sales through time and calculate whether any change occurred at the time of the campaign. However, a campaign may be counted a success even though it had relatively little direct impact on sales volume. Indeed, in many cases sales volume might be a completely inappropriate way of measuring success, for example, in the case of government advertising designed to raise awareness of the benefits of a low-fat/high-fibre diet. For this reason, many communications campaigns are supported by primary market research projects designed to establish the attitudes of the target market before and after the campaign (known as pre- and post-campaign research). Market research will be used to establish the *unprompted awareness* (for example 'What factors do you think are important in a healthy diet?') and *prompted awareness* (for example, 'would lower consumption of fatty foods contribute to a healthier diet?') among the target market. A campaign will be judged a success if awareness amongst the target market is significantly greater after the campaign than before.

Personal selling

The final element of the communications mix to consider is personal selling. This occurs in many guises, and at many different levels of sophistication. Even in the case of retail sector, there is a wide variety in the selling tasks undertaken by retail assistants, from the kind of 'consultancy' performed by assistants in specialist hi-fi and computer stores to a few simple words of encouragement in a mass market clothing store. The telephone and the computer are increasingly important tools in the selling task. *Telesales*, simply the process of selling goods and services over the phone, represents a seemingly ever–increasing component of sales activity. Teleselling is normally associated with a computer database system which enables the salesperson to access needed information rapidly (whether on the customer or on the product) and to record the customer's response for subsequent action.

Personal selling is particularly important in the field of business-to-business marketing. In such markets there are normally comparatively few customers compared to a typical consumer goods market, and the sales value of each customer is typically higher. Business is often transacted on the basis of developing a relationship between the salesperson and the client, with the client sharing information on future business plans, and the salesperson endeavouring to fit in with those plans in order to maximise sales. In such circumstances sales people do much more than simply sell, they gather market intelligence, provide after-sales support, plan the development of customer accounts and keep the customer informed of new product developments. However, the fundamental reason for the existence of a salesforce is to sell, and industrial selling is a demanding process requiring salespeople to have:

- detailed understanding of their own company's marketing, sales, stock-holding and production processes, and how these can best be used to satisfy the customer
- detailed knowledge of their own company's products and services, of competitor products and services, and of their relative strengths and weaknesses
- a good grasp of the nature of the business undertaken by actual and potential customers, and of the marketing environment in which they operate
- well-developed professional selling skills.

Professional selling skills are those skills which are involved in the process of creating and closing a sale. This process requires the salesperson to:

Step 1 identify a specific customer need
Step 2 interest the customer in the product by demonstrating how it can satisfy the need
Step 3 anticipate and overcome objections raised by the customer
Step 4 identify the signals from the customer that the time is right to 'close the sale'.

For example, the salesperson may be aware that an industrial client requires a new set of illuminated exit signs to satisfy health and safety regulations. Having explained the range of signs available, and how they meet all domestic and European safety regulations, the salesperson should expect some objections – customers very rarely say 'yes' without a fight. Objections frequently concern the price and competitor offerings: 'Yes, I agree you've got a good range, but you are more expensive than your competitors'. Good marketing, which is an essential support to successful selling, should ensure that the salesperson has ready-made answer to such standard questions. In this case, perhaps the product has been designed to be more durable, or more visible, than competing products.

MARKETING CHANNELS

KEY CONCEPTS

- **distribution for services as well as goods**
- **direct distribution compared to the use of intermediaries**
- **fundamental trade-off: wide availability versus the cost of distribution channels**
- **institutions: retailers, distributors, agents, brokers, franchisees and franchisors**

- the shifting balance of power in the FMCG distribution chain
- the role of private labels (own brands)
- the return of the discount grocery shop
- the controversy over out-of-town shopping centres
- teleshopping and telebanking

The importance of effective distribution

While it is obvious that distribution is an essential component of the marketing mix, particularly where it is physical goods that are being sold, it is perhaps less obvious that distribution can make the difference between marketing success and failure – and that it can do so for services as well as goods. However, distribution is essentially to do with the provision of two key benefits to consumers, the benefit of *place*, and the benefit of *time*. It takes only brief reflection to realise that these benefits are equally important to consumers of services as to consumers of physical goods. The consumer wants a hairdressing salon to be located conveniently (perhaps near to public transport, or by a carpark), and wants it to open at convenient times. Increasingly, it is recognised that these benefits are not just valued by consumers who pay directly for goods and services, but that they are equally of importance to citizens who wish to use, for example, local authority advice services.

The UK's retail banking industry has seen revolutionary changes in the 'distribution' element of the marketing mix as a result of changes in the marketing environment over the last decade. Two changes have been particularly influential – aggressive competition from building societies, and the development of the technology which has made automatic teller machines (ATMs or 'cash machines') possible. These two trends have both encouraged and enabled the major UK banks (National Westminster, Barclays, Midland and Lloyds) to extend the service they offer to customers, most notably by having bank branches open for longer hours and by making a wide range of services available 24 hours a day through ATMs. Whether it is tangible goods or intangible services (like banking) which are being marketed, the purpose of the distribution element of the marketing mix is to make the product available to customers at a time and a place which they find convenient.

The distribution chain

The distribution chain is the series of institutions which exists to convey the product to the final consumer. In some cases there is no chain and the producer sells directly to the consumer. For example, in the motor insurance market, intermediaries (insurance brokers) have been the traditional method of delivering the product to the customer. However, the most successful UK motor insurance company of the 1990s has been Direct Line, which distributes its service directly to customers using direct selling over the telephone, supported by large-scale television advertising.

There is a strong logic in attempting, like Direct Line, to reduce the number of institutions in the distribution chain. Each institution in the chain incurs costs, and (if independently owned) must make a profit margin. The basic trade-off in the design of a distribution network, therefore, is between the increased availability of the product to customers by extending the distribution channels, and the increased costs incurred by having more links in the chain. One example of the way in which distribution channels contribute to the final retail price of a product is illustrated in Table 1.5.

Table 1.5 shows that of the final retail selling price of a Nissan car in the Netherlands, 18 per cent went to pay the costs of running the dealer's business and profit margin, 12 per cent went to pay the costs of running the distributor's business and profit margin. Only 70 per cent of the final value of the car was retained by Nissan. The transportation cost is also, of course, a cost of distribution. Broadly defined, therefore, the distribution costs attributable to Nissan cars in the Netherlands market amount to about 34 per cent of the price of the car. This is not far short of the cost of parts and materials involved in manufacturing the car.

In practice, most products do pass through the hands of intermediaries en route to the final customer. The most familiar intermediary is the *retailer*, who

Table 1.5 Cost structure of Nissan for selling in the Netherlands

	Nissan Bluebird[a] UK made %	Nissan New Micra[b] UK made %	Nissan's Japan made cars (average %)
Retail price	100	100	100
Dealer margin	18	18	18
Distributor selling price	82	82	82
Distributor margin	12	12	12
Nissan selling price	70	70	70
Transportation cost	3.5	4	8
Duty	0	0	10
Labour cost	8	10	12
Parts and material cost	39	40	32
Overhead and selling cost	12	10	3

Note: Figures are a percentage of retail price, excluding taxes other than duty.

[a] 1988 figures

[b] Estimated figures for the year production began

Source: Kyoichi Ikeo and John A. Quelch, *Nissan Motor Co Ltd: Marketing Strategy for the European Market*, Boston: Harvard Business School, case N9-590-018. Copyright © 1989 by the President and Fellows of Harvard College. Reprinted by permission.

sells direct to final customers. *Wholesalers* are also independent businesses, but their customers are other business organisations (frequently retailers) rather than consumers. *Distributors* are companies which operate on behalf of a single company, or a limited number of companies, buying from the manufacturer and selling on to third parties – car distribution and petrol retailing are examples of this arrangement. Retailers, wholesalers and distributors all make money on the basis of buying goods or services at a lower price and selling at a higher price. Technically, they 'take title' to the goods or services, that is to say that they take ownership before selling on to someone else. Other institutions, known as *agents* or *brokers* operate in the distribution chain without taking title to the goods or services which they sell. Insurance brokers, for example, never own the insurance they sell, and estate agents never own the property they sell. An increasingly important institution in the distribution chain is the *franchise*, where a complete business idea is devised, proved to work and then sold to other business people who wish to run their own companies. Most of The Body Shop International outlets, for example, are franchises. Other well-known franchise operations include Tie Rack (clothing retail), Prontaprint (high street printing) and Wimpy (fast food).

Trends in Retailing

The manufacturer-retailer balance of power

The most significant trend in grocery retailing over the last two decades has been the shifting balance of power between the supermarket chains and the manufacturers of branded consumer goods. In the 1960s consumer good manufacturers (known as 'fast-moving consumer goods' (FMCGs)) were powerfully placed because they owned the brands which consumers insisted on purchasing. Many of these brands, such as Daz, Nescafe and Fairy Liquid, are still successful today. However, retailers have developed their own–brand (or 'private label') alternatives to many of the major brand names, and have had considerable success in persuading consumers that their private label products are as good as the market leading brands. According to *Admap* (March 1994) private label sales accounted for 20.9 per cent of the UK packaged grocery market in 1976, 28.9 per cent in 1986, and this had risen to 34.9 per cent by 1993. Comparatively recently, in the UK, private label products were perceived to be cut-price, low quality copies of manufacturer brands. This is no longer the case. Private label products now vie for a range of market positions from 'premium price and quality' to 'cheap and basic'.

Competition in the grocery retail market

While the shift to private labels has increased the power of the major grocery chains at the expense of FMCG manufacturers, the supermarkets themselves have come under pressure in the 1990s from new entry competition. The 1980s saw several of the major UK grocery chains taking advantage of economic growth to improve their profit margins by offering a wider range of products,

MICROCASE 5

Private labels at Tesco

The supermarket chain Tesco is a fascinating case study in itself. Tesco's origins lie firmly in cut-price grocery retailing – the 'pile 'em high, sell 'em cheap' philosophy. In the late 1970s and, particularly, in the 1980s, Tesco changed its marketing strategy and aimed to compete much more directly with the market leader, Sainsbury's. This involved redesigning store layouts to make them more attractive, stocking higher quality produce, selling at higher prices, and using advertising to alter the consumer perception of Tesco as a 'cheap and cheerful' retailer. Facing increasingly intense competition from cut-price retailers in the 1990s, however, Tesco launched a range of 'value lines' in August 1993. This was a separate range of private label products priced at a considerable discount to Tesco's standard private label range. By December of 1993, their value lines amounted to 11 per cent of Tesco's entire sales of packaged groceries, while the standard private label range contributed a further 36.1 per cent, so that over 47 per cent of Tesco's packaged grocery sales were 'own brands'.

Question
Carry out a survey of the price of a standard 200g jar of instant coffee in three different local supermarkets. Identify the different brands (including private labels) and different product varieties available (decaffeinated, freeze-dried, etc.). How do private label prices compare to manufacturer brands? Does the price of the same manufacturer brand vary between stores?

---

including an increasing number of 'value-added' and premium products, in increasingly attractive stores. The case history of Tesco, for example, shows that it managed successfully to reposition itself as a high quality store. These moves by the market leaders left a partial vacuum at the 'cheap and cheerful' end of supermarket retailing which a number of foreign retailers are now seeking to fill. The German retailer Aldi and the Danish company Netto have already opened stores in the UK, offering down-to-earth levels of customer service, but competing very aggressively on price.

Out-of-town retailing

In many cases retailers have responded to changes in their marketing environment – notably increasing car ownership – by altering the location and average size of retail outlet. This is the case in supermarket retailing, where an ever–increasing proportion of sales is handled by out-of-town superstores. It is also the case in electrical goods retailing. The market leader in the UK electrical retailing business is the Dixons Group, which owns the Dixons and Currys chains. The Dixons chain is positioned as the high street retailing arm of the Dixons Group, and the average sales area of a Dixons shop is 2 200 square feet, while Currys concentrates on out-of-town retailing through superstores with an average sales area of 6 601 square feet. In the early 1990s the Dixons Group was opening an average of 20 new out-of-town Currys superstores each year.

Are out-of-town shopping centres a good thing? Retailers such as Tesco, Sainsbury and Dixons argue that they are simply responding to customer demand when they open out-of-town outlets. However, there is a growing public lobby to reduce the rate at which out-of-town centres are growing, or to halt their expansion altogether. The main arguments deployed against out-of-town shopping centres are environmental and social:

- They promote environmental damage, both by encouraging shoppers to travel by car and by using large quantities of land, for the shopping malls themselves and for their enormous car parks.
- The growth of out-of-town centres has attracted so much valuable trade away from town centres that many high streets are in serious decline; those members of the population who do not own cars (disproportionately the elderly and people on low incomes) find that their level of choice has been severely restricted.

Home shopping and home banking

Virtually all households in the UK now have a television set, and 90 per cent of households are on the telephone. Both Direct Line insurance and First Direct have exploited these facts to achieve success in their markets. Direct Line used the television to promote its motor insurance service and the telephone network to handle customers. First Direct is a home banking service launched by the Midland Bank in 1989, which had achieved 400 000 customers by 1993 and expects to have over 1 million by the year 2000. Customers carry out most of their transactions over the telephone, and have access to the Midland network of ATMs where necessary (for example, to obtain cash).

It makes sense that home shopping has been developed most successfully, so far, in the area of intangible services like banking and insurance. The tangible things which are associated with these services are such things as policy documents and bank statements, which are easily sent at low cost through the conventional mail. The target markets for both First Direct and Direct Line are relatively affluent consumers, who value highly the time that they save by accessing services from home. In contrast, the older mail-order industry has had the bulk of its success amongst socio-economic groups C2 and D, and much of its attraction is based on the ease with which credit can be obtained on mail-order purchases.

PRICING

KEY CONCEPTS

- economic factors: role of demand and supply
- a marketing model of price: costs, customers, competitors
- the costs floor and penetration pricing
- the customer value ceiling and price skimming
- interdependence of competitors in markets with few competitors (oligopolies)
- elasticity of demand with respect to price (price elasticity)
- perfectly inelastic, inelastic, unitary elasticity, elastic
- sales revenue and price elasticity
- elasticity and product differentiation

A simple economic analysis of price

The price at which a product or service is sold has traditionally been central to the study of microeconomics, that is, the economics of individual markets. It is supposed that as the price of a product rises so consumers will want to buy less of it, and firms will be willing to provide more of it. The prevailing market price is the price at which the amount consumers want to buy and the amount firms want to supply is exactly equal – if the price were a little higher, firms would be unable to find buyers for everything they produced, if the price were a little lower, there would be a shortage and consumers would bid the price up. In other words, price is a matter of supply and demand.

If the world really worked this way, there would be hardly be a pricing decision to make at all, since the price would be set by the market. In practice, while the forces of supply and demand are important, and probably underlie the broad trends which we see in price levels, managers often have considerable latitude when setting prices. There was no denying the impact of the forces of supply and demand in the coffee market in July 1994 when it was announced that the Brazilian coffee harvest had been damaged by severe frost and would be 20 per cent less than expected. The price of coffee on the world commodity markets rose by 30 per cent in a single day, and retail prices began to rise almost immediately. But in deciding to raise the price of a standard jar of instant coffee to wholesalers and retailers, the coffee manufacturers were not responding blindly to a market signal, but were carefully calculating the likely impact of a price rise on their competitive position in the market and on consumer demand.

A marketing model for pricing decisions

Thomas Nagle (1987) proposes that pricing decisions should be based on an assessment of the costs of provision, the likely reaction of competitors, and the price sensitivity of customers. These factors are the *three Cs* of pricing (*see* Fig. 1.4).

In most pricing decisions, *costs* play the role of a floor beneath which price

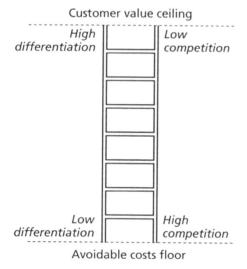

Fig. 1.4 The pricing ladder

must not be allowed to fall – although there are exceptions where, for example, a product is being used as a 'loss leader' or where the government subsidises the price of something which it regards as socially useful (such as dental hygiene). A complicating factor is the fact that costs often vary with the volume of a product that is manufactured, so that the unit cost of production for a small firm is greater than for a large firm. For this reason, when introducing new products, firms often follow a 'penetration pricing' strategy, meaning that they keep prices relatively low in order to grow the level of sales and production quickly, so that they can achieve an advantage over competitors in the form of lower costs.

Customers play the role of a ceiling on pricing decisions. Even in the absence of any competition there is a maximum value which customers would place on the benefits derived from the product or service which we are selling, and we will never be able to sell it for more than that. In practice, of course, the maximum value placed on a product or service will vary from one market segment to another and, as long as it is possible to prevent too much 'arbitrage' – buying at a lower price and reselling at a higher price – we can charge different prices to different segments. For example, students travel cheaper on the UK rail network than businesspeople. Where there are marked differences in the price sensitivity of different market segments, it is possible to pursue a policy of 'price skimming'. When Pentax introduced the Pentax Zoom – the first automatic compact zoom camera – to the British market, they priced it at £199 in the belief that there was a group of consumers who valued the benefits of the camera sufficiently highly to pay this price. Subsequently, the price of the Pentax and of similar products introduced by competitors fell rapidly to less than £100. But for a considerable length of time Pentax were able to make very attractive profit margins through a skimming strategy.

Competitors are a factor which determines where, between the floor of costs and the ceiling of customer benefits, the price will actually be fixed. In a highly competitive market, where there are many firms offering products between which consumers can perceive few differences (low differentiation), the firms will all charge much the same price and that price will offer only a modest profit margin on costs. In a market with few competitors, or in which the competitors have successfully differentiated their products in the minds of the consumers, prices will exceed costs by a greater margin. In markets with comparatively few competitors (known as oligopolies) an important consideration in the pricing decision will be the likely reaction of competitors to a price change. Any gain of market share is won at the very obvious expense of the competitors. The European market for new cars is an example. Each national market is dominated by two or three major producers; for example, Volkswagen, General Motors and Ford dominate in Germany, Peugeot and Renault in France, Ford, General Motors and Peugeot in the UK. A decision by Ford to reduce its prices in the German market in order to increase sales, for example, would probably provoke a price-cutting response from Volkswagen and General Motors. Ford may well end up selling no more cars, but charging less for each car it sells – not a happy outcome.

A note on price elasticity of demand

For most goods and services we would expect that a rise in price would provoke a decline in sales, and a fall in price would provoke a rise in sales. Obviously, the critical question is by how much will sales volume rise or fall when the price changes? The standard method of measuring sales volume changes which occur in response to price changes is the 'elasticity of demand with respect to price' (or 'price elasticity of demand'). The easiest way to think about price elasticity of demand is as the answer to the question: 'By what percentage would sales volume decline if there was a one per cent increase in the unit price?', or the equivalent question, 'by what percentage would sales volume increase if there was a one per cent decline in the unit price?' The answer to this question may fall into one of four categories, which are defined in Table 1.6.

There are certain types of product for which demand is usually inelastic; these are 'necessities' such as basic foodstuffs and essential services like gas

Table 1.6 Price elasticity of demand

Percentage sales volume decline (for 1% price rise)	Term used for this size of volume change	Impact on sales revenue of a price cut
0	Perfectly inelastic	Declines
0–1	Inelastic	Declines
1	Unitary elasticity	No change
>1	Elastic	Increases

and electricity. Demand for 'luxury' goods and services, such as personal stereos and cinema tickets, would usually be elastic. It is also to be expected that the elasticity of demand for something will be affected by the number of alternative products which are available, and the degree to which consumers regard the alternatives as good substitutes. For example, London Underground is the only company running underground trains in London, and the demand for underground train tickets is fairly inelastic – there is no really good substitute if you want to travel quickly and fairly cheaply around London. However, buses, taxis and walking are all partial substitutes for the underground. If London Underground raised their prices too far, some customers would walk (if their journey was short) and others would switch to bus or taxi.

The concept of price elasticity provides a rather comforting feeling that, by means of a simple calculation, the impact of a price change on demand and total sales revenue can be established. Unfortunately, life is seldom that simple, for a number of reasons:

1 It is very difficult to disentangle the effect of price from the effects of the other marketing mix variables. For example, if there was a change in advertising activity alongside a change in price, it would be difficult to tell what proportion of a sales volume change should be attributed to price, and what to advertising.

2 The price elasticity of demand for large price changes is likely to be different from the elasticity for small changes. So even if we know that a one per cent cut in price leads to a 0.5 per cent increase in sales volume, we cannot conclude that a 20 per cent cut in price will lead to a ten per cent increase in sales volume. This was the type of situation for London Underground described above.

3 Competitor activity also affects sales volume. As a general rule, the price elasticity of demand for the product of a single company in an industry will be higher (more elastic) than the price elasticity for the industry as a whole. So, if Ford alone were to cut the prices of its cars, it might see demand increase considerably as consumers switched from competitor models. But if all car manufacturers cut their prices, demand for cars will be seen to be inelastic with respect to price.

MARKETING PLANNING AND STRATEGY

KEY CONCEPTS

- marketing audit and SWOT analysis
- generating strategic options from the SWOT
- Ansoff's and Porter's generic strategies
- market penetration, product development, market development, diversification
- cost leadership, cost focus, differentiation, differentiation focus
- the 'Boston Box'

- cash cow, star, question-mark, dog
- the marketing budget

The marketing planning process

The concept of the marketing mix makes it clear that the many factors at the disposal of the marketing manager must be combined in a coherent way. It is intuitively obvious, for example, that putting an unusually low price on a product which is distributed through exclusive stores and which has been advertised as a top quality brand will create confusion, or perhaps suspicion, in the minds of consumers. It is equally obvious that to proceed with a substantial promotional campaign for a new product without first ensuring that the distribution channels are in place would be foolish. Such marketing *faux pas* are by no means unknown. In order to avoid this kind of problem, and to ensure that all components of the marketing mix are combined most effectively to pursue an organisation's objectives, many organisations develop marketing plans. The most frequently cited approach to marketing planning in British marketing practice is that developed by Malcolm McDonald (1991), who proposes the following steps in the process:

1 marketing audit
2 SWOT analysis
3 assumptions
4 marketing objectives
5 marketing strategies
6 marketing programmes
7 monitoring.

This marketing planning process can be summarised as the process of gathering and analysing information (Steps 1 to 3), setting objectives and devising strategies to achieve them (Steps 4 and 5), implementing the strategies and evaluating the results (Steps 6 and 7).

Gathering and analysing information

The *marketing audit* is the process of analysing the current situation in order to establish realistic objectives and strategies. The audit is informed by market research, by competitor analysis and by evaluating the success of prior marketing plans. The results of the audit are summarised in the form of a *SWOT analysis*. SWOT stands for 'Strengths, Weaknesses, Opportunities and Threats', and this has been found to be a particularly effective method of categorising the key factors influencing the development of the marketing plan. Strengths and weaknesses are factors internal to the organisation which it does better (strength) or worse (weakness) than its major competitors. For example, the British retailer Marks and Spencer is renowned for its excellent customer service, where it holds a clear advantage over its rivals. The leader in the UK telecommunications industry, British Telecommunications, found itself at a cost and price disadvantage (weakness) with respect to its rival Mercury Communications, and embarked on a strategy to overcome this. Opportunities and threats are factors in the marketing environment which are potentially beneficial (opportunities) or damaging (threats) to the organisation. When the British Government introduced a policy of forcing local authorities to put leisure services out to competitive tender ('compulsory competitive tendering') this was a threat for the leisure teams which had previously managed the service, but an opportunity to outside leisure companies who obtained a new market to address.

No matter how much information is gathered, there are always some unpredictable elements in the marketing environment which will affect the success of a marketing plan. This accounts for the use of assumptions in the marketing planning process. The nature of the *assumptions* will depend on the organisation concerned. In the public sector of the economy, for example, assumptions concerning future government policy are normally indispensable. In the private sector, government action is not normally so central to the planning process (although it can be – consider the impact of government plans for the armed forces on private defence contractors such as GEC-Marconi). However, assumptions must be made about the future of the economy in general, of specific industry sectors, and about competitor plans.

Setting objectives and devising strategies

While the members of an organisation may have aspirational objectives, in the absence of a situation analysis such as the marketing audit it is not possible to formulate realistic objectives. A national charity may aspire to increase revenue from private donations by 15 per cent within a year, but if the marketing audit identifies that other charities have greater skills in direct marketing and promotions, and that personal disposable incomes are expected to remain static over the period, it may conclude that such an objective is unrealistic. As a general rule, objectives should be realistic but still fairly demanding. In other words, the members of the organisation should feel that they can achieve the objective if they perform to the best of their abilities. Objectives should also, as far as possible, be stated in quantitative terms. While 'to achieve a successful launch of new product X' is, in general terms, a desirable objective, it would be difficult to say whether or not it had been achieved. Such an objective could be restated as 'to achieve for new product X a 10 per cent share of the national market within one year', and it would then be possible to establish whether or not the objective was achieved.

Once realistic objectives have been set, marketing strategies can be developed to achieve them. A marketing strategy is, in essence, simply a combination of marketing elements (a marketing mix). For many products and services it be unnecessary to amend the current strategy very much, if at all. In such cases the marketing audit has simply confirmed that the strategy (mix) which was in place for the product was fundamentally sound, and only needs to be adapted to recent changes in the market. For products which are clearly not meeting their objectives, a wholly new strategy may be considered necessary. Normally, a range of alternative strategies would be developed, and the strategy considered most likely to succeed would be selected from the alternatives. However, rational analysis may fail to provide a conclusive answer regarding the 'best' available strategy, and in these circumstances the marketing manager is called upon to use professional judgement based on experience of the market.

Identifying strategic options using SWOT

Marketing managers can identify the alternative strategies available to them from a number of sources. The SWOT analysis itself contains the seeds of strategic options. For example, when faced with the threat of new competition, and having identified the weakness of relatively high costs and prices, British Telecommunications plc exploited the strengths of its strong positive cash-flow and well-known brand name to develop a new corporate image and corporate advertising campaign. The promotional strategy emerges logically from the SWOT analysis. In general, organisations can ask themselves how to:

- exploit their strengths
- eliminate their weaknesses
- exploit environmental opportunities
- avoid or avert environmental threats.

Directly comparing the *internal* factors (strengths and weaknesses) with the *external* factors (opportunities and threats) is a method of generating further strategic options. There are four logical pairs of comparisons:

Strengths/Opportunities	Can strengths be used to exploit emerging opportunities?
Strengths/Threats	Can strengths be used to avoid emerging threats?
Weaknesses/Opportunities	Can an opportunity be exploited to correct a perceived weakness? Or is there a risk that an opportunity may be missed because of a weakness?
Weaknesses/Threats	Where a threat interacts with a weakness this could be a particularly serious matter for the organisation, demanding urgent action.

Identifying strategic options using generic strategies

Ansoff's growth vectors

A further source of strategic options is the generic strategies proposed by some management theorists. For example, Igor Ansoff (1987) suggested four alternative 'growth vectors' for a firm's future business (*see* Fig. 1.5).

Product Mission	Present	New
Present	Market penetration	Product development
New	Market development	Diversification

Source: Igor Ansoff, *Corporate Strategy*, Rev Edition, p 109 Penguin Books Ltd.

Fig. 1.5 Growth vector components

A firm pursuing a *market penetration strategy* aims to increase its market share in its existing markets and with broadly the same product range. Should this prove insufficient to achieve the firm's objectives, then it may consider a *product development strategy* or a *market development strategy*. In the former case new products are developed, but they are sold into markets which the firm already addresses – so much of the existing database of marketing research is relevant. *Market development* means that the firm pushes into new markets, but with broadly the same products. In this case it needs to research the new markets, but understands the product technology involved. Finally, if the firm decides to enter new markets with new products, this is known as a *diversification strategy*. By definition, both the market and the product are unfamiliar when diversification is pursued, so that the managers of the firm have to gain experience of both new markets and new products simultaneously. In consequence, diversification can be regarded as a relatively high risk strategy.

Porter's generic strategies

While Igor Ansoff's growth vector matrix proposes alternative future directions for the business, Michael Porter (1985) focused on the limited number of ways in which an organisation can achieve a competitive advantage over its rivals. Fundamentally, he argued, competitive advantage is achieved either by having lower costs than competitors, or by differentiating the product by offering consumers something which they value and which is not offered by competitors (*see* Table 1.7)

Table 1.7 Michael Porter's generic competitive strategies

Competitive advantage	Competitive scope	Strategy description
Lower cost	Broad target	Cost leadership
Lower cost	Narrow target	Cost focus
Differentiation	Broad target	Differentiation
Differentiation	Narrow target	Differentiation focus

Relative market share and market growth rate

Relative market share means your share of the market divided by the share of your largest competitor, for example:

> if you have 25% of a market, and your largest competitor has 20 per cent then your relative market share is 1.25

> if you have 10 per cent of a market, and your largest competitor has 30 per cent then your relative market share is 0.33

> if you have 30 per cent of a market, and your largest competitor has 30 per cent then your relative market share is 1.00.

Market growth rate means the annual rate of growth of the market in which you are competing, and might be quite different from the rate of growth of your SBU. For example:

Market sales grew from £15 million to £20 million last year, while you increased your sales from £1 million to £2 million – the market grew at a healthy 33 per cent, but your business grew by 100 per cent. (Incidentally, you increased your absolute market share from 6.6 per cent to 10 per cent, but we don't have enough information to calculate your relative market share.)

The basic competitive advantage achieved by an organisation can be applied either to a broad target market or to a single market segment. The two dimensions of competitive advantage and competitive scope yield four strategic alternatives – differentiation, cost leadership, differentiation focus, and cost focus. For example:

- Marks and Spencer aims to differentiate itself on customer service across a variety of products and to a fairly broad target market (differentiation).
- Kwik-Save supermarkets aim for a no-frills, low-cost service across a broad geographical market in the UK (cost leadership).
- Morgan motor cars are manufactured in very small numbers and marketed to a narrow segment of sports car enthusiasts on the basis of their traditional styling (differentiation focus).
- Direct Line insurance offers motor insurance policies to drivers who have a good 'no claims' record, and maintains a cost advantage over traditional providers by operating on a direct, telephone sale basis (cost focus).

The 'Boston Box'

One of the most famous techniques in marketing and business strategy is the growth/share matrix, proposed by the Boston Consulting Group, and affectionately known in marketing circles as the Boston Box. The Boston Box evolved from the use of portfolio models in financial management, where different types of financial security were compared using the two criteria of risk and return. It became very popular with American corporations in the 1970s, as a quick and easy method of gaining an insight into the complicated business of running several parallel businesses. Just like the financial models from which it originated, the Boston Box uses two main criteria to analyse a portfolio – which may be made up of products, or of businesses known as 'strategic business units' (SBUs). The two criteria are *relative market share* and *market growth rate*. Market share is used to indicate the degree of power which an SBU has in a given market – the higher is the market share, the greater is the power. The market growth rate is used to indicate how attractive a market is – the faster a market grows, as a rule, the easier it will be to make profits in it. So these two factors, relative market share and market growth rate, between them give an indication of how strongly you are placed in a market, and of how attractive that market is.

The Boston Box itself summarises the information on relative market share and market growth rate in a two-by-two grid (or matrix), as shown in Table 1.8

Colourful names are attached to the four sections of the Box, and these names indicate the type of strategic options which might be considered for SBUs holding such positions. A cash cow should be used as a source of money to reinvest in faster growing markets. Stars should be provided with sufficient investment funds to maintain their strong position in a fast-growing market. Question-marks should either be developed to become stars (through aggressive marketing aimed at increasing market share), or should be abandoned (sold-off) if this cannot be achieved. Dogs are prime candidates for divestment, that is, being sold off.

The Boston Box does not have the influence it once did. Certainly, the sort of naive strategic recommendations outlined in the preceding paragraph are no longer regarded as remotely adequate. However, this kind of analysis can be useful, as long as it is applied alongside some of the other techniques described in this chapter (and along with some healthy common sense). Probably the main problem with the Boston Box was found to be the classification of a high proportion of SBUs as dogs (since there are all too few markets growing at more than 10 per cent, and there can only be one SBU in any market with a relative market share greater than 1.0). Clearly, not all of these dog businesses either could, or even should be sold off. Peter McKiernan (1992)

Table 1.8 The Boston Box

High relative market share (>1.0%) High market growth (>10%)	Low relative market share (<1.0%) High market growth (<10%)
Star	**Question-mark**
High relative market share (>1.0%) Low market growth (<10%)	Low relative market share (<1.0%) Low market growth (<10%)
Cash cow	**Dog**

has devoted much of a book to explaining the many creative management strategies that can be used to obtain good economic performance from SBUs classified as dogs.

Implementing strategies and evaluating results

A 'strategy' is a fairly broad statement of the way in which marketing resources will be deployed to pursue objectives. In order to implement the strategy the broad statement must be translated into concrete action plans. Individuals must be made responsible for identifiable components of the strategy, and clear deadlines placed on the completion of allotted tasks. An important component of this task is the calculation of and allocation of the marketing budget. The ideal method of budget allocation, it could be argued, is a 'zero-based' approach whereby resources are allocated purely on the basis of the objectives and strategies specified in the marketing plan. In practice, of course, there is an existing organisational framework and an historical pattern of budget allocation which constrains the process. A certain degree of inertia within the budget allocation process is probably a good thing, remembering that it is people, not robots, who are employed in marketing organisations. While change is inevitable given the changing marketing environment within which most organisations operate, it is possible to demand too much change too rapidly and so to demoralise the people who have to implement the marketing plans. The evaluation of the marketing plan is a process which is virtually continuous, and not something which merely happens once a year. Every piece of market research, every report from a sales executive, every piece of feedback from a customer (satisfied or dissatisfied) represents an opportunity to evaluate success. It may also be necessary to commission specially a limited amount of market research to identify whether or not a key marketing objective has been met (for example, 'Have we achieved an increase in unprompted brand recognition from 15–30 per cent amongst the target market?'). However, the normal sources of marketing information, if used sensibly, should give a clear indication of the extent to which the plan is meeting its objectives.

Marketing planning and strategic management

In the preceding section it was emphasised that effective marketing is likely to follow from a planned and integrated approach to the marketing mix. Despite the undoubted importance of effective marketing to virtually all business organisations, it is important to realise that the marketing effort itself must be integrated with the other activities of the organisation. The purpose of an organisation's strategic planning process is to bring about this kind of functional integration.

Figure 1.6 shows an idealised view of the way in which a corporate strategic planning system works. If there is a similarity with the marketing planning process outlined above, this is not surprising. Planning, in virtually any field, can be summarised as the process of answering three questions:

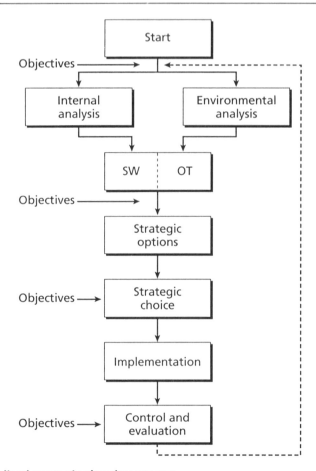

Fig. 1.6 Idealised strategic planning process

1 Where are we now?   **Situation audit**
2 Where do we want to get to?   **Objectives**
3 How will we get there?   **Strategy**

In the idealised strategic planning process of Figure 1.6, the *situation audit* comprises the steps of internal analysis, environmental analysis, and the now familiar SWOT. These steps are much more broadly based than the SWOT analysis of a marketing plan, however. The internal analysis ranges over all of the organisation's activities, identifying strengths and weaknesses in, for example, human resource management, operations management and financial management. Ambitious marketing plans, for product or market development, might have to be curtailed in the light of weaknesses such as poorly trained staff, inadequate production capacity, or insufficient working capital.

The *strategy* component of Figure 1.6 comprises the steps of strategic options, strategic choice and, to some extent, implementation. Again, while the marketing planning process focuses largely on product/market development and positioning, in the broader strategic planning process the strategic options will extend to alternative financing plans, options for extending production capacity and so on.

Objectives have been indicated at several points in Figure 1.6. Clearly, objectives have an important part to play in the planning process, but to suggest that they are just one component of the process would be naive. At the start of the planning process it is likely that the members of the organisation will have aspirational objectives, that is to say objectives which they hope the organisation will be able to achieve. However, only once an analysis of the business environment has been completed can a realistic view be taken on the opportunities open to the organisation. And only once an internal analysis has been completed can an objective view be reached on which opportunities may be realistically pursued, and which are beyond the organisation's competence. Objectives appear a third time during the process of strategic choice, since the most elementary method of choosing between strategic alternatives is on the basis of their ability to deliver the desired objectives. Finally, objectives appear once more under 'control and evaluation', where the overall degree of success of the plan can be evaluated by comparing the outcomes achieved against the desired objectives.

This is not a book on strategic planning and so this has been only the very briefest of introductions to the subject. A much more extended treatment of the subject, supported by a range of case studies, is provided by Colin Clarke-Hill and Keith Glaister (1995).

References

Ansoff, H. J., *Corporate Strategy*, Rev edn, Penguin Books Ltd, 1987.

Baker, M. J., *Marketing: An Introductory Text*, 5th edn, Macmillan, 1991.

Borden, N. H., The Concept of the Marketing Mix, *Journal of Advertising Research*, June, 1964.

Bowles, T., Issues Facing the UK Research Industry, *Journal of the Market Research Society*, 33(2)

Chisnall, P. M., *Marketing Research*, 4th edn, McGraw-Hill, 1992.

Clarke-Hill, C. and Glaister, K., *Cases in Strategic Management*, 2nd edn, Pitman Publishing, 1995.

Dhalla, N. and Yuspeh, S., For the Product Life-cycle Concept, *Harvard Business Review*, January/February, 1976.

Dibb, S. and Simkin, L., Implementing the Problems in Industrial Market Segmentation, *Industrial Marketing Management*, 23, 1994.

Drucker, P.F., *The Practice of Marketing*, Harper & Row, 1954.

Grönroos, C., Quo Vadis, Marketing? Toward a Relationship Marketing Paradigm, *Journal of Marketing Management*, 10(5), 1994.

Gross, A.C., Banting, P.M., Meredith, L.N. and Ford, I.D., *Business Marketing*, Houghton Mifflin, 1993.

Keith, R.J., The Marketing Revolution, *Journal of Marketing*, January, 1960.

Levitt, T., Marketing Myopia, *Harvard Business Review*, July/August ,1960.

McDonald, M. H. B., *The Marketing Planner*, Butterworth-Heinemann, 1991.

McKiernan, P., *Strategies of Growth: Maturity, Recovery and Internationalization*, Routledge, 1992.

Mercer, D.A., A Two Decade Test of Product Life-cycle Theory, *British Journal of Management*, December 1993.

Nagle, T. T., *The Strategy and Tactics of Pricing*, Prentice Hall, 1987.

Porter, M. E., *Competitive Advantage*, Free Press, 1985.

Smallwood, J., The Product Life-cycle: A Key to Strategic Market Planning, *MSU Business Topics*, Winter, 1973.

Vink, N., Historical Perspectives in Marketing Management: Explicating Experience, *Journal of Marketing Management 8(3)*.

Worcester, R. and Downham, J., *The Consumer Market Research Handbook*, 3rd edn, McGraw-Hill, 1989.

Answer to Microcase 3: New product options for Megafax plc

Criterion	Weighting	Dictionary of Quotations		Electronic organiser	
		Score	Weighted Score	Score	Weighted Score
Market attractiveness	50%	8	4	4	2
Product fit	20%	4	0.8	8	1.6
Research & Development	10%	1	0.1	6	0.6
Production	20%	2	0.4	8	1.6
Totals	100%		5.3		5.8

CHAPTER 2

The analysis of marketing case studies

Karin Newman and Ross Brennan

KEY CONCEPTS

- marketing case studies usually have no clear 'answer'
- defining the problem
- identifying sub-problems
- the process of analysis
- identifying and evaluating alternative solutions
- recommending action
- selling your ideas through effective presentation

WHY CASE STUDIES?

Case studies are written descriptions of realistic marketing situations and problems. Most of the cases in this book concern real marketing situations which were faced by real organisations. The case study gives you an opportunity to develop skills in problem identification, market analysis and decision making in a simulation of the marketing management process.

Most people taking courses in business or management will encounter case studies in a variety of different areas, such as operations management, accounting and finance, and human resource management. This is a book of marketing case studies, so the main emphasis is on identifying customer needs, segmenting markets, developing products, devising communications plans, and so on. However, when tackling such case studies it is important to remember that marketing does not take place in a vacuum, but has to be integrated with other aspects of the management of organisations. You may find that your analysis of a case study throws up interesting issues relating to the management of operations, of money, or of people. Although it may not be appropriate to analyse such issues in depth for a marketing class, it is important to demonstrate that you understand the wider business context within which marketing activity takes place. If you are already an experienced manager you will recognise that, in reality, management problems tend not to come in neat packages labelled 'finance', 'human resources', or 'marketing'!

The underlying problem in the case studies will not be defined. It is up to you to identify the problem. What you will find in the case study is a description of a marketing situation, with a certain amount of information about the problem situation. Just as in real life, you should expect the information to be incomplete in some areas, irrelevant in others, and perhaps excessive in still other areas. The information in the case study may well be ambiguous, capable of interpretation in two or more different ways. Case studies are usually written in narrative form. They are not organised analytically for your convenience, nor are they necessarily organised chronologically, with the various events described following each other in a logical pattern. In other words, it is up to you to organise the facts in the case. Sometimes you will find that the problem situation is described in the terms of one of the actors in the case study, but it is up to you to separate fact from opinion. It is a fact of managerial life that you will encounter people with strong opinions, who may well contradict the opinions of others who appear equally well informed. Do not be surprised if you see this aspect of managerial life simulated in front of your eyes during the discussion of these case studies.

To analyse cases, and to learn successfully from them, requires you to involve yourself in them. In many cases you are allocated a particular role, such as that of a consultant, or of a marketing manager. Try to think about the case situation as though you actually filled that position, and apply the theoretical concepts and techniques of marketing from the point of view of that role. You will find that while the nature of the problems underlying the case studies in the book is varied, there are common decision-making approaches which can be applied. Perhaps the most important lesson to learn is that the problem should be clearly defined, and the data carefully inspected, before more detailed analysis is carried out and proposals for action emerge.

LEARNING FROM CASE STUDIES

Much of the responsibility for learning from case studies rests with you. It is up to the tutor to guide you by identifying appropriate cases to use at different stages and for different topics within your marketing course. Where case studies are discussed in class, the tutor will encourage participation and the evaluation of alternative proposals, but will not usually provide an 'answer'. The tutor generally facilitates a case study class by encouraging people to summarise the discussion at appropriate points and by leading the class through the following general process:

1 What can be learnt from this case study?
2 What generalisations emerge from the case that can be carried forward to other cases?
3 Was the approach adopted to this case productive? Could it be improved upon?
4 What marketing concepts and techniques helped understanding and analysis of this case?

In the early stages of a marketing course, when only a few case studies have been tackled, you may feel a sense of frustration. Case discussions can seem disorganised and often fail to reach a clear conclusion. When dealing with marketing case studies, the tutor will normally refrain from providing a 'solution', on the grounds that there is no single correct answer to a marketing case study. This may be contrasted with the kind of case studies which are used, at an introductory level, in accounting and finance, for example. Such cases usually do have an answer, and you know whether you got it right or wrong. However, even in accounting and finance, as the cases become more complex and a better simulation of real-world decision making it becomes ever more difficult to provide a single right answer. In marketing you are unlikely ever to have the luxury of knowing that your proposed solution was clearly right.

As you progress through your marketing course you will find that the process of case analysis becomes easier, and seems much better organised. You will learn to tolerate the fact that there is no single right answer, and will find that you can present your own conclusions with great conviction, while understanding that others may come to different conclusions on the basis of the same data. Indeed, these are some of the very skills which the case study method of instruction is designed to teach you. The skills of developing a feasible solution, presenting it to a professional audience, and defending it against reasoned attack are some of the most important skills for a marketing manager to possess.

THE ROLE OF THE STUDENT

It follows from the preceding discussion that a great deal of the responsibility for learning successfully from case studies lies with you. When you are preparing a case study for discussion in class the following are your general responsibilities:

1 To prepare in advance for the class discussion. This means carrying out all the steps outlined below, so that you have something meaningful to contribute to the discussion.
2 To participate actively in the discussion, by:
   - sharing the results of your analysis
   - asking pertinent questions posed by the case
   - listening carefully to other peoples' contributions
   - adapting your analysis on the basis of what you hear
   - posing rational challenges to the analyses of others, based on contrary evidence in the case study
   - assisting the discussion by occasionally summarising the analysis as a basis for further progress.
3 At the close of the discussion, to share responsibility for reviewing the analysis and identifying lessons which can be learned for the future.

THE ANALYSIS OF MARKETING CASE STUDIES

Getting started

1 It is a good idea to prepare a written report on the case study even where this is not formally required. As a minimum, prepare outline written notes prior to attending a class discussion session.
2 Where possible, arrange an informal group discussion prior to a full class discussion.

Initial impressions

1 As a first step, read the case study as though it were simply 'a story'. This will enable you to get an overall impression of the marketing situation.
2 At the second read-through you should start to identify some key factors, and to make notes. Consider the following issues:
   - Who is the decision maker?
   - What are the key facts?
   - What are the symptoms?
   - What solutions come to mind?
   - What are the case questions, if any?
3 One word of warning – beware of the highlighter pen. Reading through a case and marking the 'key sections' with a highlighter can give a sense of security which is almost always false. It is absurd to think that at a first, or even a second, reading you can identify the key facts, opinions or actions in a case study. Furthermore, once you have marked the case study with a highlighter you will find it difficult to read the case again with an open mind, even if you subsequently decide that your first thoughts were quite wrong.

Analysis

Analysis is the process of defining an underlying problem and organising the facts at your disposal. The process of analysis can be tackled in five stages, which are illustrated in Fig 1.7.

Diagnosing the problem

Begin with a preliminary diagnosis, and then test it along the following lines.

(a) **Relate to symptoms**. Does your problem as stated match the list of symptoms that you developed earlier? Does your problem statement explain all or most of the symptoms? If not, revise it until it does.
(b) **Determine what has changed**. A problem usually occurs because something in the organisation or in the environment has changed. List the changes. Could one of these be responsible for the symptoms observed? If so, revise your problem statement.

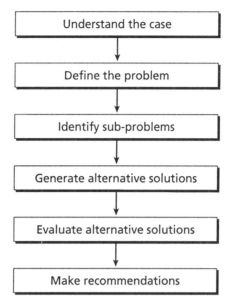

Fig. 1.7 The process of cases study analysis

(c) **Relate to intuitive solution**. Compare your first 'off the top of your head' solution with the problem statement. Does the solution meet the problem that you defined? If not, does it help you towards redefining the problem statement?

(d) **Ask – what is the cause?** The problem definition must deal with the underlying problem rather than with the symptoms alone.

(e) **Relate to case questions.** Compare your problem definition with the case questions. Does your problem statement incorporate these questions?

(f) **Write a final version** of the problem and note the evidence that you found that will justify your problem definition.

Define the sub-problems

Try to break up the problem into smaller bits and arrange them in order of importance. Most marketing case studies, like most practical marketing problems, contain several problem elements (or sub-problems). A few of the cases in this book – especially the microcases in Chapter 1 – have been designed to contain only one problem theme. The majority of the case studies however, are more complex.

Analyse the sub-problems

Using the facts and data from the case study, identify the plausible solutions to each sub-problem. This process is similar to the process of generating strategic options discussed in Chapter 1. It is designed to answer the question 'What *could* we do?', not 'What *should* we do?'.

Evaluation of alternative solutions

List all of the solutions which you have identified, and weigh them up in terms of:

- effectiveness in meeting goals
- cost
- time scale
- likelihood of success
- acceptability to affected parties.

This process is similar to the process of choosing between strategic options discussed in Chapter 1. It is designed to answer the question 'What *should* we do?'.

Make a final recommendation

Almost invariably, you are asked to conclude your analysis of a case study with a recommendation. It is not enough simply to outline the various alternatives, with their pros and cons, and leave it at that. You should select your preferred alternative and forecast the likely outcome of adopting this decision, in whatever terms seem appropriate given your definition of the problem. In proposing a solution, take into account the problems which might be encountered in implementing it, for example, resistance from consumers to a brand repositioning, or the likely response of a key competitor to a price change. One of the most common mistakes in the presentation of case study reports is failure to relate clearly the recommendations to the analysis of the facts of the case. Take care to explain how your recommendations emerge logically from your analysis.

Generalising from the case experience

Generalisations from marketing case studies can be drawn at two levels: the first level of generalisation concerns marketing concepts. In defining and analysing sub-problems, you may have been introduced to a new marketing concept. Try to define the concept and the criteria for future reference. You will also have used familiar marketing concepts. Think about the way in which you applied familiar concepts to the case study, and how it has extended your understanding of the marketing concept involved. This will assist you in developing skill in selecting and applying the correct marketing tools and concepts to case studies and, subsequently, to real-world problems.

There is a second level of generalisation which requires a review of how the class discussion of the case study proceeded. Where did the discussion start? Was a problem clearly defined? Did the problem definition help to direct the discussion? Was a decision ultimately reached? Were certain plausible solutions analysed and rejected? Why?

Perhaps the most important thing to bear in mind is that learning to analyse case studies and to make marketing decisions is partly a matter of trial and error. The learning process is speeded up when you consciously try to learn from each experience of case study analysis.

COMMUNICATING THE RESULTS OF YOUR ANALYSIS

One of the most important skills which the case study method allows you to practice and improve is the communication of your findings and recommendations through a written report or an oral presentation. One way of looking at this process is as an exercise in selling – selling yourself and selling your ideas. It is not enough simply to believe you have the best analysis. Even if this is true, a poor sales job could spoil all your hard work. It is definitely worthwhile putting in the effort required to produce a well-written and convincing report, or to develop a coherent and persuasive presentation. In order to do this, aim to achieve the following:

1 Your recommended decision must be presented clearly and succinctly.
2 The logic by which you arrived at your recommendation must be made clear.
3 The recommendation should be supported by facts developed from the case. You must do more than simply list the case study facts after each element of the problem. The data must be intelligently manipulated. Calculations, tables, graphs and diagrams should be used to bring out the significance of the facts.

The above three points apply regardless of whether you are writing a report or making an oral presentation. The objectives of both methods of communication are the same, namely to gain acceptance for your arguments and recommendations. Where you have to give a formal oral presentation there are a number of further points to bear in mind.

Oral presentations

Use of visual aids

Probably the most common medium in use for business presentations today is the overhead transparency. While flip charts and white boards can be useful for small-scale presentations, they are more appropriately used for recording group meetings and brainstorming sessions than for actually making a presentation. Overhead transparencies have many virtues:

- Computer-generated graphics and text can be printed directly on to transparencies, or transferred from paper via a photocopier.
- Good software for the production of overhead transparencies is readily available for all popular personal computer formats – modern word-processing packages have a wide variety of font sizes, graphics packages and desk-top publishing packages provide huge creative scope, while spreadsheet packages enable data to be easily converted into charts and diagrams.

- Colour printers (and photocopiers) are now quite widely available and, in the absence of a colour printer, a black and white image can be improved with the use of colour pens.
- The medium is flexible enough to be used with a small audience for an informal presentation, or with an audience of hundreds.
- Increasingly, for professional presentations, the paper or acetate stage is being missed out as many consultants and marketing professionals carry their presentations on floppy disks and output their pre-prepared slides directly to the overhead projector.

However, despite improvements in the supporting technology, the basic principles of good visual aids remain much the same:

- They should contain a very limited amount of text, or an easily legible chart or diagram.
- The information should be well organised, to help the audience understand your argument.
- Well-designed, logical visual aids which are carefully hand-written will be much more effective than poorly designed visual aids produced on the latest technology.

Presentation style

Those who are inexperienced at giving presentations, regardless of age, are almost always very nervous. If you have not had much experience of giving presentations then you will find that rehearsals really do help. When rehearsing your presentation, take care to simulate the real thing as closely as possible, with a friendly audience if one is available.

1 Time your presentation, to make sure that it is of the right duration.
2 You will probably find, for the first few presentations you give, that you need to refer to notes. A method which many people find effective is to put key words for each section of their presentation onto a postcard. Cards are easier to handle than paper when you are feeling nervous in front of an audience.
3 Resist at all costs the temptation which you may feel to read a pre-prepared presentation verbatim. This method is guaranteed to bore your audience. It prevents you from achieving any eye contact with the audience and from conveying enthusiasm for the subject.

Handling questions

Just as it is your responsibility to convey enthusiasm, so it is your responsibility to encourage the audience to ask questions or to make comments:

- It should be possible to predict at least some of these questions in advance – where it took you a long time to figure out a particular issue in the case study, it is likely that other people encountered the same difficulty.

- All presenters have the choice of whether or not to allow questions during the course of the presentation. Unless you are very confident of your presentational abilities, only allow questions once you have completed your presentation.
- If you have carried out your case study analysis effectively, you will find that answering questions is stimulating and enjoyable.
- You should, as a minimum, expect and prepare for questions which challenge your understanding of the underlying marketing problem, which suggest alternative solutions to the one which you recommend, and which challenge the basis for your own recommended solution.

Timekeeping

You should know how long you have available for your presentation, and whether or not this includes time for questions. Only with practice will you gain a feel for how long a presentation will take. Even experienced presenters often find that they are trying to pack too much presentation into too little time. Having too much to say, rather than too little, is the most common misake to make. Whatever you do, make sure that you keep to the time allotted for the presentation.

Giving and receiving feedback

In addition to comments on the quality of the ideas which you present, you should also receive feedback on the effectiveness of your presentation style. This feedback may come from a tutor, or from other members of your class. If done well, this feedback will be an invaluable method of improving your performance for the future. If you are already a manager, the benefits of this should be obvious. If you are a student intending to embark on a management career, bear in mind that an increasing number of employers value – and sometimes even test at interview – good communication ability. You should also be able to provide useful feedback to your colleagues in class. The elementary rule to bear in mind is 'do as you would be done by', in other words provide feedback to others in the same way that you expect them to treat you.

Criteria for evaluation and feedback on presentations

Apply the principle 'do as you would be done by':

- provide encouragement as well as criticism, tell people what was good, as well as what they could have improved;

- phrase your criticisms positively, explain how something could have been done better, not just that it was done badly;

- use tact and common sense – if a presenter's first language is not English or if the presenter was ill or was clearly suffering from severe stage-fright, then take these factors into consideration before making your comments;

- at all times treat the presenter with respect, since he or she is a human being with feelings.

The following criteria will assist you in evaluating presentations made by others:

- Did the presenter establish a reasonable degree of eye contact with the audience?

- Did the presenter convey a sense of enthusiasm for the subject?

- Was the audience interested in what the presenter was saying? Were people constantly attentive, or were there signs of boredom?

- Did you, at all times, know how particular points related to the overall structure of the presentation? Was there a clear structure?

- Was the presentation delivered audibly and clearly, and at a speed which you found comfortable? (Allowing for language difficulties or physical impairments.)

- If visual aids were used, were they clearly legible? Did they assist you in following the logic of the presentation?

- If visual aids were not used, why not? Would the presentation have been better with such aids?

- Did the presentation run to time?

- Were you invited to contribute by asking questions?

- Were the questions asked handled well?

Table 1.9 A process for case analysis

Step 1: Define the problem	Step 2: Define sub-problems
● relate to symptoms	● what do I need to know?
● determine what has changed	● use decision-making concepts
● relate to your intuitive solution	● use the marketing planning process
● ask 'what is the underlying cause?'	
	● use sub-problems to suggest further sub-problems
● relate to the case questions	
● should the problem be narrowed, or broadened?	● arrange sub-problems in order; look for gaps
● classify the problem	● incorporate marketing concepts.
● utilise marketing concepts	
● determine other goals/constraints on your solution.	

Step 3: Analyse sub-problems	Step 4: Analyse alternatives	Step 5: Make a final recommendation
● order the sub-problems	● identify alternative solutions	● draw together tentative decision(s)
● pick a sub-problem	● assess relative effectiveness in meeting goals	● project outcome
● determine the applicable marketing concept		● compare outcome to problem and refine
	● assess relative cost	
● search for information	● estimate time scales	● develop recommendation
● analyse the data	● estimate relative likelihood of success	● define implementation.
● write a conclusion	● consider acceptability to affected parties.	
● pick another sub-problem and repeat the process.		

Table 1.10 A checklist of marketing concepts for case study analysis

1 The customer
- ☐ Customer satisfaction
- ☐ Delighted customer
- ☐ Dissatisfied customer
- ☐ Identify current and potential customers
- ☐ Identify customer needs and expectations
- ☐ Lifetime value of a customer
- ☐ Measuring customer perceptions
- ☐ Responding to customer requirements
- ☐ Retaining customers
- ☐ Satisfied customer

2 Situation analysis
- ☐ Competitive market structure
- ☐ Environmental variables (PEST)
- ☐ External influences on consumers
- ☐ Marketing concept
- ☐ Marketing planning process
- ☐ Marketing research process
- ☐ Price elasticity of demand
- ☐ Product life-cycle

3 Market positioning
- ☐ Competitor positioning
- ☐ Demographic segmentation
- ☐ Geodemographic segmentation
- ☐ Psychographic (lifestyle) segmentation
- ☐ Repositioning
- ☐ Segment evaluation
- ☐ Target marketing

4 Marketing programmes
- ☐ Advertising budgeting
- ☐ Advertising effectiveness
- ☐ Advertising media selection

- ☐ Brand loyalty
- ☐ Brand switching
- ☐ Branding of products
- ☐ Channel management
- ☐ Channel selection
- ☐ Customer service
- ☐ Database marketing
- ☐ Direct versus indirect distribution channels
- ☐ Fixed versus flexible pricing
- ☐ Marketing mix
- ☐ New product development
- ☐ New product introduction
- ☐ New product pricing
- ☐ Penetration pricing
- ☐ Perceived value
- ☐ Personal selling
- ☐ Price and value ratio
- ☐ Price determinants
- ☐ Price skimming
- ☐ Promotional mix
- ☐ Quality and price ratio
- ☐ Recruiting and selecting sales personnel
- ☐ Responding to competitor price changes
- ☐ Sales promotion
- ☐ Salesforce organisation
- ☐ Salesforce training
- ☐ Service delivery
- ☐ Service environment
- ☐ Service product
- ☐ Service quality components

5 Evaluating outcomes
- ☐ Ethical evaluation
- ☐ Legal requirements
- ☐ Marketing research
- ☐ Projecting outcomes of decisions

SECTION 2

Cases in consumer goods marketing

Market research brief – London Electricity plc: appliance retailing business

Ross Brennan

KEY THEMES

- market research process
- secondary marketing research
- primary marketing research
- market segmentation
- marketing strategy
- competition in retailing

BRIEFING NOTES (Chapter 1)

- Buyer behaviour and market segmentation (pages 13–15)
- Managing market research (pages 17–21)
- Trends in retailing (pages 37–39)
- Gathering and analysing information (pages 44–45)

You are invited to submit a proposal to London Electricity plc for a research project to assist in formulating a strategy for the appliance retailing side of the business. This brief provides sufficient background information to enable market research agencies to formulate an initial research proposal.

BACKGROUND

London Electricity supplies electricity to nearly two million customers in Greater London. The company was incorporated as a public limited company on 1 April 1989, and, on 31 March 1990 the property, rights and liabilities of the London Electricity Board were vested in the Company.

In the year to 31 March 1992, London Electricity's turnover was £1 347.1 million, on which it made an operating profit of £137.3 million, profit before tax of £142.5 million and profit after tax of £103.5 million. The average number of employees in 1991/92 was 6 581, down from 6 691 in 1990/91.

The Company's principal activities are the distribution and supply of electricity to industrial, commercial and domestic consumers, electrical contracting and appliance retailing. Of these areas of business, the largest is electricity supply in which the company has a statutory monopoly to supply residential and small business premises within its operating area. Large business customers (using loads of over one megawatt) may choose to be supplied by another regional distribution company, or buy electricity directly from one of the national electricity generating companies (PowerGen or National Power). Electricity distribution is known as 'regulated business' since business practice is monitored by OFFER, the Office of Electricity Regulation. Business activities other than electricity supply (i.e. contracting, retailing and minor activities) produced £67.4 million turnover in 1991/92, on which a loss of £26.8 million was incurred. The retailing business alone lost £11.5 million in 1991/92 (including provisions for further rationalisation of the retailing business).

RESEARCH OBJECTIVES

The purpose of the research is to assist London Electricity in devising an effective marketing strategy for the appliance retailing business.

This is not a regulated business and is in direct competition with other major high street electrical retailers such as Comet, Rumbelows and Dixons. London Electricity is prohibited by law from cross-subsidising the appliance retailing business from profits on regulated business. The appliance retailing business must, therefore, stand or fall on its own merits. In recognition of this the appliance retailing business is in the process of a turnaround strategy, including the opening of Powerstore concessions within Debenhams department stores. The retailing business has suffered from the decline in the overall market resulting from current economic conditions.

Key sub-objectives are seen as:

- to estimate market share in the relevant geographical market
- to establish consumer perceptions of London Electricity compared to other major appliance retailers
- to define effective bases of segmentation in the appliance retailing market.

TYPE OF RESEARCH ENVISAGED

It is expected that an initial phase of secondary research will lead to an understanding of the dynamics of the appliance retailing business. Primary research will focus on customer perceptions. It is anticipated that major consumer decision-making criteria will be identified, and that perceptual mapping of the appliance retailing market will form part of the output.

The agency is invited to specify in more detail the research methodology and outputs in its proposal document.

QUESTION AREAS TO BE COVERED

This is also a matter for discussion with the agency. The secondary research will assist in the identification of appropriate question areas, and in the formulation of appropriate questions for the primary research. The hypothesis suggested by the Company is that there are major differences in consumer perception between what are still commonly referred to as the 'Electricity Board shops' and the other major high street electrical retailers. In particular, it is believed that consumers perceive London Electricity shops to price higher and offer narrower choice than competitors. It is hypothesised that a London Electricity shop is not the first place that the typical consumer thinks of when deciding on a major appliance purchase. Indeed, it is as though London Electricity shops were still perceived as falling within the 'public sector', epitomised by such customer-unfriendly organisations as British Rail and the Department of Social Security.

   However, these are merely hypotheses which may assist agencies in preparing a research proposal.

MARKET DATA

One of the purposes of the research is to identify parameters which can be used effectively to segment the appliance retailing market. Clearly, in contrast to other components of London Electricity's business, this is entirely a consumer market. Reasonable hypotheses may be made about the market, but these need to be tested:

- purchases of electrical appliances are positively correlated with household income
- certain types of purchase are highly correlated with family life-cycle stage (for example, clothes dryers with the 'full nest 1' stage)
- purchases of high-price/high-quality items are associated with consumers of high socioeconomic status.

It is not possible, therefore, at this stage to specify which target groups within the community should be researched most extensively. The research target group may be defined as all consumers who purchase electrical appliances from London Electricity or its competitors.

   A limited amount of general background information on the market is provided in Tables 2.1, 2.2 and 2.3.

Table 2.1 Value of selected UK domestic appliance markets, 1990

	£m
Audio systems	540
Camera recorders	287
Colour television	806
Cookers, electric	150
Dishwashers	107
Fridges	120
Kettles, electric	80
Microwave ovens	161
Tumble dryers	74
Vacuum cleaners	284
Video recorders	563
Washing machines	540

Table 2.2 Household penetration of selected consumer durables, 1990

	%
Clothes dryer	44
Colour television	94
Dishwasher	13
Electric freestanding cooker	36
Gas freestanding cooker	43
Refrigerator	99
Vacuum cleaner	98
Washing machine	89

Table 2.3 Selected electrical retailers, number of branches, 1990

Comet	282
Currys	530
Dixons	348
Eastern Electric	130
London Electric	61
Midlands Electric	81
Rumbelows	441
South Eastern Electric	73
Southern Electric	94
Tandy	350

Advertising the Autostore

Ross Brennan

KEY THEMES

- demographic segmentation and target marketing
- reaching a target market through advertising
- evaluation of the effectiveness of alternative advertising media

BRIEFING NOTES (Chapter 1)

- Buyer behaviour and market segmentation (pages 13–15)
- Advertising (pages 29–30)
- Market research, target markets and marketing communications (pages 31–33)

Autostore Ltd has developed a new motor accessory product (the 'Autostore'), which will be distributed through local car-parts stores and national chains, such as Halfords. Market research has indicated that many drivers regard the storage capacity within a typical motorcar cabin as inadequate and inconveniently located. Your product is a multipurpose locking container which can be attached (using velcro fasteners) practically anywhere on the interior of the car, and which will hold small items such as sun-glasses, a wallet, or some small change and a set of keys. The product will be sold in a variety of sizes, all in bright colours and designs. It is expected to become something of a fashion statement, particularly amongst young, male drivers.

The initial market research suggested that the primary target market should be AB males aged 25–40, living in London and the South-East of England. There is some debate about the most effective method of communicating with this audience. Figure 2.1 shows an initial quantitative analysis carried out by your advertising manager, comparing two alternative media – Capital FM (radio) and *What Car?* (magazine). Your advertising manager has briefed you on her analysis:

> It is estimated that 9.7 million adults listen to Capital FM at one time or another, of whom 20 per cent are in the target group. So, by advertising on Capital FM, you would reach 1.94 million people in the target group (called prospects). But on average each advertising slot will only be heard by 4 per cent of them (78 000).
>
> Since the objective is for the advertisement to be heard by 80 per cent of the target group, I've estimated that we would need 40 slots on Capital FM. At first sight this looks odd, since 40 slots at 4 per cent per slot multiplies up arithmetically to

*160 per cent of the audience. But remember that many members of the target group
(perhaps those who always drive to work listening to Capital) will hear the advert
several times. If you only booked 20 slots (on the basis that 20 times 4 per cent
equals 80 per cent) then considerably fewer than 80 per cent of the target group
would hear the advert even once. Of course, on each occasion that the advertisement is broadcast approximately 4 per cent of the target audience will hear it, but
many of them will have heard it before. I went for 40 slots because on average I
would expect to reach 2 per cent new listeners per slot (the first slot reaches many
more new listeners than this, but each subsequent slot will reach fewer and fewer).*

*The costs of preparing an advertisement for Capital FM are estimated at £1000,
and to advertise for 30 seconds at the peak 'drive-time' costs around £1 800. So a
campaign of 40 slots would cost about £73 000. Now, I've assumed that 1 per cent
of the people who hear the advert will actually go out and buy the product, in other
words 1 per cent of the 80 per cent of people we reach will buy – which is about
16 000 sales. Divide £73 000 by 16 000 sales and you get a cost of about £4.60 per
sale. The same analysis for* What Car? *suggests a figure of about £4.19 per sale.
But an awful lot depends on our assumption on the conversion rate.*

	Capital FM	*What Car?*
Universe	9.7 m	1.8 m
Penetration	20%	60%
Prospects	1.9 m	1.08 m
Costs		
Preparation	£1 000	£5 000
Per insertion	£1 800	£5 000
Objective	80% aware	80% aware
Insertions needed	40	8
Total cost	£73 000	£45 000
'Aware' prospects	1.6 m	0.86 m
Cost per 'aware'	£0.046	£0.052
Conversion rate	1.0%	1.25%
Buyers	16 000	10 750
Cost per buyer	£4.60	£4.19

What Car? 1.8 million readers, each reads 1 issue in 5, hence 20 per cent
prospects reached on each insertion
Capital FM on average 4 per cent of listeners are listening at any one time

**Fig. 2.1 Autostore advertising alternatives: Advertising a motor accessory to
AB males, aged 25–40, living in London and the south east**

Castlemaine XXXX

Ross Brennan

KEY THEMES

- **demographic and lifestyle segmentation of consumer markets**
- **designing messages for target markets**

BRIEFING NOTES (Chapter 1)

- Buyer behaviour and market segmentation (pages 13–15)
- Advertising (pages 29–30)
- Market research, target markets and marketing communications (pages 31–33)

The total volume of beer consumed by British drinkers declined by about four per cent between 1982 and 1992. There was a shift in favour of the consumption of other alcoholic beverages, notably wine, but also cider. However, within the slowly declining UK beer market there was a marked shift away from the traditional British ales (bitter and mild) in favour of lager. By 1992, lager accounted for about 46 per cent of all beer consumed in the UK, with bitter a long way behind in second place at 35 per cent. This represented virtually a reversal of the shares of the market held by these products in 1982. Clearly, it was the lager sector of the market which had commanded the attention of the big brewers during the 1980s. This sector had seen frequent new product launches, supported by expensive and aggressive advertising campaigns designed to differentiate brewers' products in their key growth market. One success of the 1980s was Castlemaine XXXX ('Four-ex').

In 1984 Allied Breweries decided to promote Castlemaine XXXX aggressively in the UK market. The brand has since become the most successful new lager launch in UK history. No other brand was selling more at the end of its first three years. Castlemaine XXXX was Allied's answer to the challenge of the early 1980s when it was recognised that new brands were needed to move the sector forward as there was a new generation of image-conscious younger drinkers waiting for modern alternative brands to replace those lagers that had been around since the 1960s. Castlemaine XXXX fulfilled the requirement, being a standard strength 'session' lager that was positively differentiated in image terms from existing standard brands.

MARKET SHARE

In 1992 the draught product was the fifth ranked lager brand in the UK in sales terms, behind Carling Black Label, Heineken, Fosters and Carlsberg, with 7.9 per cent of the market.

DISTRIBUTION

Castlemaine is sold throughout the UK, and has been launched in bottled form in Europe. Within the UK, XXXX is sold through brewery-owned pubs, tenancies and free-trade outlets (e.g. free-house pubs, working men's clubs, sports and social clubs, night clubs, student unions). Castlemaine XXXX is also sold through regional brewers estates such as Greenalls, Boddingtons and Youngs. Castlemaine XXXX is available through wholesalers and in all types of off-trade outlets.

BRAND POSITIONING AND TARGET MARKET

The brand is positioned as a quality standard-plus lager with an authentic Australian heritage appeal, played upon by strong overtones of machismo and irreverence. These images of Castlemaine XXXX are essential to its positioning since its consumers identify with the brand's trendy Australian sense of humour. Castlemaine XXXX is seen as a lager that real Australians value above and beyond anything else, hence the advertising expression 'Australians wouldn't give a Castlemaine XXXX for anything else'. Considerable use has been made of the promotional opportunities offered by visiting Australian sports teams. Everyone knows that Australian national cricketers and rugby players epitomise rugged masculinity!

The core target market for Castlemaine XXXX is males, aged between 18 and 24, socioeconomic groups C1C2D, who enjoy quite heavy lager and spend approximately £8 a week on drink. The broader target market would encompass 18–24 year-old-males, BC1C2D, who will drink any standard lager.

The profile of the standard XXXX drinker is of someone who lives life to the full, is good humoured and one of the lads. He is sociable and active, spending time with his friends in the pub or watching and participating in sport. He is both aware of, and a purchaser of, brand names (like XXXX and Reebok) which he believes will contribute to his image – which is important to him. He is likely to be a skilled, blue- or white-collar worker, who continually aspires to improve the quality and enjoyment of his life. The typical XXXX drinker would secretly like to be a bit of a yuppie. He lives on a housing estate or in a terraced house in London, Yorkshire or in the north west. He drives a second-hand car with some 'pose value': an XR3i perhaps; and plays football at the weekend. His favourite television programmes are *The Chart Show*, *The Cosby Show*, *Saint and Greavsie*, and *Hale and Pace*. He reads the *Sun* or *Today* newspaper.

Ice-cream wars: The UK ice-cream market in 1990

Ross Brennan

KEY THEMES

- segmentation and target marketing in a consumer goods market
- market and product development strategies
- price sensitivity in different market segments
- the threat from new entry competition

BRIEFING NOTES (Chapter 1)

- The marketing mix and the marketing environment (pages 6–7)
- Buyer behaviour and market segmentation (pages 13–15)
- Setting objectives and devising strategies (pages 45–46)
- Identifying strategic options using SWOT (page 46)

Until the 1980s certain aspects of the UK ice-cream market were regarded as unchanging. Ice-cream (including ice lollies) was predominantly sold to children, UK consumers preferred a product made largely from vegetable fat rather than dairy fat, ice-cream was a highly price sensitive 'commodity' product, and the ice-cream market was incorrigibly seasonal. Yet all of these assumptions have been challenged or overturned in the latter 1980s, and the nature of competition in the 1990s may be expected to be quite different.

Figure 2.2 shows UK consumption of ice-cream by volume from 1984 to 1989.

After some reasonably good summers in 1982, 1983 and 1984, 1985 was a poor summer and ice-cream sales suffered. It was not until 1988 that sales volume recovered to the level of 1984. The value of ice-cream sales (*see* Fig 2.3) showed a similar dip in 1985, but recovered much more rapidly, showing an increase of 55.5 per cent between 1985 and 1989. Even after allowing for inflation, there was a substantial increase in the retail value of each litre of ice-cream sold between 1984 and 1985. Clearly something revolutionary was happening in the market.

Demographic trends necessitated some change in ice cream marketing strategy. The number of people in the principal target market, children aged 5–14, declined from 8.42 million in 1980 to around seven million in 1989. In order to maintain and grow sales, an appeal had to be made to the adult market,

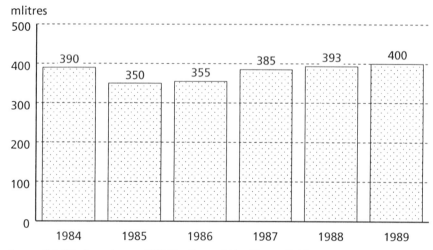

Source: Retail Business, January 1990 (The Economist Intelligence Unit).

Fig. 2.2 Volume consumption of ice-cream in the UK, 1984–89

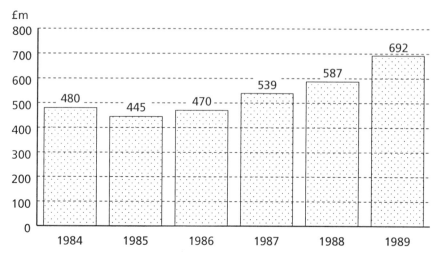

Source: Retail Business, January 1990 (The Economist Intelligence Unit).

Fig. 2.3 Retail sales of ice-cream in the UK, 1984–89

but this would not be achieved with the relatively unsophisticated products preferred by children. So, with a shift in marketing emphasis towards a new target group, came a shift in product strategy, towards higher value products with adult appeal

UK manufacturers were encouraged by the knowledge that per capita consumption of ice-cream in the UK is much lower than in a number of other developed countries. Figure 2.4 shows UK per capita consumption of ice-cream at about seven litres per head per year, compared with over 20 litres per head in the USA.

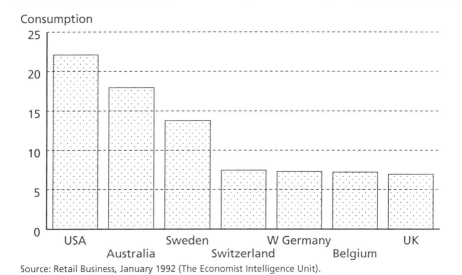

Consumption

Source: Retail Business, January 1992 (The Economist Intelligence Unit).

Fig. 2.4 International ice-cream consumption, 1987 (litres per head)

Along with an appeal to adult consumers 'snacking' on impulse purchase ice-cream bars, the ice-cream industry sought to exploit growing penetration of freezers in UK homes (*see* Table 2.4) by selling take-home packs. The take-home market is made up of multipacks of wrapped ice-cream bars, bulk packs of ice-cream and a growing market for complete ice-cream desserts such as Wall's Viennetta (the market leader).

Table 2.4 Household penetration of fridges and freezers

% owning	1986	1987	1988	1989
Separate freezer	39	37	38	37
Fridge/freezer	42	44	47	49

Source: *Marketing Pocket Book*, 1992, NTC Publications.

SECTORS OF THE MARKET

The ice-cream market can be subdivided into the impulse sector, the take-home sector and the catering sector. The take-home sector accounted for 53 per cent of the market by value in 1988, the impulse sector for 41 per cent and the catering sector for six per cent. The largest component of the take-home sector is still standard ice-cream in bulk packs, but an increasing share is taken by premium ice-cream. Premium ice-cream is rich in dairy fat, is made from quality ingredients, and has a higher overall fat content than standard or economy ice-cream. The American company Häagen Dazs is probably the best-known brand in the premium ice-cream market, but small British manufacturers such as Loseley Dairy Products and New England also specialise in premium ice-cream. Nevertheless, the major manufacturers (Wall's and Lyons

Maid) and supermarket own-label ice-cream dominate the premium ice-cream market.

The impulse sector of the market is more seasonal than the take-home sector. Purchases peak during hot weather. And while the development of new products is important throughout the ice-cream market, in the impulse sector product development is particularly important. A great deal of marketing effort goes into devising new product concepts, developing packaging that will sell products and promoting the new lines. The children's market used to be the focus for most of this effort, but increasingly promotion is directed at adults.

COMPETITION IN THE MARKET

Figure 2.5 shows the major competitors in the ice-cream market, together with their shares of the two key market sectors – take home and impulse – in 1988.

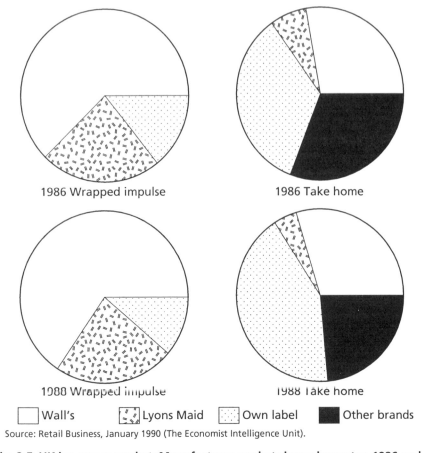

Source: Retail Business, January 1990 (The Economist Intelligence Unit).

Fig. 2.5 UK ice-cream market: Manufacturer market shares by sector, 1986 and 1988

Wall's Ice Cream Ltd and Lyons Maid dominate the wrapped impulse sector, with a minority share for supermarket own labels. In the take-home sector, however, Wall's has less than a third of the market, with the largest share controlled by own-label products. Advertising activity in the ice-cream market is substantial (*see* Fig 2.6). After only slow growth in advertising in the mid-1980s, there was very rapid growth in 1989 and 1990 following the entry of Mars into the market.

Wall's Ice Cream Ltd

Wall's Ice Cream Ltd is a subsidiary of Bird's Eye Wall's which, in turn, is part of Unilever plc. Unilever is a multinational consumer goods company incorporated in the Netherlands (Unilever NV) as well as the UK. The Wall's portfolio of ice-cream products runs to over 70 lines, with a major presence in the children's market, the adult impulse market (e.g. Romero, Feast, Sky) and the take-home market (e.g. Gino Ginelli, Viennetta). Unilever is recognised as a highly professional and aggressive marketing organisation and Wall's conforms to this pattern. In addition to developing new products to exploit growth sectors of the market, Wall's consistently outspends its competitors on advertising (*see* Fig 2.7). A notable advantage which Wall's holds over its rivals is ownership of many freezer cabinets in small confectionery, tobacconist and newsagent shops (CTNs). Generally, CTNs cannot afford the space to have more than one freezer cabinet, and if Wall's is allowed to continue to prevent the products of other companies from being kept in the freezer which it supplies then it holds an important distributional advantage. This advantage affects the impulse sector in particular.

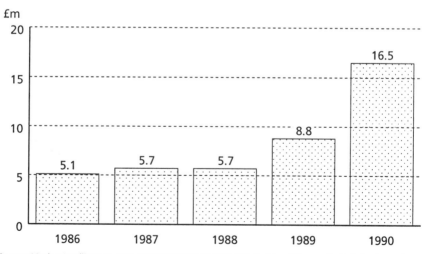

Source: Market Intelligence, June 1991 (Mintel Publications Ltd); Advertising evaluated at rate card costs.

Fig. 2.6 Main media advertising expenditure 1986–90: UK ice-cream and ice lollies

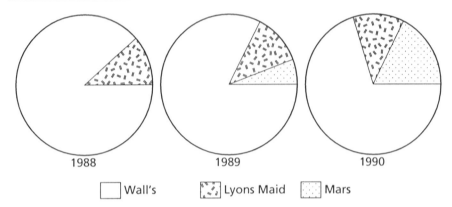

1988   1989   1990

☐ Wall's   ⬚ Lyons Maid   ⬚ Mars

Fig. 2.7 Advertising expenditure on ice-cream: Share of major manufacturers, 1988–90

Lyons Maid

The second biggest ice-cream brand in the UK, Lyons Maid Ltd is a subsidiary within the foods division of Allied Lyons plc. Allied Lyons has interests in beer, retailing, spirits and wine, as well as owning a number of well-known food brands (including other ice-cream brands such as Mister Softee and Baskin-Robbins). Lyons Maid's major strength lies in the impulse sector of the market, where in 1988 it achieved a share of 23 per cent. This success was built on well-known products such as King Cone, Figaro and Mivvi. However, as number two in a market dominated by Wall's, and facing aggressive new competition from Mars, Lyons Maid found itself in an uncomfortable position in the late 1980s.

Mars

Mars identified the adult ice-cream market as a growth opportunity in the late 1980s and successfully entered the market in 1989 by exploiting its well-known confectionery brands (e.g. Mars, Bounty) together with the renowned Mars marketing machine. Product launches in the market were directed explicitly at the fast-growing market for premium, adult ice-cream products. Market entry was supported by large-scale mass media advertising. From a standing start, Mars spent £0.5 million on advertising ice-cream in 1989, and increased this to £3 million in 1990, heavily outspending Lyons Maid in that year. Mars expected to achieve ice-cream sales of £75 million in 1990. In 1990 the Mars Bar ice-cream cost 60p each, or £1.99 as a multipack of four.

Niche players

Small specialist companies producing premium ice-creams, generally distributed on a narrow geographical basis, have made little impact on the market so far. They specialise in high quality dairy ice-cream, generally appealing to consumers on the basis of 'wholesomeness'. English firms include Loseley Dairy Products of Guildford, and New England of Newton Abbott. A rather different niche player is Häagen Dazs, an American company which, in 1990, sold 'super premium' ice cream at around £2.89 per half-litre tub (this is about eight times the unit price of a four-litre tub of economy ice-cream).

MARKET TRENDS

Many of the changes in the market observed in the late 1980s are expected to continue as longer term trends. Ice-cream is increasingly being sold as an all year round product, particularly in the take-home market but also for impulse purchase. Although an element of seasonality will inevitable remain in ice-cream sales the vulnerability of the market to climatic factors will decline.

A strong trend in the market is towards relatively expensive premium, dairy ice-cream products. This trend is closely associated with the development of the adult market, and the belief that the UK ice-cream market is far from being saturated. The take-home sector of the market is likely to show the most rapid growth, with the emphasis on premium ice-cream sold in relatively small volume 'bulk' packs (around 1 litre). On the other hand the market for complete ice-cream desserts (e.g. Viennetta) is seen as relatively mature, with little prospect of rapid growth.

The growth in premium dairy ice-cream products means that the value of the ice-cream market will continue to grow faster than volume. It is likely that the volume of sales of economy and standard quality bulk ice-cream, typically sold in large containers of 2 litres or more, will decline.

Marketing activity, stimulated by the entry of Mars, will continue at a high level. The emphasis will be on the development of new products, using innovative packaging and design, promoted by substantial mass-media advertising expenditure. It remains to be seen whether own-label products can maintain their position in the take-home sector as an increasing number of premium branded products (e.g. Gino Ginelli) are promoted aggressively in this market. Another factor which is difficult to predict is the success of the niche players.

The ultimate impact on the market of the entry of Mars is also an imponderable. In the short term Mars has made impressive inroads, and there is no reason to doubt that Mars will maintain their commitment to the market through product development and promotional expenditure. This has fundamentally altered the nature of competition in the market, which has not yet reached a new equilibrium.

A case of too many cooks? The UK electrical goods retail sector

Ross Brennan

KEY THEMES

- competition in a static/declining market
- marketing of high technology consumer goods
- the trend towards out-of-town shopping
- macroeconomic factors and consumer durable spending

BRIEFING NOTES (Chapter 1)

- The marketing mix and the marketing environment (pages 6–7)
- The product life-cycle (pages 22–23)
- Trends in retailing (pages 37–39)
- Setting objectives and devising strategies (pages 45–46)
- Identifying strategic options using SWOT (page 46)

Electrical goods retailing in the UK became an increasingly cut-throat business in the late 1980s and early 1990s as economic growth dried up, interest rates rose sharply and the housing market collapsed. Just as these adverse economic factors took effect, virtually eliminating growth from the market, the nationalised regional Electricity Boards were being privatised. Despite the prevailing conditions in the market, the new Regional Electricity Companies (RECs), far from withdrawing from the electrical retailing sector, have chosen in several cases to make themselves far more competitive. Even though some growth in the market is to be expected in the mid-1990s as the UK economy recovers, there are clearly too many competitors competing aggressively for market share. This case study examines in some detail the UK electrical retailing market and the major players within it.

THE MARKET: SIZE AND GROWTH

Sales turnover and volume trends

The value of sales of electrical and music goods in the UK in 1992 was £7.8

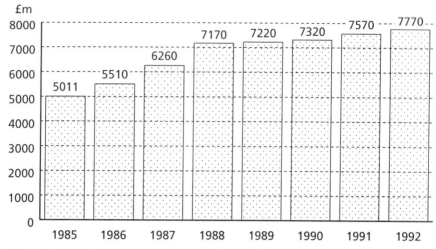

Fig. 2.8 Electrical and music goods retailers: value of sales turnover, 1985–92

billion, compared to £5.01 billion seven years earlier in 1985. A brief glance at Fig 2.8 shows that the growth of this sector in recent years divides into two quite distinct periods. From 1985 to 1988 the value of sales increased by 43.1 per cent, a compound annual growth rate of nearly 13 per cent. From 1988 to 1992 however, sales value increased by only 8.4 per cent, an annual growth rate of 2 per cent.

The sharp decline in the growth rate of sales can be split into the two components of price and volume. Figure 2.9 illustrates the comparative growth of sales volume and sales value. Over the seven-year period illustrated, while sales value increased by 55.1 per cent sales volume grew by 52 per cent, indicating a very modest overall increase in the price of goods in this sector, and a sectoral rate of inflation far below that of the general index of retail prices. Once again, it is helpful to consider the two periods 1985–88 and 1988–92 separately. In the former period, volume growth actually exceeded sales value growth, indicating an absolute decline in the level of prices. Between 1989 and 1992, on the other hand, sales value growth did outstrip volume growth, so that when price changes are removed from the data the sector showed only 4.1 per cent growth over the four-year period.

This, then, is a sector of the retail economy where prices are declining sharply relative to prices elsewhere in the economy, and where business volume grew by 46 per cent in the three years before 1988, but by a mere 4.1 per cent in the four years after 1988.

Interpreting the growth trends

Electrical goods, particularly high technology 'brown' goods such as video-recorders and camcorders, have benefited from rapid technological advances and declining manufacturing costs as sales volume has increased. In a less competitive sector of the economy at least a part of these gains in efficiency

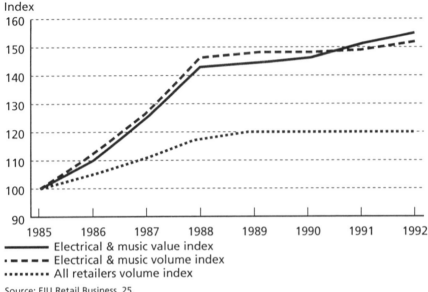

Source: EIU Retail Business, 25.

Fig. 2.9 Electrical and music goods retailers: Sales value and sales volume indices, 1985–92

might have been appropriated by the manufacturers and distributors. However, the electrical goods sector is characterised by intense competition in both manufacture and distribution, and the main beneficiary of technological and manufacturing advances has been the consumer. From January 1989 to January 1992, the average price of electrical appliances rose by 4.7 per cent, while the average price of audio-visual equipment *declined* by 7.3 per cent. The comparable rate of general inflation, measured by the retail prices index, was 22.1 per cent.

The route to success for a manufacturer in such a market is to produce a constant stream of product innovations and to persuade the consumer to invest in new products (such as the camcorder in the period 1985–1992) and to upgrade old products at more frequent intervals. Retailers may try to keep at the forefront of the market, aiming for a market of innovative, younger consumers and trying to forecast which product innovations will succeed and which will fail – the strategy chosen by Dixons – or can concentrate on more slow moving, but relatively stable markets. The latter was the strategy adopted by the regional electricity boards prior to privatisation, when they concentrated almost exclusively on white goods (i.e. domestic electrical appliances such as washing machines, cookers and fridges).

The late 1980s saw a steady stream of important product innovations such as personal stereo equipment, CD players and camcorders, which generated much of the growth in the sector. On the other hand, a number of the fast-growing products of the early 1980s were entering the maturity stage of the life-cycle by 1990, for example, the microwave oven, video-recorder and tumble dryer. However, even in these maturing markets consumers were, until 1989, prepared to replace their durable goods relatively frequently.

In 1989, however, rapidly increasing interest rates simultaneously cut the discretionary income of people with mortgages, brought about a collapse of the UK housing market and raised the price of credit to buy durables. Electrical goods in general have a high income elasticity of demand since they are perceived to be luxuries, and even those which are perceived to be necessities (such as the washing machine and fridge) are replaced less frequently in times of financial stringency. The result was the transformation in the growth of sales of electrical equipment which took place in 1989.

THE MAJOR PLAYERS

The latest data available, for 1988, show that there were 11 485 electrical and music goods retailing businesses, and that the average number of outlets per business was 1.6 – a total of 18 622 outlets. The great majority of electrical retailers are, therefore, single-shop businesses. In contrast, the market leader Dixons Group had 857 outlets in November 1992. On the basis of sales turnover, the Dixons Group is comfortably the market leader, with an estimated market share of 14.9 per cent in 1991, split between Dixons (8.4 per cent) and Currys (6.5 per cent). Comet was second in the market with an estimated share of 6.6 per cent, and Rumbelows third with six per cent. In 1991 Clydesdale claimed fourth position in the market with a share of around 1 per cent. However, following developments in the market between 1991 and 1993 E & S Retail Ltd (joint venture between Eastern and Southern RECs) probably holds third place in the market with around a three per cent share.

Dixons Group

The Dixons Group trades in the UK electrical retail sector through the Dixons and Currys chains, owns the UK-based Supasnaps film processing chain, and is involved in the US electrical retailing business through Silo.

In the 1991/92 financial year the Group's UK retailing operations generated £1.2 billion sales turnover, contributing to Group turnover of £1.86 billion. Group pre-tax profits were £70.3 million.

The Dixons chain focuses on the brown goods market and is positioned as the high street electrical chain within the Dixons Group, while Currys sells a broad range of brown and white goods and is positioned as the out-of-town superstore chain within the Group. Currys high street outlets are gradually either being closed down or converted into Dixons stores, while around 20 out-of-town Currys superstores are being opened each year. In 1990/91 Currys contributed 56 per cent of sales turnover from the Group's UK electrical retailing activities, and Dixons 44 per cent. As at November 1992 there were a total of 857 Dixons and Currys stores, of which 128 were Currys out-of-town superstores. The average sales area of a Dixons store in November 1992 was 2200 square feet, that of a Currys high street store was 1890 square feet, and that of a Currys superstore was 6601 square feet. In contrast the average sales area of each of the 352 Supasnaps outlets was 321 square feet.

The Dixons Group became the UK market leader in 1984 when Dixons acquired Currys and retains that position today. In 1986 Dixons failed in a bid for Woolworths (now Kingfisher) which would have given it control of Comet, the second largest electrical goods retailer in the UK.

Comet

Comet is one of four retail chains owned by Kingfisher (formerly Woolworth Holdings), the others being B&Q, Superdrug and Woolworth. The Comet chain is the least profitable of the Kingfisher businesses and is less profitable than Dixon's UK chains. Comet generated sales turnover of £501 million in 1990/91, with operating profit of £7.6 million. In 1990/91 Comet accounted for 16.1 per cent of total Kingfisher turnover.

Comet started as an electrical discount warehouse in the 1960s, and is today the leading out-of-town electrical chain in the UK. In February 1992, the chain comprised 275 outlets in all, of which 80 were high street stores and 195 out-of-town superstores. The few remaining trappings of the 1960s discount warehouse will be eliminated in the early 1990s as further investment is made in both improving the shopping environment and in staff training.

Clydesdale

Clydesdale is an electrical retailer with approximately 130 outlets concentrated in Scotland and the north of England. Like other players in the electrical retail market, Clydesdale has concentrated most of its recent store development in the superstore category. Ten Clydesdale superstores were opened in 1992 taking the total to 31. The average sales area in Clydesdale high street stores is 1300 square feet, and in superstores 4450 square feet. Despite its limited geographical base Clydesdale was firmly in fourth place as a UK electrical retailer behind Dixons, Comet and Thorn EMI (Rumbelows/Atlantis) in 1991. Thorn EMI's move out of electrical retailing would have promoted Clydesdale to third place, but the launch of E & S Retail (an Eastern Electricity/Southern Electric joint venture) relegated Clydesdale once again to fourth place.

Thorn EMI

Until 1992 Thorn EMI Home Electronics operated in the UK electronic equipment rental business and, through Rumbelows and Atlantis, in the electrical retailing business. In February 1992 Thorn EMI announced that it was pulling out of electrical retailing in the UK and concentrating on the hire business. The 450 Rumbelows outlets would either be sold or converted into electrical equipment hire shops. Rumbelows had been making losses for several years and Thorn had been looking for a buyer. Scottish Power purchased 17 high-street Rumbelows stores in Scotland from Thorn EMI in April 1992, together with eight Atlantis stores. The Atlantis chain was Thorn's electrical superstore chain, with 32 outlets as at February 1992, but the chain is being sold off piece-meal. Another regional electricity company, Norweb, purchased 20 Atlantis stores (four of which were later sold) in June 1992.

The regional electricity companies

Prior to privatisation the emphasis in the retailing arms of the then regional electricity boards was on the sale of white goods. At the time of privatisation two major strategic options were suggested for the retailing operations. One option was aggressive expansion of the retailing activities as part of a broad-er diversification strategy to reduce dependence on the core distribution busi-ness which had become subject to competition. The second option was to exit from electrical retailing entirely, in order to concentrate on those aspects of the business in which the regional electricity companies could claim unique competence, namely the distribution of electricity. Given the difficult economic circumstances of the early 1990s, the intensity of competition in the electrical retailing sector and the relative inefficiency with which the electricity boards had managed their retailing operations, the option to exit had to be taken seri-ously (in practice, only London Electricity appears to have chosen this option). The most likely strategy was presumed to be somewhere between the two extremes, involving a rationalisation of the retailing operations and the clo-sure of unprofitable outlets with the objective of becoming more effective com-petitors in electrical goods retailing.

At the time of privatisation, there was considerable regional variation in the penetration of the retailing sector by the electricity companies – in 1990 London Electricity had 57 outlets producing sales of £33.4 million, while Eastern Electricity had 124 shops generating turnover of £96.3 million. And, in prac-tice, the response of the RECs to privatisation has varied from company to company. For example, NorWeb (operating in the north-west of England) have expanded their interests in electrical retailing with the acquisition of the Atlantis stores from Thorn EMI. Scottish Power, as noted above, acquired 25 electrical retailing outlets (17 Rumbelows and 8 Atlantis) from Thorn EMI in 1992.

Another strategy has been adopted by several other RECS, which have formed alliances with RECs serving other geographical areas, to strengthen their position in the retailing business. The advantages of this approach are expected to accrue in terms of economies of scale, in particular the ability to concentrate buying power.

MERGERS AND ALLIANCES

Following its acquisition of Currys in 1984 which made the Dixons Group the largest electrical retailer in the UK, Dixons attempted to acquire Woolworths in 1986. The attempt failed to gain the backing of Woolworths largest institutional shareholders. Subsequently, in 1989, Kingfisher made a hostile bid for the Dixons Group. This bid was ultimately blocked by the Monopolies and Mergers Commission on the grounds that combining the operations of Dixons, Currys and Comet in electrical retailing would significantly reduce competition and be against the public interest.

Since the privatisation of the regional electricity companies, three major retailing alliances have been formed, and it is to be expected that there will be further such activity as the RECs attempt to make themselves effective competitors. Eastern Electricity and Southern Electric formed a 50:50 retailing joint venture which began trading in April 1992 under the name E & S Retail Ltd, with 227 outlets across the south and east of England. Subsequently, Midlands Electricity became the third partner in E & S Retail by acquiring a 28 per cent stake in the venture, and the 82 Midlands Electricity stores were transferred to E & S Retail from April 1993.

South Western Electric and South Wales Electric (now Swalec) merged their retailing activities from April 1992, in a joint venture (SWEB Retail) 80 per cent owned by South Western. SWEB Retail had 67 outlets when it began trading, and expected to achieve £70 million turnover in its first trading year.

East Midlands Electricity and Yorkshire Electricity announced in November 1992 that they were to merge their retailing and appliance servicing operations in a 50:50 joint venture which will have around £125 million annual turnover.

Clearly the RECs are aiming through alliances to build retailing operations which can match the scale of their competitors.

PROFITABILITY

The profit margins on electrical goods are slim, and retailers rely on the sale of extended product warranties to boost profits – in 1989/90 the Dixons chain generated profits of £48.9 million, of which £37.8 million was from the sale of warranties. The most recent figures available, for 1988, show that the average gross profit margin in electrical goods retailing was 31.8 per cent, slightly higher than the equivalent figure for 1986 (30.8 per cent) but below the gross margin achieved in the household goods sector as a whole (34.1 per cent). The operating profit margin achieved by the market leader, Dixons Group, on its UK electrical retailing operations rose from 3.1 per cent in 1990 to 5.0 per cent in 1991 and 6.0 per cent in 1992. Comet, operating the second largest chain in the sector, achieves lower operating margins than Dixons – an operating profit of £7.6 million in turnover of £501.7 million yielded an operating margin of 1.5 per cent. Meanwhile, Thorn EMI decided to divest themselves of Rumbelows, the third largest electrical retailing chain, because it has made consistent losses.

THE MOVE OUT-OF-TOWN

In common with other retailing sectors, most notably the large supermarket chains, there has been a trend away from the high street towards large out-of-town stores. Superstores (with around three times the selling space of a high street store) at out-of-town shopping centres can offer the customer a wider choice of merchandise, and fit into a consumer lifestyle which is increasingly based around the car. The Dixons Group are developing Currys as an out-of-town superstore chain, and now have 128 superstores out of a total of 857 Dixons and Currys outlets. Comet is the leader in out-of-town electrical retailing, having 240 out-of-town superstores. Three-quarters of Comet's sales area was in out-of-town stores by 1992, with a continuing drive towards superstores and away from high street outlets

CONFRONTATION BETWEEN THE MARKET LEADERS AND THE RECs

In the difficult trading conditions of the early 1990s, the market leaders in the electrical goods retailing sector – Dixons and Comet – must have hoped that the newly privatised Regional Electricity Companies would slowly withdraw from the retailing business. Certainly, *The Financial Times* (4 November 1992) failed to see the logic in the expansionist strategy of the RECs towards the retail sector:

> *given the very tough market for electrical goods the electricity shops look increasingly like spoilers which can afford to stay in the game only because they have rich parents.*

However, several RECs have already demonstrated their commitment to aggressive competition in electrical retailing. In addition to the acquisition of new stores and the formation of retailing alliances, the product mix in REC stores is moving away from the traditional emphasis on white goods to a more balanced white and brown goods mix. According to the Norweb Annual Report and Accounts for 1992/93:

> *NORWEB has a long record of success in retail. Its historic strength has been in white goods (cookers, freezers, washing machines), where we have always had a significant share of the local market. We have considerably expanded our presence in the important brown goods market (audio goods, televisions, camcorders) . . . Our range now includes most of the leading brands, and we more than doubled sales of brown goods during 1992/93.*

The decision by the RECs to compete more aggressively in retailing has prompted their major competitors to claim that the RECs are competing unfairly. Retailing is a comparatively small part of the overall business of the RECs, which make much the largest share of their revenue from the distribution of electricity. Although electricity distribution is being slowly opened to competition, for the majority of customers the REC remains a monopoly supplier.

It has been claimed that the RECs are cross-subsidising their retailing activities from their monopoly electricity supply business. This is a difficult charge to refute, since the primary purpose for the high street presence of the RECs was originally to provide a 'front office' function for the electricity distribution business. Electrical appliance retailing was a secondary activity which helped to spread the cost of maintaining a high street presence. Naturally, the RECs claim that there is no cross-subsidisation, and that the retailing operations are bearing the full cost of their operations. However, it is difficult to disentangle the costs involved where, for example, the REC provides bill-paying facilities in a retail outlet and the distribution business pays a transfer charge to the retail business for the use of the space.

SHAKEOUT?

Most economic forecasters expect the UK economy to grow slowly in the mid-1990s, with no return to the boom conditions of the late 1980s. Consumer confidence – an intangible factor, but one which greatly affects the demand for consumer durables – shows signs of a fragile recovery in the short term. The demand for durable goods is likely to grow only slowly in the next few years. It would take rapid growth to save the sector from some kind of shakeout – whether in the form of a major competitor directly exiting the industry, or a merger taking significant sales capacity out of the system.

The 'quality' newspaper price war of 1994

Ross Brennan

KEY THEMES

- price competition
- price elasticity
- market segmentation and target marketing
- managing distribution channels

BRIEFING NOTES (Chapter 1)

- Buyer behaviour and market segmentation (pages 13–15)
- The importance of effective distribution (page 35)
- A marketing model for pricing decisions (pages 40–42)
- A note on price elasticity of demand (pages 42–43)

> *The dust is beginning to settle in the price war. All the gains that could be made appear now to have peaked. Similarly, according to the latest Audit Bureau of Circulations, all the falls have bottomed out.*
>
> (The *Guardian*, 17 October 1994)

By October 1994, the *Guardian* thought it safe to suggest that the virtually unprecedented price war among British 'quality' newspapers had come to an end. Only virtually unprecedented, since, more than 60 years before, the *Daily Telegraph* had marched into battle against *The Times* by announcing a price cut from 2d to 1d (that is, from roughly 1p to 0.5p). It has been suggested that the man who initiated the price war of 1993/94, Mr Rupert Murdoch, owner of *The Times* and the *Sun*, was inspired by the success of that precedent. The *Daily Telegraph* almost doubled its sales within two months in 1930, with most of the new readers coming from its main rival, *The Times*. If the dust had, indeed, settled by October 1994, then who might be judged the winners and the losers of this modern-day price war?

THE UK NEWSPAPER MARKET

The British are internationally famous for their adherence to the idea of 'class'.

Perhaps nowhere else is the notion of class so well represented as in the newspaper market. The 'middle classes' (broadly, socioeconomic groups ABC1) buy 'quality' newspapers which are typically produced in broadsheet format, and the 'working classes' (socioeconomic groups C2DE) buy 'popular' newspapers produced in the more convenient tabloid format. Between the qualities and the popular newspapers there lies a small group of middle-market newspapers. Table 2.5 indicates the extent to which these stereotypical views of newspaper readership are supported by the facts.

Table 2.5 UK national newspaper circulation (January–June 1993)

	Daily circulation (000s)	ABC1 % readership
Popular newspapers		
Daily Star	773	22
Sun	3517	22
Daily Mirror	2680	28
Today	538	43
Daily Express	1497	56
Daily Mail	1775	61
Quality newspapers		
Guardian	416	77
Independent	347	81
The Times	366	84
Daily Telegraph	1025	84
Financial Times	290	88

Source: *Marketing Pocket Book*, 1994, NTC Publications.

DISTURBING TRENDS IN THE MARKET

British newspaper proprietors faced a challenging marketing problem in the 1990s. Although costs were being controlled by investing in new technology and by overcoming restrictive labour practices (and, in the process, moving the heart of the industry from its famous home in Fleet Street to Wapping in East London), no formula had been found to overcome a downward trend in sales (*see* Table 2.6).

One or two titles seemed capable of avoiding the trend in the market, but the overall picture was clear. While loss of circulation is bad enough in its own right, the problem is magnified in the newspaper business where sales of advertising space are closely tied to circulation figures. When a single newspaper loses circulation to its rivals, its position in the market for advertising can be seriously compromised. The consequences of a general decline in newspaper circulation are no less serious for newspapers in general. Proprietors of alternative advertising and promotional media, such as specialist magazines, radio stations and poster sites, are quick to point out when the audiences reached by newspapers are in decline. The position of *The Times* was doubly

Table 2.6 National newspaper circulation trends 1987–92

	1987	1988	1989	1990	1991	1992
Daily Star	1 137	967	891	912	838	798
Sun	4 045	4 219	4 107	3 855	3 665	3 544
Daily Mirror	3 128	3 157	3 092	3 083	2 881	2 762
Today	340	548	589	540	460	545
Daily Express	1 690	1 637	1 575	1 585	1 519	1 512
Daily Mail	1 810	1 759	1 723	1 708	1 684	1 737
Guardian	460	438	431	424	410	413
Independent	361	387	412	411	372	368
The Times	447	436	428	420	387	379
Daily Telegraph	1 169	1 127	1 103	1 076	1 058	1 036
Financial Times	307	278	288	289	287	286
Total	14 894	14 953	14 549	14 303	13 561	13 380

difficult in that it seemed to be slowly losing market share in the declining market. Perhaps one of the reasons for *The Times'* bold price-cutting strategy can be found here.

WAR AMONGST THE QUALITY PAPERS

The Times is owned by Rupert Murdoch's News Corporation, which also owns the *Sun*. In July 1993 the News Corporation had instigated a price war in the tabloid newspaper market by cutting the price of the *Sun* from 25p to 20p. Over the subsequent months the circulation of the *Sun* increased, adding daily sales of 400 000 between July and December 1993. In August 1993, *The Times* carried out an experiment in parts of Kent, selling the newspaper at 30p (rather than 45p), and seeing sales increase by 14 per cent as a result. Armed with this research, on 6 September 1993 the price-cutting strategy was extended nationally, with the price of the daily newspaper cut from 45p to 30p, and the price of the Saturday issue cut from 50p to 40p. It had been virtually an article of faith in the newspaper business that people do not buy papers on price. Readers were believed to select their paper on the basis of its editorial coverage and political leanings, and price was thought to be very much a secondary consideration. So the decision of *The Times* to opt for a discount price was contrary to the conventional wisdom of the industry. The objectives of *The Times* in pursuing such an aggressive strategy were not entirely clear. While it might seem obvious that the aim was to generate an increased share of the market, which would largely be won at the expense of the market leader – the *Daily Telegraph* – it was also suggested that *The Times* might be aiming to force the *Independent* out of business. The News Corporation strategy appears even bolder when one considers that the general trend in newspaper prices had been upwards. The *Daily Telegraph* increased its price from 45p to 48p in February 1993, the *Guardian* went from 40p to 45p in March, and both the *Daily*

Mail and the *Daily Express* increased price by 2p during the summer of 1993.

The response of rival newspapers to the price cuts at *The Times* was to claim that it was a short-term and desperate measure, that readers did not buy on the basis of price, and – in the case of the *Independent* – to claim that the action was anti-competitive (a charge later rejected by the Office of Fair Trading). What rivals pointedly avoided, at least in the short term, were price cuts. However, it turned out that British newspaper readers were perhaps not so insensitive to price as had been thought.

Table 2.7 shows comparative circulation figures for the six-month period within which the price war started, and for the comparable period one year earlier. By comparing the same six-month period of the year it is possible to avoid the problem of seasonality in newspaper sales. However, since there is a trend in the data (broadly, the volume of newspapers sold is declining over time) it would be slightly misleading simply to compare the two periods directly. The total volume of newspapers sold declined by about 0.6 per cent between the two periods, which is slightly less than would have been expected on the basis of the long-term trend in sales. In other words, the total market for news-

Table 2.7 Changes in newspaper circulation

	Circulation average, August 1993–January 1994	Circulation average, August 1992–January 1993
Daily Star	763 308	704 631
Sun	3 833 581	3 552 749
Daily Mirror	2 544 731	2 743 384
Today	563 138	539 907
Daily Express	1 409 665	1 510 898
Daily Mail	1 710 816	1 743 588
Guardian	399 508	415 970
Independent	316 623	364 721
The Times	430 388	376 956
Daily Telegraph	1 019 449	1 038 104
Financial Times	287 039	287 321
Total	13 278 246	13 278 229

Source: Audit Bureau of Circulations data.

papers would probably have declined further but for the price cuts at the *Sun* and *The Times*.

To talk of a price war implies some shots fired by more than one side. Belatedly, the *Daily Telegraph* and the other quality newspapers responded in kind. In April and May 1994, estimates put the circulation of the *Daily Telegraph* below 1 million for the first time in 40 years. The cover price of the *Telegraph* was cut from 48p to 30p on Thursday 23 June. The *Independent*, known to be financially less stable than its rivals, experimented with a cut in price to 20p (from 50p) for one day only on 23 June. For that one day, the *Independent* claimed a 15 per cent increase in circulation. The *Daily Telegraph* claimed that its price cut resulted in a 10 per cent boost in circulation. However, it is unlikely that either the *Telegraph* or *The Independent* expected to see such a rapid and aggressive response from *The Times*. On Friday 24 June the cover price of *The Times* was cut from 30p to 20p, where it remained in October 1994 when the *Guardian* suggested that the price war was at an end.

FALL-OUT FROM THE PRICE WAR

The Times ensured that newspaper vendors did not suffer financially as a result of its price-cutting strategy. Had the vendors been expected to contribute to the price cut by accepting a lower profit margin, they would have had less incentive to sell *The Times* and this might have adversely affected sales. Once the June 1994 price cut had been implemented it is estimated that News Corporation was receiving only 2.5p for every copy of *The Times* sold, with the remaining 17.5p of the cover price going to the news trade. Before the price war began News Corporation received 27.5p out of the cover price of 45p, with the trade margin still at 17.5p.

However, the fall-out affecting the middle market newspapers appears to have been much more serious. While the *Daily Telegraph* and the *Independent* are considered to be the closest rivals to *The Times*, and were expected to suffer in the price war, both the *Daily Mail* and the *Daily Express* also suffered circulation declines. The original price cut from 45p to 30p made *The Times* cheaper than both the *Mail* and the *Express* (at 32p). The further price cut to 20p meant the 'quality' paper was more than a third cheaper than the two middle-market tabloids. At the same time, of course, the price of the *Sun* had been cut to 20p in July 1993. While both *The Times* and the *Sun* primarily target different readers from the *Express* and the *Mail*, the suspicion grew that some middle market readers were moving 'up' to *The Times*, and others were moving 'down' to the *Sun*.

Although it appears that a transfer of readers between newspaper 'categories' may have taken place, from the *Mail* and the *Express* to *The Times* and the *Sun*, it is interesting that two of the 'quality' papers were largely unaffected. Both the *Guardian* and the *Financial Times* stood aloof from the price war, and neither of them seems to have suffered as a result. The *Financial Times* is, arguably, a very specialist newspaper which offers unique benefits to a well-defined target market. The loyalty of *Guardian* readers is perhaps a little more surprising, since one might characterise it as a direct rival to *The Times* and the *Daily Telegraph*. However, the *Guardian* is unique amongst British quality newspapers in adopting a left-of-centre political stance. The evidence of the price war of 1993 and 1994 is that *Guardian* readers are particularly loyal, which suggests that the newspaper is, for them, differentiated from its rivals in some important way.

WHO WON THE WAR?

News Corporation has invested considerable sums of money in the newspaper price war. A 5p cut in the price of the *Sun* costs around £200 000 a day in lost revenue; at 30p the revenue generated from sales of *The Times* was around £120 000 per day, compared to £180 000 per day at a cover price of 45p. As economic theory suggests, the price cuts have boosted sales to some extent, by an estimated 23 per cent in the case of *The Times* and an estimated 10 per cent for the *Sun*. For the national newspaper industry as a whole, Harry Henry, writing in *Admap*, (April 1994), concluded that:

> It is not difficult to work out . . . that for the national dailies together, with circulation increased by 1.0 per cent and cover price decreased by 3.9 per cent, total consumer expenditure on the purchase of those national dailies has decreased from the 'expected' level by three per cent.

Even though *The Times* did manage to boost its market share, each percentage point share of the market was bought at great expense. Opinion within the industry was that any increase in advertising revenues attracted by the boost in circulation would be dwarfed by the revenue lost through the cover price reductions.

Just as in the case of many other wars, it is not difficult to find losers, but trying to identify winners is a more difficult task. Nor does it appear that the long-term trend decline in the sales of newspapers has been significantly affected. Perhap the only group which had unambiguously benefited was newspaper buyers.

Taiwai SA

James Patterson

KEY THEMES

- distribution channels for consumer goods
- market development strategy
- identifying and communicating with target markets
- marketing planning

BRIEFING NOTES (Chapter 1)

- Market research target markets and marketing communications (pages 31–33)
- Trends in retailing (pages 37–39)
- The marketing planning process (page 44)
- Identifying strategic options using SWOT (page 46)

Taiwai SA is a South Korean conglomerate which was only included in the Fortune 500 for the first time some five years ago, but which now stands at a ranking position of 73rd.[1] The range of products manufactured and distributed by the company is considerable, although very little up to now has been sold under, and therefore been identified with, the company name, even within its own country. Its products therefore reflect little or no corporate identity, relying rather on a variety of brand names. The main areas of business tend to be in consumables and in consumer durables, but as with many companies of this type, there are interests in banking, shipping, freight forwarding, hotels and tourism and even in coal mining. Historically, the company is relatively young as it developed through a number of brilliant acquisitions. Its component companies are household names in South Korea having been both successful and profitable for the past 30 years, principally in the clothing industry.

For the purposes of this analysis, the main interest is in a recent major acquisition of a prominent sports shoe manufacturer. This company has very modern and profitable production facilities just outside the capital city of Seoul located some 200 miles from their own head office and major warehousing and distribution centre. This company has been absorbed within the Taiwai organisation, which is now most anxious that this new acquisition should not only continue but surpass its own very profitable performance.

THE NEW SPORTS SHOE DIVISION OF TAIWAI SA

The sports shoe division was formed two years ago when Taiwai bought out the Yan San Shoe Company, merging it with a smaller operation it already owned and which also manufactured sports shoes and components. Both these companies are near to each other and have a very skilled and loyal workforce.

Details concerning the past five years of operations are given in Table 2.8, as well as current projections for the market. Export sales are illustrated in Table 2.9. Although there were different accounting periods and practices in the two companies, these have been taken into consideration and the consolidated figures are reasonably accurate.

The takeover was harmonious, as demand remained buoyant and apart from some management changes and retirements, the staff have not been affected. Order books have remained full and present customers seem to have remained loyal and unaffected so far by the changes.

THE PRODUCTS

The company makes an extensive range of sports shoes including football and rugby boots, tennis, badminton and squash shoes as well as special sports shoes and trainers of all types. It makes shoes in all price ranges and to

Table 2.8 The Taiwai company

Year end December	Turnover £000	Pre-tax profit £000
1988*	47 300	3 457
1989*	53 100	3 799
1990*	59 010	4 335
1991	86 311	6 429
1992	97 000	8 325
1993 (projected)	110 000	10 150

* Combined figures for Taiwai and Yan San Shoe Co.

Table 2.9 Taiwai SA: Sales by destination, 1992

Country	Sales £m
S Korea	29.1
USA	21.3
UK	13.6
Other W European	11.6
SE Asia	9.7
Others	11.7
Total	97.0

different quality specifications. The company boasts that it is in the forefront of technology and that it is able to react as quickly as any of its rivals to changes in taste, fashion need or craze.

All of its products carry other firms' brand names abroad. In South Korea, products bear the brand names owned by the companies it has taken over. They are made to designs and rigid specifications negotiated with international buyers. These buyers are many and varied but as the setting up costs of manufacture tend to be very expensive their orders must be large enough to justify this, otherwise changes in the production process become uneconomical.

MARKET RESEARCH

Since the takeover and the function of the Sports Shoe Division, Taiwai, in the realisation of fow far it is from its main markets, has been conducting extensive worldwide research of this market to:

1 familiarise itself with the market;
2 attempt to identify any general trends, changes which may occur in the near future.

The major findings which cause immediate concern have been identified as follows:

- All the products are 'own' brand with the exception of the Korean market, which represents about 30 per cent of the division's sales. These own-brand products have no consumer identification of the manufacturer but have the buyer's brand on them and are often endorsed by local sporting heros in their appropriate sports.
- Buyers have little loyalty to their suppliers if they are not able to get what they want at the right price and could, with little or no notice, move their business to a cheaper country/source of supply.
- Buyers can also go bust and are of course subject to economic ups and downs in their own countries.
- Taiwai knows very little about what happens to its products once they leave the factory especially as most are bought on terms 'ex factory gates' or 'ex works'. The company therefore has no practical knowledge about foreign markets, wholesalers, retailers, trading terms, conventions, the distribution structure or trading laws. Even the UK, where it has been doing business for over ten years with increasing success, is still a completely unknown market.
- A good, rapid and accurate distribution service in this global market is the key to successful marketing. If the right goods are not in the right place at the right time, the best advertising and promotion in the world will not make the sale.

MANAGEMENT ACTION

In view of the above findings, management as a priority has made the following decisions:

1 The company should launch its own brand of sports shoes at the middle to upper end of the market in both price and quality. This is not because it wishes to either upset or harm its customers' own markets but
    (a) as an insurance should one or some of its major customers move their business elsewhere;
    (b) to gain a more intimate knowledge of the market, retailer and consumer trends and
    (c) to publicise its own new brand name 'Athletico'.
2 It should enter the British market first, even though it is not the biggest for the company's products. It does take the widest variety and is not as competitive as other markets. The company also feels that by starting here it will be able to retain other national markets should the venture be unsuccessful, so limiting any damage to this one area.
3 This operation should be undertaken as soon as possible as there are already indications that buyers are looking elsewhere for supplies, particularly in the Republic of China and Indonesia.

As a first stage in the implementation of the objective of entering the British market, the company has decided to set up a subsidiary in the UK with a small office in the City of London, near the Tower of London. This British-registered company would be able to share office space, at least initially with the branch of the shipping and forwarding operation of the parent company. The latter has been established in the city for at least seven years.

Although the above mentioned is a British-registered company, all the shares are owned by the parent company. However, it has been made clear that as soon as possible it should be able to stand on its own two feet and be a profit centre.

All shoe products destined for the British market should therefore in future be channelled through this new office, whether they be branded or unbranded (customer own-branded) products, which would give it some very useful information about customers and market trends. The company should always deal 'at arms length' with the parent, buying as a customer but on most favoured terms.

This will enable the subsidiary to:

- buy and sell currency forward on the money market should that be advantageous, especially in times when there are major fluctuations in the value, even though most of the company transactions are carried out in dollars
- invoice its customers according to British conventions, in sterling and with the appropriate VAT as required
- communicate and negotiate in English from a local base
- act as a conduit between the manufacturer and the customers providing clearing and forwarding facilities in UK.

For the above purposes it was considered essential to hire a top-class British team to run Taiwai (UK) Ltd or TUL as it soon became known.

THE TUL MANAGEMENT TEAM

Fred Uppers had for many years worked for a major shoe company. Aged 45 years, he was looking for a career change especially now that his daughter had recently been married and there were just him and his wife left to look after. Although he was looking for a change, he was also a realist and knew that with 20 years experience in the shoe business ending as Footwear Sales Manager (south east region), he wanted to capitalise on that knowledge and experience.

Looking through the trade press, he spotted the job advertisement inserted by Taiwai for the position of Managing Director of the UK operation, with a very attractive remuneration package including fringe benefits. As a young man he had served in the Intelligence Corps in the army in Korea where he had learnt both Korean and Chinese, which enhanced his suitability for the position.

Fred Uppers was offered the post on a five-year contract (renewable) and started as soon as he could, after negotiating severance from his previous employer, on 1 May 1994. He was to report directly to the main board but had the services of a senior Korean accountant as his number two and fellow director. At the start-up they decided to share a secretary and employed an office junior as well. They were advised to increase the staff as and when it became necessary.

Fred was determined that TUL should first, and foremost, be a marketing organisation and that therefore the first new recruit should be a marketing person to help establish the company on that track. He chose Fiona Sole, a recently qualified marketer with an impressive academic record as well as good practical marketing experience with one of the major FMCG manufacturers, as his assistant. He also recruited William Slipper to handle all the current business as well as any future own-label business as a full-time administrator who would eventually take over all the documentation, clearance invoicing and payment aspects of the business.

Apart from these appointments, he was reluctant to add any more staff, especially as their premises were not exactly palatial and additional staff might mean that he would have to move. This would result in higher running costs and as he was on an earnings-related bonus it would affect him personally, and he had to remember the keen prices the company was offering, the consequent low margins and the high cost of market entry with the branded range Athletico.

Fiona Sole's initial responsibility was to undertake some desk research to ascertain the trends in the market in order for Fred to prepare a report considering the various options open to the company in setting up a distribution system, both to the UK and also within the UK, with recommendations to present to the board.

Taiwai internal memo

From	: Fiona Sole
To	: Fred Uppers
Date	: 12 March
Subject	: Report on size of footwear market

The size of the UK footwear market is approximately £4 billion per annum. Per capita expenditure on footwear has increased steadily over the past five years. Last year spending was just under £63.00 per head.

More than three-quarters sold by volume is imported, a proportion that has been increasing over the past five years. The need for UK manufacturers to source products from overseas has been driven by the increased competition from imported goods. It is not only at the lower end of the market that this has been occurring. Foreign shoes, particularly those from countries such as Italy, are perceived to be of better quality than UK manufactured products, and demand for these goods is quite high.

The average increase in the value of footwear imports has fluctuated around 12 per cent over the last five years. Last year, however, the figure was approaching 20 per cent, denoting a significant rise. HM Customs and Excise figures suggest that given the current trend, imports are likely to grow by at least 10 per cent in value terms next year.

This trend is apparent when examining the change in the market by volume. The exception was in 1989, when imports fell due to over-supply at the lower end of the market. This was in sharp contrast to the following year when growth of just over 19 per cent was achieved. (See Table 2.10.)

Table 2.10 Sources of footwear imports (last year)

	Million pairs	%	£ million	%
Italy	50.5	19.3	372.3	26.8
South Korea	24.6	9.4	158.7	11.4
Spain	26.4	10.1	152.5	11.0
Portugal	13.4	5.1	109.0	7.8
Taiwan	15.3	5.8	83.5	6.0
Brazil	10.1	3.9	59.1	4.3
Thailand	16.0	6.1	40.6	2.9
France	4.6	1.8	39.5	2.8
Indonesia	21.2	8.1	39.4	2.8
Germany	4.1	1.6	38.7	2.8
Hong Kong	11.2	4.2	12.5	0.9
China	4.6	1.8	4.2	0.3
Other	59.6	22.8	277.5	20.0

Fred knows that the company is keen to catch major sales and is already tooling up for the new range. The company is also prepared to speculate a considerable amount on advertising the new brand. However, Fred knows that the existing prices and products have been well tested in the market, although under different brand names in a wide variety of outlets.

Taiwai internal memo

From	: Fiona Sole
To	: Fred Uppers
Date	: 15 March
Subject	: Analysis of market by sector

I have managed to obtain the following information from various industry sources and publications. It relates to the market breakdown by sector.

The recession has affected the footwear market quite badly. Particularly hard hit was the women's sector. In general the children's sector remained relatively buoyant. As the country has slowly eased out of recession, it is the women's market that has experienced the most significant growth.

Demographic projections indicate that the number of children in the key 0–5 age bracket is set to increase in the next five years. This, coupled with the expected growth in disposable income, is likely to be responsible for increased growth in the women's sector. It is also anticipated that they will tend to trade up to higher quality brands.

Year-on-year analysis of the value of the market share by each sector shows that the women's shoe sector accounts for about 43 per cent of the market, men 47 per cent and children 10 per cent. Segmenting by volume shows the reverse picture, women's shoes (47 per cent) account for a larger proportion than men's (43 per cent). This indicates that women buy more pairs of shoes than men per year, but men are prepared to pay more per pair.

Interestingly, if trainers are taken out of the equation, the analysis is different. In volume terms, 40 per cent of the men's shoes by value are in the trainer category, 10 per cent of women's, and 15 per cent of children's. The sports shoe sector is still experiencing significant growth (about 15 per cent per annum), although this has slowed compared to the early 1990's when growth peaked at 24 per cent (1990/91). This trend corresponds to the rise in popularity of the sports shoe for leisure wear, rather than sport use. Sports shoes now account for just over one-third of all sales.

Taiwai internal memo

From   : Fiona Sole
To   : Fred Uppers
Date   : 23 March
Subject   : Consumer profile of footwear expenditure

I have managed to locate the following figures for 1993 and 1994.

Average weekly expenditure on footwear was £3.48 per household in 1993 and £3.65 per household in 1994.

This can be broken down by household income category as shown in Table 2.11.

Mean weekly expenditure was £2.74 in households without children, and £4.97 in households with children.

Looking at regional expenditure patterns, it seems that levels are on average 15 per cent higher in Greater London than elsewhere, reflecting both the greater level of prosperity and the higher retail outlet rents. Scotland and Northern Ireland also have high levels of spending on average. Expenditure is lowest in the south west.

Table 2.11 Footwear expenditure by income category

Gross weekly income	Footwear expenditure (average weekly) 1993	Footwear expenditure (average weekly) 1994
less than £45	1.02	0.75
£45 to £59.99	1.41	0.76
£60 to £79.99	1.41	1.44
£80.00 to £99.99	1.64	1.44
£100 to £124.99	2.21	1.76
£125 to £174.99	2.40	2.34
£175 to £224.99	2.78	2.34
£225 to £274.99	2.90	3.94
£275 to £324.99	3.70	3.46
£325 to £374.99	4.03	4.04
£375 to £424.99	4.30	4.74
£425 to £474.99	5.12	4.48
£475 to £549.99	6.19	5.57
£550 to £624.99	6.07	5.93
£625 to £749.99	5.58	7.02
greater than £750	7.90	6.96

Taiwai internal memo

From	: Fiona Sole
To	: Fred Uppers
Date	: 26 March
Subject	: Report on retail distribution

There are over 12 000 retail outlets in the UK, operated by just under 4000 businesses. The majority of outlets are independents, there being only 10 significant multiple retail groups in this market. These specialists account for 60 per cent of the market by value, independents 10 per cent, and department stores 15 per cent. The British Shoe Corporation is the largest multiple retailer, operating twice the number of shops of its nearest rivals, C&J Clark and Oliver.

Expert product knowledge and the necessity for fitting skills are attributed to the preponderance of specialist outlets. This is particularly evident in the children's market, where correct fitting is perceived to be essential. This is interesting, in the light of a recent *Which?* report which demonstrated a substantial degree of variability of standards between fitting 'experts' in a sample of shops. The value attributed to correct fitting has led department stores to encourage the opening of in-store concessions such as Dolcis and Saxone. In the summer months, when the majority of sales are sandals and canvas shoes, the share of sales made by non-specialist outlets increases.

Mail order accounts for 10 per cent of the market. This proportion is unlikely to increase since customers strongly prefer to try before they buy.

Sales of sports footwear by outlet follows a different pattern. This is mainly due to the role of specialist sportswear chains, both retail outlets and concessions within department stores, such as Olympus and Champion.

The growth in the wearing of sports footwear for leisure purposes has resulted in a swing of sales towards the department stores, in particular to high street clothing stores operating concessions within their shops. Despite this, specialist shoe retailers remain dominant in this sector as well.

Outlet type	per cent Sales by value
Shoe shops	36
Sports shops	24
Department stores	26
Mail order	9
Other	5

Taiwai internal memo

From	: Fiona Sole
To	: Fred Uppers
Date	: 30 March
Subject	: Details on brands and manufacturers

As requested in your memo dated 26 March, I have been able to locate the following information to expand on the previous information.

There are over 750 footwear manufacturers in the UK. The UK output is relatively low on an international scale. Each British manufacturer accounts for only a very small proportion of total production.

In the past footwear retailers and manufacturing groups were closely tied together. However, following the sale of British Shoe Corporation's (BSC) manufacturing interests to a management buy-out this has changed.

BSC has slowly been losing market share to competitors. Its main problems stem from the large number of outlets and staff. It is interesting to note the continued growth of Marks & Spencer's market share, now standing at around 7 per cent.

There are very few established brands in the market. Perhaps only Clark's (C&J Clark) and Hush Puppies (BSC) are really well known. Even these are sold within the manufacturing companies' outlets. Clark's is particularly strong in the children's sector where, like Startrite Shoes, its name is associated with quality. The majority of shoes are sold under the name of the individual retailer selling them. The only exception is the sportswear market, where brands do predominate. Three companies are battling for leadership, namely Reebok, Nike and Hi-Tec. All three hold similar market shares of about 15 per cent. Recently, Hi-Tec has edged ahead as consumers have tended to trade down to cheaper models.

Taiwai internal memo

From   : Fiona Sole
To   : Fred Uppers
Date   : 2 April
Subject   : Advertising

I hope that this information does not come too late to be collated in your final report, it was quite difficult to find.

Media advertising exceeds £10 million annually. The balance of advertising spending has shifted from general shoes to sports shoes. This has been in response to the massive advertising campaigns led by Reebok and Nike in the early 1990s. Spending for these companies last year stood at over £3 million each. There is additional spend in the specialist sports press on advertising sports-specific footwear. This is not accounted for in the statistics. An example would be football boots.

Clarks and K Shoes (both C&J Clark) brands are advertised most heavily in the non-sports sector. Spend last year stood at approximately £2 million on each.

Please let me know if you require any further information. I realise that time is short, but I have amassed considerable amounts of documentation and some useful contacts.

---

1 The Fortune 500 is an annual ranking of the top 500 international companies conducted by *Fortune* magazine in the USA. Recently an increasing number of companies from the newly developing economies of the world have featured in this ranking, demonstrating their penetration of global markets.

Famagusta Bakery Ltd

Ghalib Fahad

KEY THEMES

- marketing in small and medium-sized enterprises
- marketing objectives and strategy
- market segmentation and target marketing
- pricing strategy

BRIEFING NOTES (Chapter 1)

- Buyer behaviour and market segmentation (pages 13–15)
- Market research, target markets and marketing communications (pages 31–33)
- A marketing model for pricing decisions (pages 40–42)
- Setting objectives and devising strategies (pages 45–46)

DEVELOPMENT OF THE COMPANY

Famagusta Bakery Ltd was founded in 1956 by Mr Georgiou Kyriakos, two years after emigrating to England from Cyprus. Georgiou, who was born in the beautiful town of Famagusta in Cyprus in 1922, came to England to work in his uncle's grocery corner shop in Finsbury Park in north London. This period was to see large immigration to the UK especially from former colonies and the Commonwealth. Many of the Greek cypriots who migrated to England seem to have headed for north London.

While working for his uncle, Georgiou realised that many food items were imported either from Greece or Cyprus. The goods often took time to arrive and, when stocks ran out, customers simply had to wait until they arrived. Many were happy to wait since they considered the food items from the 'old country' to be superior and were those that could not be directly produced by British manufacturers. Items which young Georgiou felt he would be able to duplicate almost like the home-recipes were the manufacture of Greek pitta bread and sweets. Before joining his uncle in England, Georgiou had worked for a traditional baker in Cyprus who was renowned for making the finest bread and sweets in Famagusta. On joining the old baker, Georgiou was made to take an oath that he would not disclose the baking recipe used nor would he, while the old baker lived, directly set up a bakery in competition.

One Sunday without telling his uncle, Georgiou decided to visit a friend whereupon he set out to bake some bread using the old recipe taught him by the old baker. Despite the limitation of having to work with ordinary utensils and cooker, he was able to produce some pitta bread and sweets almost exactly as had been shown him by the old baker. At dinner that evening, young Georgiou brought out the sample of bread and sweets and asked his uncle and wife and their two boys for their opinions. His uncle upon tasting the bread admonished the young man for having spent so much money on what he considered to be expensive items. That evening was to mark the start of the Famagusta Bakery because having convinced his uncle of the fact that he baked and produced the items, it was agreed that young Georgiou would bake a few items each week for sale in his uncle's shop.

Thus in July 1956, Georgiou began producing pitta bread and selected Greek sweets in the shed behind his uncle's shop. The bread and sweets proved to be a success with the few customers who were willing to give the new products a trial. A few months after starting, word-of-mouth recommendations produced a few more customers and it was then that both Georgiou and his uncle decided that it was time to hire a shop that would be more appropriate to the business.

In November 1956, with a loan of £500 from his uncle and on condition that he took one of his uncle's sons Theo as a partner, the Famagusta bakery was born. The bakery was only some 500 yards away from his uncle's shop and within easy reach of other major Greek shops. Georgiou decided that in order to break into this ethnic market, it was best to keep production to pitta and other types of bread that were much in demand. He immediately set about convincing local shop owners to accept his bread by lowering his prices but not the quality of his bread. At the same time, Georgiou realised that many of the immigrants were steeped in Greek traditions and their observation. So it was that whenever he heard of an occasion, Georgiou would send gifts of pitta bread and specially made sweets to the organisers of such festivities.

By the end of 1957, most small shop-keepers within north London were stocking Famagusta bread and sweets. This was the result of the policy by Georgiou to deliver fresh-baked bread directly to these shop-keepers as and when needed. By this time, the second of his uncle's sons, Peter, had joined the company bringing the total number of people to five. At the end of that year, Famagusta Bakery realised sales of some £7500, of which 85 per cent were for bread products.

In 1960, Georgiou realised that sales were levelling off at about £25 000 per annum and that the company had secured most of the market in north London. Also, two or more competitors had entered the market and were producing very similar products to the company. He felt it was time to expand the company in order to counter the competition and consolidate his position in the marketplace. In that belief, Georgiou approached his bankers, the Bank of Cyprus in Finsbury Park, for a loan to move to bigger premises. A loan of £15 000 was made to him by the bank which allowed him to convert an old building within Finsbury Park and to purchase new equipment. Despite his busy schedule, Georgiou still found the time to marry a girl whom had been recommended by his uncle and aunt. His wife's relations were relatively well-off and owned a number of grocery stores both in north and south London and in Birmingham.

By 1965, the company had some 20 employees and a turnover of about £75 000. Through his wife's relations, Famagusta Bakery had been able in 1964 to secure the custom of a number of Greek and Asian shop-keepers in Birmingham where the pitta bread was finding a ready-made segment in the form of new Asian migrants. It is in this new segment of the market that Georgiou hoped his company would achieve growth and which would allow it to become the major player in this niche market.

Throughout the 1970s, the company continued to expand both in terms of sales and number of employees. By 1975, the company had annual sales of £550 000 and a workforce of 35 full- and part-time employees. In keeping with Georgiou's philosophy, the office staff had been kept to a minimum with only one full-time secretary to look after the entire communications of the company and a part-time accountant to look after the wages and taxation. Georgiou believed that management had to be close to its employees and therefore ensured that the two-roomed office was close to the factory floor.

However, by the early 1980s it had become clear that the present accommodation was not sufficient for the type of expansion envisaged for the company. The company capitalised on the local authority policy of helping with relocation and expansion costs by moving to specifically designed council premises in 1986. With demand buoyant, the company continued to increase its labour force and today employs some 70 full- and part-time staff.

MANAGEMENT AND ORGANISATION

From the very start of the company, Georgiou ensured that he was fully in charge of not just the day-to-day running of the company but all the major decisions. Even when his two cousins joined the company, they were more like employees than equal partners.

In the first four to five years of the company's existence, absolute control by Georgiou was seen as essential since all the company's product emanated from him. Indeed, Theo would be the first to recognise that at the initial stages all the successes were due to the far-sightedness of Georgiou. This encompassed the products that were produced as well as the way customers were secured for the company. Even the first loan granted to the company was secured on the understanding that Georgiou would remain in complete charge of the company.

By the mid-1960s when demand for the company's products was increasing, Georgiou's style of management was proving to be too much of a burden on him since he insisted in making all the decisions himself including answering customer queries. The result was that sometimes he would leave the office to go to see a customer thereby holding up production since he insisted on inspecting the quality of, for example, the dough, the level of sugar content and so on before the manufacture of each run of product.

In 1967 as a result of a confrontation between Georgiou and Theo, it was agreed that Theo would be in charge of customer queries and complaints. Initially even this delegation proved to be a problem since Georgiou insisted on being detailed on the visits and the nature of each enquiry. However, production problems soon forced him to give up this responsibility completely.

The decision to expand the company's activities in the 1970s had forced Georgiou to employ a part-time accountant but again with a limited scope of responsibility. The accountant merely prepared the accounts, wages, VAT returns and other financial reports but was not a member of the board nor was he invited to any of the decision meetings.

In 1977, as a result of the growing rift between the cousins, Georgiou decided to buy out his two cousins. The parting was amicable but left a wide gap in the company since Theo had been there from the very beginning and knew most of the intricacies of operating in this market. For a time, Georgiou had to seek the help of his wife's two younger brothers in order to successfully run the business. This period saw Georgiou positively encouraging his 15-year-old son Demitros to visit the factory since the boy had shown no inclination for school work and was by now truanting a great deal. He was heartened by the boy's interest in the business and his ability to grasp the complex nature of the market.

By 1980 Georgiou, in order to continue his consolidation of the market, agreed to employ two qualified staff: a manager to look after production, and another to look after the general administration. Both were experienced men who had been made redundant by their companies but who were now prepared to accept more constrained positions. They were both required to report directly to Georgiou who still insisted on visiting the factory and in meeting with workers personally when they had problems.

In 1982, Georgiou suffered a mild heart-attack and was compelled by his doctor to take a two-week break. On his return, he realised that his company had not been bankrupted and in fact had operated smoothly without him. It was this that lead him to convene a family meeting in which for the first time in the company's history he officially constituted a board of directors consisting of five members: Georgiou (Chairman/ Managing Director), Demitros (Deputy MD/Marketing Director), Mrs Kyriakos (Deputy MD/Finance), Stefanos (Director of Production/Operations) and Petros (Director of General Administration).

A second heart attack in June 1985 forced Georgiou to hand over the reins to his now 23-year-old son Demitros. Upon taking control of the company, Demitros reconstituted the board adding two new members: his younger brother Louisou to replace his mother in the position of deputy MD/Director of Finance and Louisou's college friend John as Director of Marketing. The others remained in their current positions.

In 1991, as a result of the departure of the director of administration a new appointment was made in the form of Nicolas who was appointed as Director of Human Resources/General Administration. As before, his brief was limited to carrying out the paternal wishes of the founding father whereby all employees are treated as part of the family and problems were to be resolved in that context. Demitros felt for the first time that his present team is the right one to launch the company into 'the big time league'.

MARKETING ACTIVITIES

From the very beginning the company was hall-marked by quality and the need to serve the customer. Although Georgiou himself had no formal qual-ifications and could barely read and write, he set up his company in the belief that it had a good product to market and as long as it remained 'close' to the customer then it would continue to be a winner.

So it was that throughout the first decade of the business marketing was more in the form of being close to the customer. Georgiou personified all the marketing required: he contacted the customers himself and depended on word-of-mouth recommendations to do the rest. His key focus was fresh qual-ity and accessibility to customers. Although he used price as an initial com-petitive entry strategy, once the company became established he made his prices more competitive rather than being cheaper.

This broad strategy was to continue until the early 1970s when stiff com-petition and a general change in eating and shopping habits forced Georgiou to adopt a more systematic and formalised approach to his marketing activi-ties. In 1972, Georgiou became determined to make his company the major player in the Greek bread market and thus set about to produce a range of products that would satisfy the diverse Greek market. Much later, through his in-laws, he realised that the Asian market was a growing one and that his company could tap successfully into this segment. Therefore, there was a need to adopt a more formalised system of contacting the customer in addition to his personal solicitation of shops who would distribute his products. Thus he started sending out letters to community group leaders whom he had identi-fied as opinion leaders, informing them of his company and its activities; this was complemented by local advertising and leaflets and other promotional point-of-sale materials. This approach to marketing was carried out through-out the 1970s.

By the early 1980s, with the growth and expansion of activities and the entry of other people into the company and stiffer competition, there was a need for a more formal approach to marketing. Demitros and his team started by fine-tuning the company goals and in 1987 stated these as being:

(a) Famagusta Bakery Ltd is to become a major national bread manufactur-er by the 1990s, catering for both the established markets and new seg-ments to be identified.

(b) The company will continue the policy of the founder of producing high-quality products across the whole portfolio range in the belief that qual-ity and premium pricing are related.

(c) The company will continue to be competitive through its differential pricing strategy, new product introductions and targeting specific identified growth markets.

(d) The company intends to establish itself as a major supplier of own-label breads including pitta, French and other breads, especially to the large multiples.

(e) The company will continue to look after the welfare of its employees across the whole organisation and will ensure that their personal needs and goals are met by the company's activities and working environment.

(f) The company will remain a family-owned business and will continue operating well into the 21st century.

With these goals, the board moulded the following approach to the marketing mix elements.

Product

From its inception until the early 1980s, the company had some 35 different products in its portfolio. This diversity meant that long-run productions could not be achieved. In 1987, it was decided to rationalise the total number of product lines to the following:

- white bread
- rolls: plain and beniseed
- beniseed bread
- pitta bread: white, wholemeal and garlic
- French sticks
- naan breads
- sesame sticks
- Greek sweets (baclava).

This it was felt was more manageable and ensured that the board's resources were capable of determining the growth and development of the product range.

Pricing

Through its formative stages, the company used price as a competitive tool for entry into the market. In keeping with the founder's goal, the aim was to price the products at a level that could be afforded by the local shop-keeper and the Greek consumer. Thus, the first decade saw the use of cost-plus pricing method.

In the early 1980s, with changes taking place in the marketplace and in the profile of consumers, together with the learning experience that had been gained over the previous two decades, the pricing mechanism became more robust, encompassing the use of several methods. Although this process did not occur overnight, it was incorporated into the activities over a period of years. Today, management sees pricing as one of the weapons that can be used to reinforce the image and quality of the products.

Promotion

When the company was first set up, the overriding concern was to make the products available to consumers. Thus, in the early days, much emphasis was placed at the retail end of the business and the use of effective packaging to promote the company's name.

In the 1970s, the company began to use more limited forms of promotion including advertising in the local press and point-of-sale promotions. In the 1980s, the company began to use more visible forms of advertising including promotion on local radios in London and Birmingham. Also, the company began to use the emerging newspapers and magazines that were targeted at various ethnic groups.

In the 1990s, the company began to use sale promotions techniques such as 'money-off', 'free product' trials, coupons, etc. in a more systematic manner. Although at the moment the company merely uses these when it feels there is a need the board realises that there was gain to be made from boosting sales of products especially when the market was sluggish or being affected by seasonal factors.

However, over the years the company has steadily increased the total amount that it spends on promotions. Furthermore, the board has become aware of the need to promote itself more vigorously alongside the major multiples for whom it may be producing own-brands.

Distribution

From the very start, the company believed in making its products available to the selected segments. Initially, this was not a problem since the company dealt with a limited market (north London). Once the company started to expand to other parts of London and Birmingham, it became necessary to obtain means of transport in order to distribute the products. By the 1980s, the company had three vans which were used for the distribution of products.

No specific policy has been developed over the years about where the products are distributed. The company regards any channel of distribution as being a legitimate target as long as they met the company's financial requirements. It was as a result of this policy that in 1991 Demitros started contacting the major multiples with a view to becoming one of the manufacturers producing own-brands. This policy has paid off in so far as Safeway has agreed a five-year contract with the company to supply Safeway own brands for its London stores.

In 1993, through a similar approach the company secured a contract with Tesco to supply own-label white bread. However, after negotiating with the company Tesco agreed that after a period of five years both parties would review their position. Tesco was of the view that a successful working relationship might convince the company to accept producing exclusively for them. Tesco, like Marks & Spencer, was interested in introducing new snacks such as sesame sticks and biscuits in its stores to cater for the more discerning and well-travelled customer.

PROFILE OF THE UK BREAD MARKET

The bakery products market, according to Mintel (1992), is one of the largest food markets in the UK. In 1990, the retail market increased by four per cent and although consumption levels have remained relatively stable, there is considerable activity in the large and relatively unsegmented white bread sector.

Although bread is the major sector, between 1986 and 1990 cakes and morning goods took a great deal of the market share. In 1990 alone cakes were the best performing market sector with a seven per cent increase in value, marginally ahead of morning goods.

By value, the manufacturing of bread increased by 21 per cent since 1985 to £1 209 million at manufacturer selling price (msp) in 1988. Industry sources suspect that at 1992 retail prices sales were close to £2 625 million. A breakdown of consumption patterns according to NFS/Mintel (1991) since 1985 is shown in Table 2.12.

Table 2.12 Famagusta Bakery: bread sales by type

	1985 £m	1988 £m	1990 £m
White large unsliced	562.5	497.7	494.2
White small unsliced	149.0	199.2	229.4
White small sliced	25.3	30.2	36.6
Brown	207.0	254.0	250.8
Wholewheat/wholemeal	194.3	274.2	285.4
Other bread (pitta, etc.)	387.7	607.0	654.8
Buns/scones/teacakes	126.6	157.4	210.9

Table 2.12 shows the growth of certain types of bread including added-value such as granary, seeded bread, French/Vienna bread and pitta bread.

The reasons for the shift are:

(a) Demographic changes and the rise in the number of 5–14 year olds most of whom require packed lunches.
(b) Increase in the number of working women who are turning to other breads and morning goods.
(c) Major changes in eating habits and lifestyles .
(d) The move towards more healthy eating habits favouring more diverse breads including foreign ones.
(e) The greater availability of convenience foods.
(f) Increased foreign travel and media influences, heightening the consumer's awareness of exotic foods.

Surveys have shown that the UK population as a whole favours eating bread in the morning or at midday rather in the evening. Furthermore, it would appear that a sizeable proportion of the population is now familiar with other breads and use these more often than the case a decade ago.

COMPETITION

The two major industrial and plant bread bakers are Allied Bakeries and British Bakeries with some 70 per cent of the market share in wrapped products. This does not cover the majority of products sold from high street bakers and shops. According to Euromonitor (1992), the major players of white bread are: Allied Bakeries/RHM (Mother's Pride 10 per cent), Allied Bakeries/ABF (Sunblest eight per cent), Allied Bakeries (Kingsmill five per cent), Allied Bakeries (Hovis three per cent), own labels (43 per cent), and others (26 per cent).

Advertising spend by the industry tends to be mainly by the big manufacturers interested in protecting their brands against the in-roads being made by own labels. Thus for example in 1992, Allied Bakeries spent some £1.5 million on Kingsmill and another £1 million on Mighty White while British Bakeries spent over £1 million on two of its major bread brands.

While initially the major bakers were not interested in the production of foreign types of bread, the growth of this sector has attracted their attention. This trend has become more pronounced in the 1990s where in order to enter the market, for example, a number of purchases of small specialised bakers has resulted.

Although Famagusta Bakery is still family owned they are now faced with stiff competition, especially as a producer of own labels where most of the growth is predicted over the next decade. Furthermore, the fact that experts are predicting that growth will continue to be dominated by value-added products and healthier foods will continue to intensify competition and investment in this sector.

THE COMPANY'S PRESENT AND FUTURE POSITION

In 1994, after undertaking additional changes to the factory building and offices with the support of the local authority the board commissioned a consultant to undertake a study of the company and its future.

The consultant produced a SWOT analysis (see Table 2.13) in which he illustrated the key points that the board would have to examine. The report noted the strong position of the company having achieved sales growth of 10–20 per cent from 1985. Thus for example sales in 1989 stood at £2 338 million, 1990 £3 113 million, 1991 £3 251 million and 1992 £4 211 million, all reflecting a healthy growth by the company. Also, the company's financial position was satisfactory as shown by the Balance sheet and profit and loss account for 1992 (see Table 2.14). The key recommendation of the consultant was the need to examine the current marketing activities and how these were carried out. He felt that the present informal approach reflected a general weakness in the organisation structure and that this was likely to prove fatal, especially in the light of current competition and the securing of major multiple retail accounts.

Table 2.13 Famagusta Bakery – summary of SWOT analysis

Strenths	Weaknesses
• The company is well established in its niche market both in London and nationally.	• The building should have been modernised at the same time as new equipment was being brought into the company.
• The family environment has meant that there is a strong employee loyalty across the whole organisation.	• The organisation structure of the company is becoming cumbersome in the light of the markets in which they are now operating.
• The range of products has ensured that the company is not affected by a downturn in any single market.	• The company's present way of gathering and disseminating information has become outdated and may prove costly in the future when adequate information will be required to counter the competition.
• The company has invested in new equipment and machinery and is in a position to enter new market segments.	
• Management has been strengthened over the years and has helped in injecting some degree of professionalism in decision-making and planning.	• The growth of the company and the lack of direct control in respect of costs may prove fatal in segments where margins are tight and cost-savings add to total profitability.
• The founding father's desire to serve the customer has continued and is reflected in new product introductions.	• The company will need to decide whether they are to continue to produce their own brands or to become solely own-label producers.
• The company has become known for the quality of its products and for the reliability of its services.	
• The company is becoming more widely known to the major multiples.	• The present image of the company as a small family-owned Greek company will have to be dealt with as this may not be suitable when dealing with the major retailers.
• The product portfolio of the company means that it has product at different development and growth levels.	

Table 2.13 (continued)

Opportunities	Threats
• The company is now in a position to become a major producer of own labels for the retail multiples.	• The last decade has seen many entrants into this lucrative market including other ethnic entrepreneurs with similar resources and seemingly better organisations.
• The company can continue the process of consolidating its position in the niche markets.	
• The continuing trend towards healthier lifestyles provides the company with the opportunity of introducing new products with minimal risks.	• The big bakers are beginning to eye this market and it is likely that with the downturn in the other bread sectors would wish to diversify into this growth sector.
• The company should explore the possibility of a joint-venture in other European countries known to have large ethnic minorities.	• The increasing profitability of this sector may mean that the major multiples setting up their own manufacturing bases or taking over successful ones.
• The company should begin examining the possibility of setting up of factories elsewhere in the UK.	• Large European bakeries may enter the niche markets that have been identified by the company.
	• Though profitable, the company may expose itself if it were to decide to become an exclusive own label manufacturer.

Table 2.14 Famagusta Bakery: Financial position

Balance sheet as at 31 October 1992		Profit and loss account from November 1991 to October 1992		
Fixed assets				
	£			£
Goodwill	10 000	Turnover		4 201 700
Freehold property	419 000	Less cost of sales		
Plant and machinery	560 427		£	
Fixtures and equipments	75 000	Purchases	1 532 076	
Motor vehicles	95 571	Packaging	497 597	
	1 159 998	Wages	739 142	
		Distribution costs	308 230	
		Heat/fuel	100 175	
				3 177 220
Current assets				
Stock	82 500	Gross profit		1 024 480
Trade debtors	625 100			
VAT refundable	33 000	Administration and overhead expenses:		
Sundry	27 250	Plant repairs	42 590	
Cash-in-hand	2 000	Plant depreciation	73 120	
	769 850	Admin and salaries	180 660	
		Telephone	13 290	
		Print-postage	10 410	
Current/long-term liabilities:		Advertising	12 810	
		Motor expenses	43 400	
Trade creditors	655 842	Canteen expenses	18 800	
Others:		General repairs	24 267	
PAYE	28 100	Professional fees	28 360	
Hire purchase	2 750	Entertainment	4 670	
Sundry	72 920	Bad debt provision	29 700	
Bank overdraft	32 186	Rates/water	30 915	
RHM mortgages/loan	195 000	Insurance	9 060	
Deferred tax	58 140	Laundry	38 362	
Corporation tax	123 200	Interest on loans	89 488	
	1 168 138	Hire purchase	5 280	
		Subscriptions	2 840	
Total net assets:	761 710	Depreciation (F&F)	8 736	
		Depreciation (vehicles)	25 129	
Financed by:		Renovation of		
Share capital	50 000	factory/offices	130 000	
Profit and loss account	711 710			821 887
		Net profit before tax		202 593

SECTION 3

Cases in consumer services marketing

Sketchley and Supasnaps: Under the same roof!

Derek Thurley

KEY THEMES

- product development, market development, diversification
- adverse marketing environment
- extending distribution channels

BRIEFING NOTES (Chapter 1)

- The marketing mix and the marketing environment (pages 6–7)
- Marketing communications (pages 29–34)
- Identifying strategic options using SWOT (page 46)

Whilst the green Sketchley logo can be found in over 500 shopping centres and towns throughout the United Kingdom it has lost some of its lustre. Radical diversifications into vending, photocopying, and ancillary goods such as umbrellas in the late 1980s had diverted management time and resources at a time when the core dry-cleaning business was in the doldrums. Poor economic conditions had reduced consumer spending and the reduction in human resources in key industries had unsettled the industrial cleaning contracts division. Unfortunately, Sketchley chose to diversify into business areas which themselves turned out to be facing poor trading conditions. The result was that 1990 and 1991 were loss making years, and a rights issue was required to raise money to salvage the core business whilst buyers were found for the loss-making acquisitions, which were sold off at discount prices.

The first priority of a radical new management was to cut costs, improve sales per store, and improve staff morale. Performance began to improve and the ability to pay shareholder dividends reflected this growing confidence. It was at this time that discussions between Sketchley and Supersnaps management took place to provide more distribution and sales per outlet for both of the companies. Supasnaps at that time was a vertically integrated film-processing and photographic accessory service operating from 353 shops in city suburbs and small to medium-sized towns in high street locations. Supasnaps had 140 branches sited in the south of England, and further branches in Scotland and Wales.

Whilst the market for dry cleaning was generally fairly static, there was a rash of entrants into the fast/overnight/one-hour express film-processing industry in the late 1980s. Supasnaps was part of this new industry and its national chain of outlets positioned it well to exploit the growing market.

It came as something of a shock to industry commentators when Sketchley announced plans to acquire Supasnaps:

> *The acquisition should add value to the Sketchley Group in two ways. First, we anticipate incremental benefits from managing and operating Supasnaps in conjunction with the dry cleaning chain. Second, there is a significant potential for cross-marketing the two businesses by offering both services through selected outlets.*

The 1994 Sketchley *Annual Report* referred to:

> *Significant geographical overlap between the two operations as Supasnaps is represented in some 150 locations where there is a Sketchley presence. The Board believes one unified management team is better able to deliver to shareholders the full benefit of this acquisition. The principal management task for 1994/95 will be promotion of a strong brand image for both operations.*

For all your photographic needs
from cameras and film to
film processing, reprint and
enlargement services, frames
and albums.

≣Polaroid

SupaSnaps 'Passport Photo Service'
is approved and recommended by
Polaroid (UK) Limited.

Polaroid is the registered trademark of Polaroid
Corporation, Cambridge MA 02139 USA

PERSONAL SERVICE GUARANTEED

Sketchley
DRY CLEANERS

Professional Dry Cleaning

Repairs & Alterations

Waxed Garment Cleaning
and Repair

Shirts & Laundry*

Scotchgard™ Protection*

Shoe Repair Service*

Suede, Leaather &
Sheepskin Cleaning

Duvet & Pillow Cleaning

Blankets & Bedspreads

Carpet Cleaning Machine Hire

Specialist Rug Cleaning

Eiderdowns Repaired & Recovered

*Available in selected Sketchley branches
Please ask for details of these and other services.

Fig. 3.1 Sketchley/Supasnaps

Table 3.1 Sketchley: financial position, 1990–94

	1990 £000	1991 £000	1992 £000	1993 £000	1994 £000
Turnover:					
Continuing operations					
Acquisitions	–	–	–	–	41 502
Other	111 045	114 197	107 081	103 964	101 408
Discontinued operations	80 229	43 723	–	–	–
Total	191 274	157 920	107 081	103 964	142 910
Operating profit before exceptional charges:					
Continuing operations					
Acquisitions	–	–	–	–	1 405
Other	7 467	4 189	8 636	5 828	5 154
Discontinued operations	(6 028)	(3 306)	–	–	–
Total	1 439	883	8 636	5 828	6 559
Loss on sale/termination of operations	(2 878)	(46 804)	–	–	–
Profit/(loss) on ordinary activities before taxation	(7 765)	(52 068)	6 015	3 111	5 060
Tax on profit/(loss) on ordinary activities	1 481	3 346	(1 504)	(279)	(1 174)
Profit/(loss) on ordinary activities after taxation	(6 284)	(48 722)	4 511	2 832	3 886
Bid defence costs	(1 771)	–	–	–	–
Dividends	(2 360)	(6)	(1 753)	(1 739)	(1 987)
Retained profit/(loss)	(10 415)	(48 728)	2 758	1 093	1 899
Shareholders funds	30 317	35 394	38 006	39 024	35 363
Net borrowings	59 864	31 595	11 903	6 921	11 311
Gearing	198%	89%	31%	18%	32%
Earnings/(loss) per Ordinary share (pence)	(14.5)	(92.3)	7.8	4.9	6.7
Dividends per Ordinary share (pence)	6.5	–	3.0	3.0	3.2

Note 1: Earnings per share have been restated as a consequence of the rights issue of Ordinary shares in August 1990.
Note 2: The 1991 figures have been changed to reflect goodwill attributable to disposals.
Note 3: All figures have been adjusted to reflect the provisions of FRS 3.

Rationing or demarketing? That is the question

Annabelle Mark

KEY THEMES

- marketing in the public sector
- demarketing
- healthcare marketing

BRIEFING NOTES (Chapter 1)

- The marketing concept (pages 4–6)
- The marketing mix and the marketing environment (pages 6–7)
- Marketing in the public sector (pages 11–12)
- Marketing services (pages 25–29)

The concept of the 'internal market' has been introduced to the UK National Health Service (NHS). Purchaser organisations (health authorities and those general practices which manage their own budgets – known as GP fundholders) buy services from providers – broadly, the hospitals. The idea behind the internal market is that competition between providers will increase the efficiency with which medical services are supplied. Provider organisations have recognised that marketing has a role to play in designing better services and selling them effectively to purchasers. But what has marketing got to offer the purchasers?

Political correctness is not only a prerogative of the left, but is now at the heart of a debate on how to manage demand or ration health care. What is needed for the sake of such political correctness in current government terminology is a way of discussing rationing without explicitly using the word and all that implies (*Health Service Journal*, 1994). Demarketing may be one solution to this problem of finding appropriate marketing concepts with which to manage the 'chronic overpopularity' (Kotler and Levy, 1971) of the National Health Service, which remains the single most difficult policy issue in spite of the reforms. Demarketing 'deals with discouraging customers in general or a certain class of customers in particular on either a temporary or permanent basis' (Kotler and Levy, 1971).

The story so far is that, given the arrival of a new mechanism for managing demand via markets rather than hierarchies, providers rather than purchasers have found a whole new discipline, that of marketing, available to them. Meanwhile purchasers have been struggling around the old disciplines of epidemiology, economics and sociology to find adequate solutions to managing demand as only one part of the need debate. Contracting meanwhile, which considers only supply and demand, has continued apace, based largely on inadequate information and hearsay. Unlike the Netherlands where the internal market's competition was based on quality and not prices (which were fixed nationally), the UK purchasers and providers have been drowned in the development of price data and contracts which so far manage mainly quantity in the supply side of the equation. However, in failing to address the issues of intervention in and management of the demand side, the customer's perception of health and the health system is left adrift in a sea of confusion about why the changes are occurring. This risks the reforms falling foul of the public's disillusion and disenchantment with changes they have yet to fully understand, let alone accept.

Providers have proved adept, in marketing terms, at promoting themselves, but often at the expense of purchasers who are portrayed as the bad guys unwilling to buy what is on offer. Purchasers are thus left starting out in a new area, without new tools to guide them and certainly few proactive mechanisms for the future management and, more importantly, development of health care, except for the removal of contracts from outdated or outmoded sources of supply, which inevitably sets them up also as the 'fall guys' of the reforms.

A review of the notion of demarketing, which has been largely ignored so far in favour of the 'fair weather activities of marketing' (Kotler and Levy, 1971) in the UK health sector, reveals that rather than being unworkable or unethical as marketers have suggested, it is perhaps another window on the issues at the heart of the rationing debate.

Let us examine the concept more closely in its four modes:

- general demarketing – shrinking total demand
- selective demarketing – discouraging certain customers
- ostensible demarketing – appearing to discourage demand as a device for increasing it
- unintentional demarketing – attempts to increase demand driving customers away.

We can see that there are some familiar elements which have been present in the rationing debate so far ignored by those who wish to believe that the price mechanism has all the answers. If cutting off supply is a way of managing demand, then general demarketing has been a major activity of the last ten years with a 30 per cent reduction in the number of public hospitals in the UK.

Selective demarketing occurs not only where purchasers refuse infertility or varicose vein treatment, which is just cutting supply again, but also through the whole health education and promotion activity where lifestyle targets, e.g. stop smoking campaigns, seek to decrease demand on health care from smoking-related diseases.

Ostensible demarketing, which occurred for many years through the long waiting lists of hospital consultants who believed it made people think they were waiting for the best, now may have transferred to a debate about access to health via the private sector when the public system provision seems unavailable. Unintentional demarketing, the most often explored aspect of demarketing in the private sector, tells us more about systems failures in, say, the provision of inappropriate care in inappropriate ways than anything else. For example, inappropriately using male doctors to provide family planning services to women from certain cultural backgrounds, whose culture demands an all-female environment for such intimate discussions.

So far the National Health Service Executive's seven stepping stones to effective purchasing have been:

- a strategic view
- robust contracts
- knowledge-based decisions
- responsiveness to local people
- mature relations with providers
- local alliances
- organisational fitness.

All are just process, or how to do it, issues and have not provided any new tools for purchasers wrestling with the 'rightsizing' or 'smartsizing' of health care which they have been given the responsibility for achieving. Demarketing may be such a tool, especially if used explicitly.

Making the demarketing activity explicit would also have ethical and political consequences, but using the idea as an instrument to examine current practice in the health sector reveals that some unchallenged ethical and political decisions are already being made. These could be more acceptable if they were explored using demarketing as a framework for understanding and debating the consequences of decisions (Mark, 1994). Purchasers would also finally have a proactive lead activity in the management of health provision.

References

Health Service Journal, Let's be frank about rationing says IHSM. 26 May, p 4, 1994.

Kotler, P. and Levy, S. J., Demarketing yes demarketing. *Harvard Business Review*, November/December, *49*(6), 74–80, 1971.

Mark, A. , Demarketing – A strategy of rationing for equity. in Malek, M. (Ed.), *Setting Priorities in Health Care*, John Wiley, 1994.

The Beaufort Hotel

Stephen Hearnden and Paola Bradley

KEY THEMES

- marketing business and consumer services
- capacity utilisation in service businesses
- researching customer service perceptions
- marketing planning

BRIEFING NOTES (Chapter 1)

- Managing market research (pages 17–21)
- Market research, target markets and marketing communications (pages 31–33)
- Marketing services (pages 25–29)
- The marketing planning process (page 44)
- Identifying strategic options using SWOT (pages 46–50)

The Beaufort is a two-star hotel situated in Harrow, a busy north London suburb within the professional commuter belt, boasting a famous public school. The town is twinned with the French town of Douai, with which there is a very active exchange programme. The hotel is very close to Wembley, site of a national conference centre, concert arena, large regional hospital and national football stadium. Four large multinational companies have their headquarters located within a two-mile radius of the hotel. The Beaufort is actually situated in the town centre close to a large modern shopping mall. Two cinemas are within five minutes walk.

There are several other hotels in the vicinity, the nearby 150 room three-star Wellington is the Beaufort's closest competitor, tariffs being set at a very similar rate. The Wellington boasts an indoor sports complex, however, making it particularly popular with families on short breaks. Not only does the Beaufort have to consider its close geographical rivals, but being so close to central London means that travellers have thousands of options when choosing a hotel. It is therefore the concern of the Beaufort management that the hotel's name is well publicised.

ACCESSIBILITY

The hotel is in a very accessible location:

- The local underground station is two minutes walk away, the journey to central London taking on average only 30 minutes.
- The main line rail station is about 15 minutes away. The journeys by train from both of London's main airports, Heathrow and Gatwick, take approximately 25 and 45 minutes respectively.
- The hotel is also very close to the M1, M40, A40 and the M25.
- There is a large 60-space car park on the premises.

ORGANISATION STRUCTURE

Rupert McIntyre, the General Manager of the hotel for the past five years, as well as having extensive experience of the hotel and catering industry, recently completed a Masters Degree in strategic marketing management with a specific focus on the marketing of services. It is this training which has caused him to reorganise the hotel and run it along strategic business unit (SBU) lines. The rooms, bar and restaurant are all run as independent profit centres.

To assist in the restructuring exercise, which took place two years ago, Rupert used his university contacts to secure employment for a one-year placement student studying on a BA Business Studies course. The result was so successful that this arrangement has remained in place. The current student/assistant is Andrew Davis, who has been helping Rupert for the past six months.

HOTEL REPUTATION

The hotel is currently recognised by the AA as a two-star establishment, whereas the British Tourist Board has awarded it four crowns. The Beaufort has also recently gained an 'Investor in People' award (recognising a commitment to the development of its workforce) and several national training awards.

As a direct result of initiatives by Andrew Davis, the hotel has managed to secure valuable contacts with three Midland-based, premier league or first division, football clubs. Both players and organised 'supporter packages' are catered for at the hotel. The Beaufort has also recently been appointed 'preferred hotel' by the nearby Northwick Park Hospital, which, as a major research centre, has to arrange or recommend accommodation to a growing number of visiting medical researchers.

HOTEL ROOM FACILITIES

The original four-floor hotel building was built in the 1930s. The majority of bedrooms are now situated in a three-storey detached block added in the 1960s.

In total, the hotel has 84 rooms, 12 of which were recently redecorated and designated no-smoking rooms. All rooms have en-suite facilities, radio, hair dryer, trouser presses, direct-dial telephones, colour satellite television sets (not remote control operated) and tea/coffee making facilities. There is no room service, lift or porterage service.

All prices are per room (1994 rates) on a bed and breakfast basis:

	Monday–Thursday	*Friday–Sunday (+holidays)*
Single	£64.00	£29.50
Double/twin	£70.00	£50.00
Executive* single	£65.00	£45.00
Executive* double	£80.00	£50.00
Triple rooms	£85.00	£65.00

* Executive rooms are considerably larger than standard rooms, however furnishings are of the same standard.

Discounts can be individually negotiated on booking, the reservations staff exercise discretion depending on the number of rooms available, whether repeat business is likely and how many nights are being booked. Large companies who use the hotel regularly for their staff are given a discount in the region of 25 per cent off the standard rack rate.

The hotel, in line with the current trend for hotels in the London region, tends to have good occupancy rates. The figure generally fluctuates around 65 per cent (*see* Appendix A).

A questionnaire is routinely left in all bedrooms. On registration guests are asked to fill in a registration form including personal details. It is mainly from these two sources that the Marketing Manager has been able to compile a customer profile, although response rates for the questionnaires are generally low at 30 per cent.

From the booking forms over the past 12 months:

- 94 per cent of customers stay at the hotel for business purposes, 3 per cent to visit relatives and 3 per cent are tourists. Of the business clients 56 per cent make their own decision where to stay, 32 per cent have no say in the matter as the company chooses the hotel, but in all cases the company reimburses the individuals fully for the cost of room and meals.
- Guests come from a large and even geographical spread: 26 per cent from the south west, 23 per cent from the Midlands, 20 per cent from the north west, 8 per cent from Scotland, 6 per cent from the south east, 20 per cent from East Anglia and 11 per cent from the north east.
- 83 per cent are male.
- 47 per cent of customers are aged 25–35, 22 per cent between 36–46 and 25 per cent older than this.
- 56 per cent are repeat customers, 40 per cent staying once a month or more frequently.

- 70 per cent travel to the hotel by car, 22 per cent by public transport and 8 per cent have taken a taxi from the airport.

From the questionnaires over the past 12 months:

- When asked to rank deciding factors in choosing a hotel, where 1 = most important, 5 = least important, the averages scored for each reason were as follows:

Convenience for travel	2.6
Quality of service	2.5
Hotel facilities	1.5
Price	2.7
Friendly atmosphere	3.5

- Average satisfaction ratings were also calculated, where 100 per cent means 'fully satisfied', 0 per cent 'not all satisfied', and 50 per cent means 'satisfied', for the following factors:

Room decor	49%
Cleanliness	62%
Room facilities	53%
Room comfort	51%
Security	44%

- With regards to the no-smoking policy, only 14 per cent responded that more than half of the hotel rooms should be set aside as no-smoking. All respondents agreed with the statement that it was important to set no-smoking rooms apart from the others.
- 91 per cent felt that they had received 'value for money' and the same percentage found the room adequate for their stay.

THE BEAUFORT BAR

The Beaufort bar is a pleasantly decorated large room located adjacent to the reception area. There is a separate entrance outside the hotel, so that it is not necessary to enter the hotel itself to gain access. There are 20 dark oak tables which can each seat four people at meal times, six if drinking only. At the bar itself, which is arranged in a typical horseshoe fashion, there are no stools.

As a separate business unit the bar is very successful, in particular due to the contribution from bar meals. Annual turnover is in the region of £280 000.

There are five permanent members of staff directly involved in running the bar. At peak periods, extra help is brought in, in particular to assist during the busy lunchtime period, when there are, on average, three times more customers than in the evening session. The opening hours are 12.00–14.00 and

17.00–23.00 for members of the public, hotel guests are able to use the facilities after hours. By far the quietest period is between 17.00 and 18.30.

The bar offers drinks at 'pub prices' and serves typical 'pub fast-food' at reasonable prices. The lunchtime trade is particularly brisk due to the good quality and value of the food served. The high levels of demand often mean that the service is slow, generating a few complaints from customers. Another source of complaint is the noise level. There are two fruit machines which are in constant use at lunchtimes and taped music is played using an inferior system with poor sound quality.

The room questionnaire indicates that 78 per cent of hotel residents use the bar, this is not surprising as there are no mini-bar facilities in the rooms. From the 'charge to room' facility, the average daily spend in the bar for residents is £4.50, and only 10 per cent eat in the bar at lunchtimes. The following satisfaction ratings were also gleaned from the questionnaire:

	Average	*Above average*
Food price	42 per cent	58 per cent
Food quality	35 per cent	49 per cent
Food range	32 per cent	38 per cent
Politeness	25 per cent	60 per cent
Speed of service	44 per cent	23 per cent
Atmosphere	32 per cent	25 per cent

In the comments section a few customers have complained about the lack of no-smoking area in the bar. This is in direct contrast to the no-smoking rooms policy, operating in the refurbished accommodation.

Six months ago, David Petts, the Bar Manager, decided to design and administer a questionnaire to customers, to establish a customer profile. Bar staff handed these out when an order had been placed. The scheme was not successful, response rates were poor, and during very busy periods the system broke down. It was then decided to leave copies of the questionnaires on the tables and along the bar, but response rates were virtually zero. For the past month bar staff have been requested to ask informal questions when serving drinks and to collate information on specially designed tally sheets held behind the bar counter. This has generated the following statistics: 45 per cent of customers were locals, of these 80 per cent were regulars coming more than twice a week. At lunchtimes 75 per cent of those eating are regular customers.

Like the restaurant, the bar's competition comes not only from the other hotels in the area, but also from public houses in the vicinity. The Moon on the Hill, a large, bright, well-appointed, modern establishment, situated half a mile away from the Beaufort, is the bar's main competitor. It offers drinks at similar prices, but a more varied menu. A major promotion offered at the Moon, for the past month, has been the 99p pint, this price being applicable at the traditionally quieter times of the day. This has been successful in terms of bringing business in, but the offer will be closed in the next two weeks. It remains to be seen whether new customers will continue to frequent the establishment and purchase as often when the offer closes. The Beaufort is unable to offer a similar loss-leader promotion because of contractual obligations with the brewery. From time to time free barrels are supplied by the brewery for promotional activities.

THE LE PRINTEMPS RESTAURANT

The 60-seat restaurant, with both smoking and non-smoking sections, is situated on the ground floor of the hotel. Unlike the bar there is no separate entrance to it. The food served is predominantly French. Marie Renault has been the manager of the restaurant for the past three years. In response to the image of hotel restaurants traditionally being rather old fashioned and uninspiring, she oversaw a major refurbishment programme completed two years ago. This and a change of name and cooking style, from traditional English fare, was aimed at attracting a greater proportion of local clientele. A young French chef who had recently completed his training at one of London's five-star establishments, was recruited to run the kitchen.

The restaurant now serves high standard well-presented meals, with a wide range of dishes catering for most tastes including several vegetarian options. This has been reflected in the local newspaper restaurant review section which consistently praises the establishment and recommends it to readers. The large amount of choice is particularly commended, but it is this which causes most friction between Marie and the chef, because of the high wastage levels necessary to maintain a large selection.

Breakfast is served between 7.30 and 9.30am, although only 60 per cent of residents avail themselves of the inclusive breakfast, which is surprisingly low. Lunch is served between 12.00 and 14.30, dinner between 19.00 and 21.30.

Between September and November last year all customers were handed a questionnaire with their bills. Just under 55 per cent completed them and from this information Marie was able to compile the following information:

- 60 per cent of customers were female
- 62 per cent of meals were eaten in the evening
- 12 per cent of customers ate alone, 37 per cent had two in their party, 42 per cent were threes or fours
- 50 per cent were over 55 years of age, 25 per cent between 35–45 and 12 per cent younger
- 58 per cent are local residents
- 25 per cent knew of the restaurant from the local paper, 61 per cent from recommendation
- 12 per cent use the restaurant regularly more than once a week, 12 per cent more often than once a month and 25 per cent more than every three months
- 50 per cent had eaten in other restaurants in the Harrow area in the past three months, of these all rated the Le Printemps as the same or better
- 50 per cent travelled by car, the rest were evenly distributed between bus, taxi and by foot

Andrew Davis, helped Marie process the questionnaire results and suggested expanding the questions asked to glean more information, particularly to focus on diners' experience of local competition. In January this year a second questionnaire was administered. Andrew also prepared a questionnaire which he used to question 40 shoppers chosen at random in the shopping centre, as well as 25 people in the waiting area and 20 members of staff at the hospital to find out whether they knew of the restaurant, had eaten there and where they usually chose to eat out. The results are given in Appendix B.

Harrow is dominated by fast-food outlets. Increasingly the town and neighbouring areas such as Wembley, Pinner and Northwood are becoming business oriented as firms move out of central London in search of cheaper premises. Initial investigations indicate that Le Printemps has failed to entice that sector of the community to eat in the restaurant.

The hotel advertises quite heavily in the local press. A few years ago a 'free bottle with meal on presentation of the advert' promotion was run, but this did not significantly increase the number of customers, so it was promptly withdrawn. Other than this the hotel relies on word-of-mouth recommendations.

APPENDIX A: DATA ON UTILISATION OF BEAUFORT HOTEL FACILITIES AND BACKGROUND INFORMATION ON THE MARKET

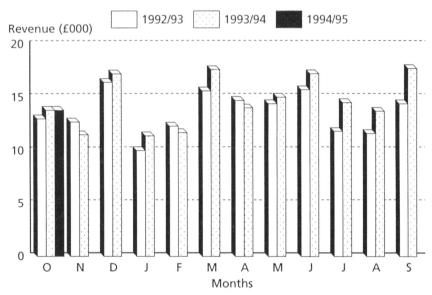

Fig. 3.2 Beaufort Hotel: Beaufort bar drinks, October 1992–September 1994

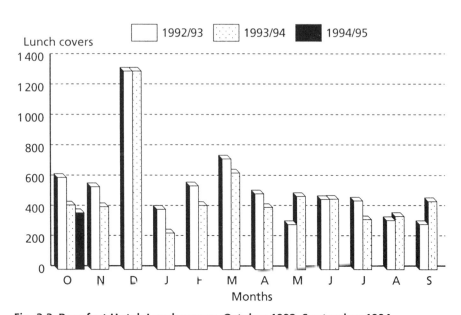

Fig. 3.3 Beaufort Hotel: Lunch covers, October 1992–September 1994

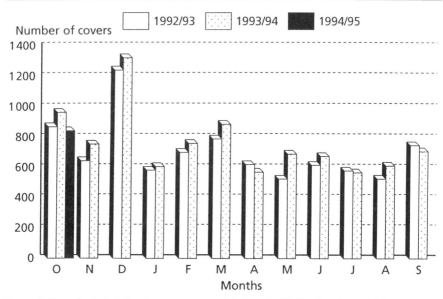

Fig. 3.4 Beaufort Hotel: Dinner covers, October 1992–September 1994

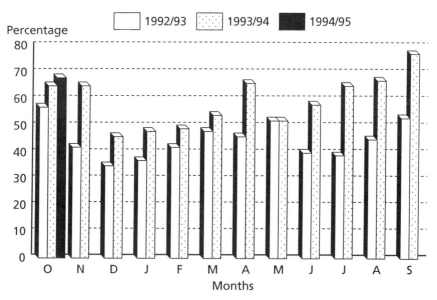

Fig. 3.5 Beaufort Hotel: Percentage room occupancy, October 1992–September 1994

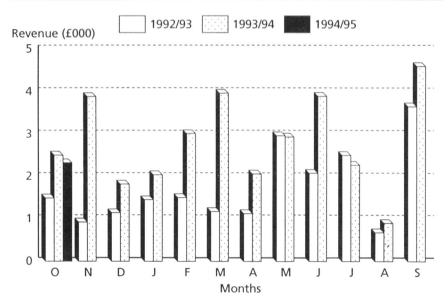

Fig. 3.6 Beaufort Hotel: Conference hire, October 1992–September 1994

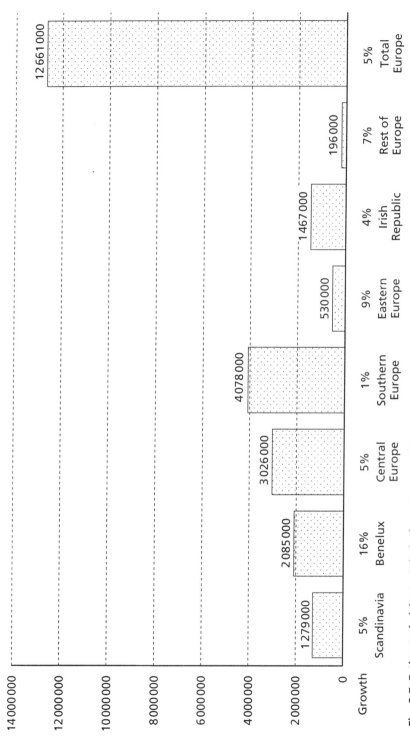

Fig. 3.7 Estimated visits to Britain from Europe, 1994

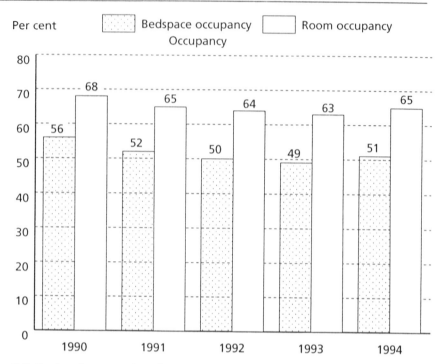

Fig. 3.8 **Regional average hotel occupancy, October 1990–September 1994**

APPENDIX B

MEMO

To:	Rupert McIntyre
	Marie Renault
From:	Andrew Davis
Date:	1 February
Subject:	*Competition for Le Printemps*

I have collated the information from the questionnaires to diners and members of the public concerning their knowledge and attitude towards other restaurants in the area. The most important findings are outlined below.

Diner's opinions
More than three-quarters of diners expressed a preference for formal restaurant eating compared with fast-food outlets. This was reflected in their choice of alternative venues. The most commonly mentioned alternative was the Canesta, the Egon Ronay noted Spanish restaurant situated about a mile away. The Doric Room at the Wellington Hotel was also mentioned several times. As expected, several other restaurants much further afield were also named, most notably by those who live locally and travelled to the restaurant by car. Business travellers staying at the hotel did not have as extensive a knowledge of competing establishments in the area.

Comparatively, Le Printemps fares quite favourably with these alternatives. A small proportion expressed an interest in a more varied menu, citing the choice of ethnic dishes available at the Doric Room. The lack of background music compared with the Canesta was also noted.

Shopper's opinions
Nearly all the shoppers questioned were aware of the hotel, but none could remember the name of the restaurant unprompted. One shopper had eaten in the restaurant three years previously, but could not recall whether the meal was enjoyable. Most easily recalled were the large fast-food outlets, local Indian, Italian and Chinese restaurants and the Canesta.

Hospital findings
Fifty per cent of hospital staff questioned had eaten in the restaurant and found it to be of comparable standard to the other establishments mentioned, although three doctors said that rated the Canesta. The responses by those in the waiting room mirrored the findings of respondents from the shopping centre. Awareness was very low, only two people had eaten in the restaurant, one of whom complained that their meal was much too rich. These respondents favoured fast-food outlets and a number of local ethnic and Italian restaurants were mentioned as preferred venues.

Could we meet to discuss in more detail the details highlighted above?

MEMO

To:	Rupert McIntyre
	Andrew Davis
From:	Marie Renault
Date:	2 February
Subject:	*Competition for Le Printemps*

Thank you for your memo dated 1 February.

   We are working 'flat out' every day in the restaurant. Before we discuss the findings from your questionnaire, I need more staff to cope with present business.

   I assume the idea of meeting is to discuss ways of increasing business. It is quite simple – more staff, more business!

The Niger restaurant

Bal Chansarkar and Ghalib Fahad

KEY THEMES

- marketing for small and medium-sized enterprises
- market segmentation and target marketing
- primary marketing research
- planning the marketing mix

BRIEFING NOTES (Chapter 1)

- The marketing mix and the marketing environment (pages 6–7)
- Buyer behaviour and market segmentation (pages13–15)
- Managing market research (pages 17–21)
- Market research, target markets and marketing communications (pages 31–33)

ORIGIN OF THE BUSINESS

In 1989, Mary Audu decided that after some ten years of working for various organisations it was time to become her own boss. It was in 1979 that Mary completed her National Diploma in Food Management at Brixton College but management jobs in the hospitality field for members from the ethnic minorities were limited and available work was confined mainly to menial jobs. It was this employment situation that caused Mary to seek a job in the retail sector where, despite her qualification, she could only find work as a shop assistant.

Mary worked in that capacity for four years before joining another large retail organisation, again as a shop assistant, in one of their branches based at Oxford street. The idea for her restaurant was germinated here because of her contact with foreign customers, especially those from West Africa. In addition to their shopping many of these customers would ask Mary about the possibility of purchasing African foods. She would guide some of these queries to one or two of the Afro-Caribbean restaurants that she knew in North London. Some of the customers on a return shopping trip would seek her out to thank her for her recommendation.

By the mid-1980s, Mary realised that fast-food outlets were springing up all over the city but very few were for the Afro-Caribbean ethnic groups. This market segment it appeared to her was still largely untapped despite the fact that from the late 1970s onwards the proportion of Afro-Caribbeans, especially West Africans, settling in the UK had increased dramatically. It was this realisation in 1988 that prompted Mary to begin thinking about setting up her own African restaurant (*see* Appendix A).

In 1989, Mary at last found a suitable place near her home in Tottenham, in north London. During the previous year, she had taken up an extra job for a few nights a week as a care assistant looking after the elderly in order to be able to put together enough savings for her business. In her spare time, she had visited her local council offices to enquire about properties and the possibility of securing some financial help. It was on one such excursion that she was informed of the availability of a property in the Tottenham high street which had previously been a bakery. The premises proved suitable, requiring minimal changes and renovation, and as a result within three months Mary was able to secure a contract on the premises.

So it was that, in July 1989 Mary was able to open her restaurant with her savings of £3500. The council had agreed to renovate the place for her and to provide a one-year rent- free lease. Mary purchased enough chairs and tables to seat some 20 customers, although the premises had the capacity to seat well over 40 customers and there was sufficient space to add a bar.

DEVELOPING A MARKETING STRATEGY

Although Mary herself would frown at the idea of her developing a 'strategy' when she first started the business, she had a clear idea about how the product should be developed and how to make it a success. Though not written down in a formal manner, she undertook the following actions to achieve her conception.

The product

From the very start, Mary perceived her restaurant to be one providing African foods, especially Nigerian foods. The choice of name was intended to reflect her roots and origin and the fact that her restaurant served some of the finest fish dishes, since that is the speciality by which that region is known. To maintain the African authenticity, Mary was determined that she would buy most of her fish and other food products directly from Nigeria and that the original cooking recipes would be diligently observed.

To that end, Mary set about decorating the restaurant in a typically African manner: bamboo shoots, palm leaves and African objects adorned the premises. Even some of the serving utensils were African in origin, such as small calabash dishes used for serving soups.

To reinforce the Africanness of the restaurant Mary designed typical Nigerian dress for the two part-time waitresses she would employ. Mary herself was responsible for the cooking of the various dishes, all of which were freshly cooked each day. To ensure high quality and freshness, customers were informed upon arrival in the restaurant of the fact that everything was fresh-ly cooked and that this may entail some extra waiting time. In keeping with African traditions, it was then expected that customers would have starters in the form of 'pepper soup' (a very hot soup).

Location

Mary was keen to be located where large numbers of people of African ori-gin lived. Tottenham, which is part of the London Borough of Haringey, was such a location.

The fact that Mary had a year of rent moratorium encouraged her to accept premises in the high street, which generally have higher surcharges and rates. The location was close to residential areas and the main shopping centres which meant easy access to the restaurant by bus and other means of trans-port. Furthermore, the area had ample parking space so that car owners would not be put off coming to the restaurant.

Price

Mary's conception of price was that her cooking must reach her intended cus-tomers. Using her own income and those of her close friends as a basis of cal-culations, she resolved that prices would be based on good value for money.

No research was carried out on what other restaurants' pricing policies were. Mary used a crude form of cost plus pricing based on her bulk buying of goods from Nigeria. Rather than itemise the cost of each item, Mary simply calcu-lated the overall cost and fixed a return she expected. This was then translat-ed into an item price.

Initially, this method worked well because of the ease of obtaining most food items from Nigeria. In time, however it became more difficult to get hold of some food items forcing Mary to look for alternative suppliers and having to pay the 'going-rate'. Mary responded by making slight changes to her prices because she felt that any further charges would simply send customers away, especially to places like McDonald's and Kentucky Fried Chicken which at this time were well established in the high street and provided direct compe-tition.

Promotion

Despite her training in food management, Mary was a great believer in the effect of word-of-mouth recommendation. She had herself experienced this in action when her African customers asked her to recommend a suitable restaurant. The multiplier effect of this method of promotion she felt would be large once she had spread the 'good news'.

When the restaurant was about to be opened, Mary contacted as many friends as she could and asked them to tell their friends both about her restaurant and the opening day. Though lessons could have been learnt from the opening day when very few friends or customers turned up, this did not deter Mary. For the following week, she hastily put together a leaflet and distributed copies of this herself around the housing estates near her restaurant. The leaflet itself was made in a personalised way, asking people to come round to see Mary's restaurant and to 'give Nigerian cuisine a trial'.

Whenever the opportunity arose, Mary also distributed business cards giving her name and the address of the restaurant and the fact that it was a Nigerian restaurant. These she distributed to all her college friends and any other Africans she came across.

Target segments

Mary expected when she started her restaurant that it would be attractive only to Africans and more especially Nigerians. Being one herself, she realised that many were very fussy about their foods, preferring to eat in a home surrounding.

Furthermore, many Nigerians are reluctant to try other foods, considering theirs to be the best. There is also the fact that there exists major cultural differences between West Indians and Africans made it difficult for many of them to visit the mainly West Indian restaurants which were to be found around the area.

Given Mary's own experience of how she came to settle in this country, she realised that many Africans were in a similar position to herself and therefore likely to welcome a surrounding that reminded them of home. It was these people at whom she aimed her restaurant and it is for this reason that she decorated the premises in a typical African manner.

DEVELOPMENT OF THE BUSINESS

Mary's overall policy was a success. Within four months of starting her business, she had to modify her product concept by taking orders for take-away foods. This resulted in her pre-cooking some food items in order to achieve faster turnround and in being able to cater for the customer.

In addition, Mary had to employ two other part-time staff in order to cater for weekend demand, when 70 per cent of her sales occurred. The revenues she realised enabled her to add more tables and chairs, bringing the restaurant up to its full complement. In keeping with restaurants back at home, the bar was merely seen as an extension to the kitchen since it is the hostess who served drinks directly to her customers.

In April 1990, almost nine months after starting her business Mary realised that she needed to keep more accurate financial records both for tax purposes and in order to determine the extent of her success. She approached a small accounting firm in her area headed by Abdul, who turned out to be a Lebanese born in West Africa. The two hit it off almost immediately and it was Abdul who ascertained that her takings were nearing £2000 per week and advised that this figure could be increased by examining price more carefully.

Mary was reluctant to alter her prices because, in 1990, she had noticed that competition was beginning to increase. Even within the north London area, some four or five African restaurants had opened up (*see* Appendix C for the trend of ethnic foods). She had investigated one or two of these places and was confident that her prices were very competitive and that overall the quality of her cooking was as yet unrivalled. It was for this reason that she was reluctant to alter prices in any significant way. Thus, while average restaurant spending at 1990 prices was £10.50 per customer, Mary's average customer spent some £4.50p per visit (eating in).

By 1991, Mary had become engaged to Abdul who now became a partner in the business. Abdul decided that for sales to increase it was necessary to advertise in the local press and to design better structured leaflets for wider distribution. This was done and contributed to the doubling of the business, so that by the end of 1991 weekly takings had mounted to £4250 per week. The cooking remained the same although, through proper costing of the food items, the prices charged became closer to those charged within the industry and the more immediate competition.

Through hard work and a combination of rapport with customers and suitable personality, the business had by 1992 become very successful with takings now reaching some £6000 per week and employing some ten full- and part-time staff. It was this that prompted Mary and Abdul to consider extending their business by opening another branch in Wood Green. Given that Mary's younger sister Sarah had now been trained to cook Mary's recipes, it was felt that she would become the chef and manageress of this new branch. However, overall control would still remain in Mary's hands and Abdul would alternate between the two places to check that all was going well.

Realising that they might have to raise some capital from the bank and in order to secure some local authority grants and concessions, Abdul decided to prepare a business plan. As a result, overall goals and objectives were specified for the company (*see* Appendix D). In addition, Abdul for the first time secured Mary's consent to carry out a literature survey on the industry and its prospects (Appendix B) as well as a small survey on the perceptions of the general public to restaurants, especially Afro-Caribbean ones (*see* Appendix E). The survey was carried out by the local college where Abdul had a business lecturer friend, whereas the literature search was done by Abdul himself.

So it was that a place was eventually found in Wood Green and in May 1992, the 'Niger Restaurant 2' as it was called was opened. Mary and Abdul had injected some £20 000 of their own money and had secured a £25 000 loan repayable over five years, from their local bank. The new restaurant looked and felt much more costly and contained many of the features which the survey had identified as being important in the choice of a restaurant. The target segment was perceived to be different, possibly younger and more affluent.

Accordingly, prices were varied to reflect this target although no compromises were made in respect of the dishes that were to be served. Mary was quite adamant about this aspect of the business which she felt was the key to distinguishing her from her competitors.

The new restaurant was much more widely publicised and promoted, and as result within a short period of time was becoming a popular visiting place for younger professional black people and other groups such as African diplomats and business people visiting London. The fact that the restaurant could accommodate up to 75 people at any one time encouraged Abdul and Mary to encourage group functions and activities. Furthermore, unlike Niger 1, the new restaurant encouraged young African artists to play their music at weekends which helped to make the place attractive. In November 1992, Niger 2 was taking some £10000 per week and employed 12 full- and part-time staff.

Some of the customers who visited the new restaurant began to seek Abdul out with a view to establishing another branch in the West End. The fact that one or two Afro-Caribbean restaurants had started to explore the possibility of franchising convinced Abdul that their track record now made it imperative to expand further. He felt that a new branch in an upmarket area such as Edgware Road (W1) would consolidate the company's position and would provide sufficient returns for the partners. This was the wedding present Abdul felt he would give Mary and so asked for a meeting to see how they could progress the idea of a new branch in the West End.

APPENDIX A: FAST FOOD AND RESTAURANT MARKET

The term fast food refers to the type of commodity provided by catering outlets which may be characterised as offering: a fast service, a limited choice menu, low or high price meals, and the option of takeaway, which is an element of pre-preparation of food. The principal catering establishments coming under this heading include fish and chip shops, pizza restaurants, fried chicken outlets and ethnic and speciality restaurants such as Chinese, Indian, and Afro-Caribbean eating houses to name but a few.

There are distinctions between the types of service offered in fast-food outlets. Some offer takeaway counter service only, some offer a takeaway service and eating area where customers have the option of eating. Systems catering outlets, epitomised by pizza restaurants, offer normal restaurant service together with a takeaway option.

In 1990, there were a total of about 46 472 restaurants and takeaway businesses in the United Kingdom, with sales turnover of over £6492 million. (*See* Tables 3.2 and 3.3).

Table 3.2 Restaurants and take-away businesses in the UK, 1980–90

Year	Restaurants	% of total	Take-away	% of total
1980	11 512	10.5	22 715	20.8
1981	11 735	10.5	24 980	22.4
1982	11 817	10.4	26 256	23.2
1983	12 119	10.6	27 049	23.6
1984	12 692	10.8	29 205	24.8
1985	13 362	11.3	28 274	24.0
1986	14 000	11.8	27 804	23.4
1987	14 846	12.2	28 092	23.1
1988	15 743	12.7	28 382	22.6
1989	16 640	13.2	28 672	23.2
1990	17 510	13.9	28 962	23.8

Source: Business monitor and retail business estimates.

Table 3.3 Estimated turnover of restaurants and take-away establishments, 1980–90

Year	Restaurants £m	Take-away £m
1980	1 431	1 103
1981	1 529	1 284
1982	1 639	1 497
1983	1 742	1 664
1984	1 900	1 869
1985	2 194	2 063
1986	2 350	2 128
1987	2 503	2 204
1988	2 845	2 442
1989	3 187	2 660
1990	3 574	2 918

Source: Business monitor and retail business estimates.

Table 3.4 shows the average weekly expenditure of consumers on the different restaurants and takeaways found in practice. The figures, although not broken down into specific types of establishment, clearly show a marked growth for the takeaway sector: a trend likely to continue in the future. When these figures are then set against the pattern of meals eaten out of the home in Table 3.5 it becomes clear just how important a shift there has been in British eating habits. Of interest is the fact that not only has expenditure increased, but so has the number of visits now made by the average person.

Table 3.4 Average weekly expenditure on restaurants and take-away meals, 1983–90

	1983 £	1984 £	1985 £	1986 £	1987 £	1988 £	1989 £	1990 £
Hot take-away food	0.00	0.35	0.55	0.70	0.85	1.35	1.65	2.00
Fish and chips	0.27	0.34	0.37	0.38	0.40	0.52	0.56	0.58
Restaurant meal	5.01	5.36	5.80	6.85	7.50	8.20	9.10	10.5

Source: Family Expenditure Survey.

Table 3.5 Number of family meals eaten outside the home per week and average spend per visit, 1983–1990

	1983	1984	1985	1986	1987	1988	1989	1990
No. of meals eaten out, per person, per week	3.21	3.29	3.23	3.37	3.54	4.00	5.21	6.23
Average spend per week (£)	5.01	5.36	5.80	6.85	7.50	8.70	9.89	10.90
Average spend per visit (£)	1.56	1.63	1.79	2.03	2.12	3.60	5.89	9.65

Source: Family Expenditure Survey National Food Survey.

APPENDIX B: FAST FOOD AND RESTAURANT FRANCHISING

Having looked at the general growth and consumer expenditure levels, it is as well to consider franchising which is an important aspect of the fast-food sector and one that has allowed many companies to expand faster than would have been possible with wholly owned company units.

At present, it is estimated that some 800 to 1000 of the country's fast outlets are operated on a franchise basis, a figure which is almost certain to increase over the next five years. Franchising is especially prevalent in the pizza, hamburger and fried chicken markets though not generally found in fish and chips and ethnic food sectors, these sectors are expected to offer many opportunities for franchising.

Many companies manage their own restaurants in addition to pursuing a franchise policy. This strategy enables them to monitor the business, train franchisees and test new products and services.

Future prospects of the food sector in general

The growth in demand for fast foods by UK consumers shows little sign of slowing down. Fuelled by increases in real disposable income, eating out in general, and eating of fast foods in particular, continue to gain in popularity.

As many women return to full-time employment, demand for restaurants and fast-cooked foods are expected to increase.

Mintel, in its 1991 report, notes that there is great opportunity for the ethnic fast-food sector to grow and expand as more and more people are now visiting ethnic restaurants, especially health-oriented fresh-cooked foods. Mintel notes that those entrepreneurs who think beyond the present limited practices to be found in the ethnic food sector are likely to reap major benefits.

APPENDIX C: THE ETHNIC FOOD MARKET

In view of the predictions of the continuing growth in ethnic foods, this appendix looks at some of the important factors which have influenced the different ethnic food markets.

Personal disposable income

High levels of growth in personal disposable income (PDI)during the 1980s (£239.8 billion in 1985 increasing to £374.4 billion in 1990) has led to an increase in discretionary spending: for example, trying new foods and eating out. This has benefited the total ethnic food market. However, the current UK recession is dampening demand on the market, although ethnic restaurants are unlikely to suffer as much as others, due to the relatively lower costs involved. As PDI decreases and eating out becomes more expensive, people will turn to creating these meals at home rather than eating out.

Population of ethnic minorities

The rising number of people within the ethnic minorities present in the UK is becoming significant (especially those born within the UK; the 1991 figures indicate that some 45 per cent of the total ethnic minority population are UK born). Over 2.6 million members of ethnic minorities were resident in 1986, rising to 2.7 million in 1988 – a group who are accustomed to a different style of cooking and thus purchase particular ingredients and products. Hence they are, by and large, the core consumers of the ethnic food market.

Table 3.6 provides a breakdown of the different ethnic groups in the UK between 1986 and 1991. It can be seen from this that, despite the overall increase in the size of the ethnic population, the composition has remained relatively stable.

Table 3.6 Population of ethnic minorities in Britain (1986, 1989, 1991)

	1986 (000s)	% of total pop'n	1989 (000s)	% of total pop'n	1991 (000s)	% of total pop'n
Indian	784	1.4	814	1.4	792	1.4
Pakistani	413	0.8	479	0.9	485	0.9
West Indian	526	1.0	468	0.9	455	0.9
Chinese	113	0.2	136	0.2	137	0.2
African	98	0.2	122	0.2	150	0.2
Bangladeshi	117	0.2	91	0.2	127	0.2
Arabian	73	0.1	66	0.1	67	0.1
Mixed	269	0.5	328	0.6	309	0.6
Other	164	0.3	184	0.3	154	0.3
All ethnic minority	2 557	4.7	2 688	4.8	2 676	4.9
Total population	54 370	100	54 662	100	54 979	100

Source: 1986 and 1989 Labour Force Surveys/Mintel and Regional Trends, 27, 1992.

This rise in the number of ethnic minorities has also caused a mushrooming of ethnic restaurants and catering outlets prompting non-ethnic consumers to widen their culinary experiences and, ultimately, to try to reproduce these meals in their own homes. This phenomenon is particularly evident in areas of high minority residency, such as Haringey, Lambeth and Hackney.

Fast-food outlets

According to Mintel's special report, *Catering for the Consumer* (1990), there were some 335 000 fast-food outlets in the UK in 1988, of which 125 000 were ethnic. The Indian fast-food market was valued at £215 million, while the Chinese market represented £470 million. In 1990, there were approximately 6000 Chinese restaurants and around 5500 Indian restaurants in the UK. Although still very underdeveloped, there is also a growing number of Afro-Caribbean and Greek restaurants, mostly in London and the south east. However, this growth is not nearly enough to match the numbers who reside in the capital.

Media exposure

Media exposure on ethnic food has had a beneficial educational effect on the public. Good food guides and critical journalism (featuring restaurants and recipes), as well as television cookery programmes and books have all contributed to making ethnic foods more popular, whether eaten within or outside the home.

Changing eating habits

Changing eating habits which reflect the nation's new health concerns, evolving lifestyles and population mix have had a big effect on the nature of the UK diet.

Alongside more informal eating trends, there has been a huge growth in snack meals, the use of convenience foods and a taste for takeaways. As a result of demand, retail distribution has altered in that major grocery multiples now allocate shelf space to the staple ethnic foodstuffs and consumers are also more willing to purchase from specialist outlets.

Market size and trends

Gone are the days when the nearest one could get to a real ethnic meal was a dehydrated curry with easy-to-cook rice. The recent influx of good quality, reasonably priced ethnic restaurants in virtually every city around the UK, has fuelled demand for better calibre and more authentic food that can be easily prepared in the home.

The ethnic food market is one of the fastest growing sectors within the total food market. Whereas in the early 1980s the ethnic food market was worth some £60 million. In 1990, the market had grown to some £240 million – a staggering 300 per cent increase over the past ten years!

The total UK retail market for ethnic food for in-home consumption is estimated to be worth £300 million in 1991, a more than doubling (in current terms) on 1986. The market boom can be attributed to several factors, in addition to the restaurant knock-on effect that have been described in the previous section.

Table 3.7 examines the total retail sales of ethnic foods. As noted earlier, this shows

Table 3.7 Retail sales of ethnic foods (1986–91)

Year	£m at current prices	Index	£m at constant 1986 prices	Index
1986	101	100	101	100
1987	121	120	117	116
1988	140	139	131	130
1989	190	188	169	167
1990	240	238	196	194
1991 (est)*	300	297	231	229

* Excludes Italian and French food
Source: Mintel, 1990.

a dramatic rise in expenditure levels and indicates clearly the prospects for new enterprises entering this sector.

With more people cooking ethnic recipes in the home, there has been a rise in demand for authentic ethnic ingredients. Growth in the ethnic ingredients market has been spurred not only by television programmes, recipe books and magazine articles, informing the public on how to cook international dishes at home, but also by factors affecting the whole ethnic food market, such as the expansion of ethnic restaurants and increased travel abroad.

Market segmentation

The retail market for ethnic food can be divided into four segments, namely: Indian, Chinese, Mexican and Afro-Caribbean/others (*see* Table 3.8).

Indian
Indian food is the largest ethnic food retail sector and in fact represents one of the fastest growing grocery sectors overall. The Indian food market was heavily dependent on ethnic minorities in the early 1980s for sales. However, consumption has seen a shift towards non-Asian groups eating Indian food, especially complete meals. An increased exposure to Indian food on television and in recipe books and the large number of people eating out in Indian restaurants and buying Takeaways has encouraged consumers to experiment with a wider variety of different Indian ingredients.

Table 3.8 Retail sales of ethnic foods by segment (1988–90)

	1988 £m	%	1990 £m	%	% change 1988–90
Indian	72	51	115	48	+60
Chinese	52	37	79	33	+52
Mexican	10	7	17	7	+70
Others (inc. Afro-Caribbean)	6	4	29	12	+383
Total	140	100	240	100	+71

Chinese food

The UK market for Chinese food became established in the late 1940s, when the first Chinese immigrants came to England, bringing with them home-cooking versions of their own cuisine. The growth of Chinese take-aways helped to spread knowledge and interest in Chinese foods, resulting in a large number of people wishing to cook it for themselves at home.

Currently the Chinese food market is valued at £79 million in 1990. Growth has been consistent at a buoyant 20 per cent, year-on-year increase, of which complete meals and meal centres represent the majority of the total Chinese complete meals market, with chilled, canned and dried meals accounting for the remaining 30 per cent.

Afro-Caribbean foods

In terms of sales to the non-ethnic consumer, the Afro-Caribbean food market is still very underdeveloped, so that there is plenty of room for expansion. At the moment there is low consumer awareness of Afro-Caribbean foods, due partly to the lack of sufficient restaurants serving Afro-Caribbean dishes. As a result, it has not been possible to introduce the variety of tasty dishes available to the non-ethnic public.

On the other hand, Afro-Caribbean fruits and vegetables have been available for some time through specialist outlets and are gradually being used in British cookery, as opposed to only supplying the large West Indian or African communities.

Future prospects

The ethnic food market is still young and growth can be expected to continue as befits a market at this stage of development. This will continue despite the recession, which has not affected the food market as much as other fast-moving consumer foods markets.

Ethnic foods have now become established as part of many Briton's everyday diets, in much the same way as canned spaghetti did 20 years ago. Mintel's 1991 consumer research shows that six out of ten housewives had eaten at least one ethnic meal in the last six months.

As in other food sectors, the long-term trend seems to be for consumers to demand quality as well as value for money, and manufacturers have developed their products in line with consumer demand.

APPENDIX D: GOALS AND OBJECTIVES OF NIGER RESTAURANT

The mission of Niger restaurant will be to set up a service operation that will become known for its high-quality service of African foods and for authentic African cuisines.

In the short to medium-term, the company aims to accomplish the following objectives:

(a) To set up a restaurant that will be run efficiently and effectively to obtain a high degree of customer satisfaction.
(b) To set up an operation that will attract highly competent and motivated staff
(c) To set up a financially viable operation that will provide returns that are deemed to be satisfactory by the owners.
(d) To set up a restaurant that will be known for its strict adherence to the health and safety regulations including those relating to food production.

In the long term, the aim will be to set up an operation that will become the prime provider of African foods in the UK. Once the concept has been fine-tuned, the prospects of taking the restaurant to other parts of the UK will be considered.

APPENDIX E: A SURVEY OF CONSUMERS

This appendix summarises the findings of a research study that was carried out by students into consumers' perception of Afro-Caribbean foods and restaurants.

The characteristics of respondents are shown in Table 3.9 and the results of the survey are reported below.

Outline of the study

Subject	Usage of restaurants
Sample size:	150
Sample type:	General consumers aged 16–70
Location of study:	Wood green, Green lanes, Manor House, Stamford Hill, Finsbury Park, Tottenham High Road

Table 3.9 Niger Restaurant: profile of respondents sampled

Age	%	Employment status	%	Marital status	%	Place of residence	%
Under 20	2	Working	57	Single	49	Haringey	45
21–30	25	Housewife	16	Married	43	Hackney	30
31–45	57	Unemployed	24	Divorced	4	Islington	10
46–55	14	Student	3	Widowed	4	Enfield	10
56+	2					Others	5

Table 3.10 Niger Restaurant: frequency and time of visits

		%
Day of visit:	Weekdays	45
	Weekends	68
Time of visit:	Afternoon (12.00–17.00)	36
	Evenings (after 17.00)	69
Frequency of visits:	Twice a week or more	25
	Weekly	56
	Fortnightly	49
	Monthly	36

Frequency of usage

When respondents were asked to state how frequently they visited various restaurants, the answers in Table 3.10 emerged.

It is clear from these answers that a substantial number of the respondents surveyed ate out frequently, with most going out in the evenings and at weekends. This finding has a major implication in that any business wishing to enter the market would have to ensure that their needs are satisfied on days and times that are convenient to them. Furthermore, it provides some indication that quick afternoon lunches could be a viable proposition although the regularity of such visits would be regulated by the cost of the lunch (*see* Table 3.11 and 3.12).

Table 3.11 Niger Restaurant: amount spent
per visit

Amount spent (£)	%
10–15	45
16–25	40
26 and above	15

Table 3.12 Niger Restaurant: type of
restaurant visited

Type of Restaurant	%
Indian	45
Chinese	35
English	20
Other (inc. Afro-Caribbean)	18
Pizza Huts	15
McDonald's	15
Kentucky Fried Chicken (KFC)	11

Average expenditure per visit

Consumers were asked to state roughly how much they spend per visit. The answers
provided were interesting in so far as they provide a benchmark of possible prices that
could be charged by the Niger Restaurant should they wish to attract some afternoon
diners.

Type of restaurants used and occasion of vists

Consumers were asked to state the type of restaurant they had recently visited and the
occasion of their visit, the results are given in Tables 3.12 and 3.13.

The answers illustrate the popularity of both Indian and Chinese foods and the in-
roads yet to be made by Afro-Caribbean outlets. Although it can be argued that this
situation is changing as evidenced by the few Afro-Caribbean eating places that have

Table 3.13 Niger Restaurant:
occasion/reason for visit

Reason for visit	%
Fresh food	52
High standard of service	50
Weekend outing	47
Convenience	41
To taste foreign food	31
Healthy eating	30
Lunch break	26
Variety of food	15

sprung up over the last five years, the numbers are not nearly enough to redress this imbalance.

The answers in respect of the visit occasion help to identify the aspects that will need to be emphasised in any future marketing namely: high-quality food/service, convenient location and a place for relaxation at weekends. These aspects can be used to not only attract certain segments but also to distinguish one restaurant from another.

Table 3.14 Niger Restaurant: location of restaurants visited

Location	%
Crouch End	25
Finsbury Park	25
Tottenham	18
City	16
Green Lanes	16
Wood Green	16
Other areas	25

Location of restaurants

Following the factors perceived as important, respondents were then asked to state the location of the restaurants visited. Their responses are shown in Table 3.14.

When the location of restaurants visited is set against the place of residence of respondents, it can be seen that most tend to visit restaurants within their residential area or that are close to their workplace. This finding carries with it the implication that communications would have to be specifically targeted not only at the identified segments but also at consumers living and working near the location of the restaurant.

Table 3.15 Niger Restaurant: important factors in choice of restaurant

Factors	%
Cleanliness/hygiene	99
Freshness of food	80
Attractiveness	63
Price	59
Variety	50

Attributes considered important in restaurants visited

Table 3.15 summarises the factors perceived to be important in restaurants visited by respondents. This finding appears to support the general literature regarding the factors which may be used by service providers to create a competitive advantage. They will need to be carefully examined by the management of the Niger Restaurant

Consumers who visited restaurants

This question was an attempt to determine the profile of people who regularly visit restaurants. The answers provide the basis for segmenting the market and indicates the marketing mix programmes that should be developed to cater for each market segment.

The answers, given in Table 3.16 indicate that a large proportion of visitors are family members and those socialising.

Table 3.16 Niger Restaurant: profile of visitors

Visitor profile	%
Privately	60
With friends	58
Family without children	55
With workmates	45
Family with children	40

Type of facilities expected

Table 3.17 shows the basic facilities expected by respondents in restaurants selected. The aspect relating to facilities for children is significant and is one that will need to be carefully considered by any venture wishing to make a significant entrance into the marketplace.

Table 3.17 Niger Restaurant: facilities expected

Facilities	%
Toilet	98
Facilities for children	70
Smoking area	68
Cloakroom	50

How they learnt about restaurants visited

This question was an attempt to solicit some of the important means by which respondents came to hear about restaurants visited. (*See* Table 3.18.)

Table 3.18 Niger Restaurant: how they heard about the restaurants visited

Method	%
Leaflets through door	40
Word of mouth	30
Local papers	20
Local radio	10

Awareness of Afro-Caribbean restaurants

The questions in this last section attempted to find out the general awareness level of respondents regarding Afro-Caribbean food outlets, whether they have ever visited such outlets and their likelihood of visiting the future. The responses are given in Table 3.19.

This answer seems surprising given the efforts that have been made over the last few years by various Afro-Caribbean restaurants within London to promote themselves, some even getting national coverage on television and one or two even capturing a largely elite clientele in the West End. Nevertheless, it points to the task that needs to be accomplished and the need not to assume that those willing to try different foods will be well informed on the cuisine they are to eat.

Table 3.20, like Table 3.19 points to the low uptake of Afro-Caribbean eating places.

Table 3.21 provides hope in that it shows that a sizeable proportion of those interviewed were not averse to the idea of visiting in the future an Afro-Caribbean eating place. The answers overall indicate that there is potential for offering Afro-Caribbean foods but major communication efforts are required to inform and educate the general public about the various tastes to be expected from Afro-Caribbean foods. This, together with other marketing strategies, is likely to increase the competitiveness of this sector of the ethnic foods market.

Table 3.19 Niger Restaurant: awareness of Afro-Caribbean restaurants

	%
Yes	30
No	70

Table 3.20 Niger Restaurant: visits to Afro-Caribbean restaurants

	%
Yes	25
No	75

Table 3.21 Niger Restaurant: whether or not they would consider visiting such restaurants

	%
Yes	48
No/Don't know	52

APPENDIX F: POPULATION PROFILE OF HARINGEY

According to the 1991 census, over 30 per cent of the population of Haringey can be classified as belonging to the ethnic minorities. The latest estimate from the Borough itself indicates that the figure is much nearer 43 per cent as evidenced by Table 3.22. These figures reflect the diverse character of Haringey's population and the potential segments that could be targeted by the restaurant.

Despite the fact that Haringey is often presented as one of the most deprived boroughs in England, the borough itself notes in its recent report that wards vary in respect of degree of deprivation. In some wards, such as Bruce Grove and Bowes Park, the numbers employed vary between 70 and 80 per cent of the population and of these a sizeable proportion were classed as professionals (16.8 per cent) and managers (7.7 per cent). This illustrates the fact that the community is not stagnant and that economic regeneration is taking place. The council's own statistics indicate that in a labour force population of 162 605 aged 16 and over, some 105 693 (65 per cent) are economically active and, of this number some 60 000 were employed within Haringey.

Furthermore, Haringey is one of the most diverse boroughs in London with some 20 languages being spoken by its people. This diversity presents opportunities in that it is more likely to encourage people to understand different cultures and try different foods.

Table 3.22 Ethnic population profile of Haringey

	Number	%
Black Caribbean	18 862	9.3
Black African	11 085	5.5
Black other	4 613	2.3
Indian	7 265	3.6
Pakistani	1 476	0.7
Bangladeshi	3 060	1.5
Chinese	2 270	1.1
Other Asian	4 571	2.3
Other (non-white)	5 465	2.7
Irish	13 139	6.5
Cypriot	11 593	5.7
Turkish	3 890	1.9

Source: *Haringey in Figures*, November 1993.

Freddy Slinger's bed and breakfast

Ghalib Fahad

KEY THEMES

- marketing for small and medium-sized enterprises
- market segmentation
- product development

BRIEFING NOTES (Chapter 1)

- Buyer behaviour and market segmentation (pages 13–15)
- The product life-cycle (pages 22–23)
- Marketing services (pages 25–29)

Freddy Slinger started his bed and breakfast business soon after he was released from the army, after the Second World War. He came to Eastbourne because his wife, Shona, was born there and had convinced him that the majority of the British people would now spend their spare time in leisure activities, making up for the time they had lost during the War.

From a six-bedroomed building, the Slingers moved to new premises in the early 1950s which gave them a total of 30 bedrooms. Throughout the early years trade was irregular, but Freddy persisted in giving his customers the so-called 'personal touch'. Though at times the majority of his custom was from newlyweds, it was not long before other young couples, not necessarily married, began to stay at the 'the Slingers' (as it was popularly called by its regulars). This period was marked by an increase in the disposable income of a large section of the population, particularly those in younger age groups who, for the first time, found themselves with money to spend. They were looking for ways to 'discover' themselves, and many felt that one way of doing so was through visiting seaside resort areas which until recently had been largely reserved for the 'gentry' classes. Seaside resorts were thought to cater for a diverse group of people, including those in search of adventure.

By the 1960s, however, the profile of guests who were attracted to Eastbourne had changed, with a higher proportion of older people among the visitors. Freddy was fortunate, since he was able to retain a substantial part of the younger clientele who continued to stay at Slingers. As a matter of fact, a few continued to visit even when they had become parents (often with one or two children). Profits had remained steady, and the Slingers were satisfied that they had maintained a low level of overhead costs. Most of the work required on the business in the off-season (decorating, repairs and so on) was done by the Slingers themselves. Freddy, being a strong believer in 'standing on your own two feet' had encouraged his three children to take an active interest in the family business. The youngest child, Stuart, had become sufficiently interested to take a degree in hotel and restaurant management.

By the late 1970s Freddy realised that it was time to hand over the family business to his son, Stuart. The other children had left to develop their own careers, one in computing and the other as a travel agent. When Stuart completed his studies in 1986, Freddy handed over the business to his son.

On taking over the business Stuart became convinced that the business could be made more profitable. Having taken a look at the accounts kept by his father, Stuart discovered that for over ten years now the business had returned a gross profit of 15 per cent on sales; in 1986 sales turnover stood at £250 000. Stuart's own research of other bed and breakfast businesses within the area indicated that some were making as much as 30 per cent return on turnover. Many of these concerns were about the same size as Slingers.

After a year of running the business on his own, Stuart began thinking of ways of completely updating the business. Though Stuart would not think of hurting his father, who called in from time to time to help with odd chores, his knowledge of marketing convinced him that the product on offer at Slingers had reached the decline stage of its life-cycle. Further, he was convinced that the product was no longer appropriate because of a number of initiatives and developments that were taking place in Eastbourne. These were aimed at attracting younger people. The activities included tennis tournaments, open-air pop concerts, fashionable nightclubs, and so on. In short, the move was towards a younger, high-spending market segment.

Stuart's ideas for the development of Slingers were as follows:

- increasing his room capacity to 55 by taking over the building next door, which was for sale
- developing a restaurant to seat about 50 people, intended for both guests and non-residents
- providing an indoor swimming pool by converting some of the space currently under-used within the old building
- finally, to convert the much-neglected space in Slingers' backyard into two tennis courts.

There was adequate space for these developments, and no difficulty was envisaged in obtaining the necessary permissions from the local council. Before finalising the financing arrangements for the work, Stuart wanted further assurance that his marketing strategy was, indeed, an appropriate response to the trends which he had identified.

London Underground Ltd: Customer charter

Simon Speller

KEY THEMES

- understanding customer requirements
- researching consumer markets
- dealing with change in the marketing environment

BRIEFING NOTES (Chapter 1)

- The marketing concept (pages 4–6)
- The marketing mix and the marketing environment (pages 6–7)
- Analysis for marketing decisions (pages 13–21)
- Marketing services (pages 25–29)

BACKGROUND TO LONDON UNDERGROUND LTD (LUL)

What LUL does

- Oldest and one of the world's largest urban rapid-transit systems:
  - 273 stations (of which it owns 247)
  - nine separate branded lines
  - 2.8 million passenger trips per average weekday, 700 million trips a year
  - busiest station is Victoria: 57 million journeys start or finish there each year
- Key Markets
  - 50 per cent of the commuters in central and outer London travel to work area, peak hours weekdays
  - leisure travellers, off peak periods
  - tourists to London from elsewhere UK and overseas.

The physical infrastructure

- Stations (see above)
- 254 miles of track, 149 miles in the open, 85 in tube tunnelling and 20 miles in 'cut and cover' tunnelling
- Rolling stock – nearly 500 trains

- Staff – 19 000
- The oldest part – Metropolitan line (1863), District line (1868)
- The newest part – Jubilee line (1977), Angel Station (rebuilt entirely in 1993)
- It is not a single railway but a series of railways, linked up to make a system. Two different basic types of train (many different ages and types), three different basic types of station.

Organisation structure

- LUL is a subsidiary of London Transport, which is responsible to the Secretary of State for Transport for providing public transport services in London.
- LUL is organised as a series of directorates, including Engineering, Human resources, Safety and quality, Development, Finance and Business planning and Passenger services.
- The Passenger Services Directorate (PSD) is responsible for the day-to-day running of train services, stations and train maintenance. Within PSD, each line is managed by a general manager responsible for service quality, safety and for meeting financial targets. The general managers are, in effect, brand managers. They have control of trains, track and stations on their line, and, in theory at least, the rest of the LUL organisation should serve and support them.

BECOMING MORE BUSINESS LIKE

The way things were

A report by the Monopolies and Mergers Commission into London Underground in 1991 referred to three decades of 'chronic under-investment.' This can in large part be blamed on government under-funding over the years. However, the London Underground management can be said to share responsibility for this. Such under-investment created in part the conditions which allowed the Kings Cross fire disaster of November 1987 to happen. On the evening of 18 November a fire, caused by a lighted match which fell through a gap beside escalator treads and ignited an accumulation of rubbish underneath, brought about the deaths of 31 people. Up until this period, the London Underground system and its services could be said to be run like a branch of the civil service, but with the difference of having a strong 'engineering' culture in the way things were done or approved. In both marketing and operational terms, London Underground could be described fairly and accurately as 'service-led' rather than 'market' or 'customer-led'.

After the Kings Cross fire – The Fennell Report

The Fennell Inquiry of 1988 looked into the causes of the Kings Cross fire. The report of the Inquiry raised many questions about the management of London Underground. It identified several areas of management complacency, for example the belief or assumption on the part of managers that fires were inevitable on an underground railway system.

The report also raised many questions about the clarity of management roles and responsibilities, and about the difficulty of introducing changes in the organisation and in services. 'Slow change' often meant 'no change'.

The re-launch of London Underground Ltd

The Fennell Inquiry led to many changes in the underground system. The priority of safety was emphasised in a complete ban on smoking on the underground and a thorough review of safety procedures. Regular stringent safety audits of the system were introduced. At the same time a reorganisation of LUL was introduced to meet the requirements of the Fennell Report. The new management structure involved creating separate business units for each of the ten underground railway lines. The lines became the 'core business'. All other Directorates became 'support functions' for them. Thus LUL was to become a 'customer-led' business which would be more accountable, efficient and effective. It was understood that safety and quality together needed to be promoted, and that there needed to be rapid change towards a quality approach of continuous improvement, culture change and greater customer focus.

A flatter management structure was thus introduced throughout the organisation. Managing Director, Dennis Tunnicliffe, also introduced a Vision and Mission statement, which can be summed up by the acronym PLEASE:

- To be a key **P**artner in London's life and its continued prosperity.
- To become once again a **L**eader in the world's underground networks.
- To provide customers with an **E**njoyable travel experience, and a similar work experience for employees.
- To provide good services, **A**ffordable to Londoners and visitors.
- To ensure that services are **S**afe for customers and staff.
- To be regarded by customers and shareholders as **E**fficient and to satisfy ourselves that we actually are so.

Business goals

The Vision and Mission statement gave LUL a context for developing the underground's business goals. Four business goals were identified to be communicated throughout the organisation, to be given the same emphasis as safety issues. The goals were :

- running the maximum number of trains, at regular intervals, throughout the peak by September 1990
- having no more than 35 escalators out of commission at any one time by April 1991
- a welcoming and customer-friendly environment
- investment into assets covering track, signalling, escalators, stations, trains and other structures.

These goals were to be achieved through the development and implementation of the Company plan, which was launched in November 1991. The plan emphasised the need to improve safety, quality, efficiency and productivity in parallel. In March 1992 a revised Company purpose and Mission statement was produced. This identified corporate target requirements described as Key Performance Indicators (KPIs) and Critical Success Factor (CSF). At the same time, the LUL vision of becoming a 'decently modern metro' was launched. This meant :

- new or refurbished trains on all lines
- more frequent services, faster journeys and less crowding
- high-quality stations providing greater capacity and better standards of service
- reliable lifts and escalators
- new travel opportunities
- rebuilt track and restored embankments, tunnels, drainage, etc.
- Better information for customers
- a safe, secure environment for customers and employees

This Vision could only be achieved if London Underground, its customers and society as a whole, through the government, all played their part. The levels of investment implied in 1992 by government spending decisions would mean a decently modern metro could not be achieved in less than 20 years.

Developing customer focus – the quality programme

The development of Vision and Mission statements and the Company plan took place over the same period as the development of a Quality strategy and programme, to be led by a Quality Council of LUL directors, meeting each quarter.
The principles of the Quality Strategy are:

- to use a quality framework based on the European Foundation for Quality Management (EFQM) model
- to support the development of performance culture
- to use a defined control process for implementation of the strategy and other Quality initiatives
- to gain maximum employee involvement in both design and implementation
- to form support groups and action groups.

This provides the context for the marketing activities of LUL.

DEVELOPING MARKETING AT LUL

Marketing activities are primarily concentrated on the regular market research surveys of various types that are undertaken either corporately or by the individual line general managers. These support in some way the Customer Charter, the customer information strategy and the Key Performance Indicators.

THE CUSTOMER CHARTER – THE SERVICE PROMISE

The cornerstone to the development of marketing activities at London Underground is the Customer Charter, first produced in 1992. This is updated and re-issued annually. The purpose of the Charter is to tell the users/customers of the underground how well services have performed over the past year, and what targets are being set for the next year. The Charter is a kind of 'service promise' to customers.

Extracts from the 1994 Charter are set out in Figs 3.9 to 3.15.

- 'Welcome' – the introduction from Dennis Tunnicliffe, Managing Director (Fig 3.9)
- 'Improving the Underground' – on reliability of service (Fig 3.10)
- 'Bright, welcoming and efficient . . . a safe environment' – on cleanliness of trains and stations, queueing for tickets, escalators and lifts, and feelings of safety and security (Fig 3.11)

Welcome

London relies on its underground. Every day more than two million journeys are made by underground. The fastest way through the city, it helps keep traffic off the roads. It delivers employees and customers to business and commerce. It keeps London's cultural and social life flourishing.

We exist to deliver the best possible service for our customers and for all the others who rely on the underground's presence. To find out whether we are getting it right, we survey 2000 customers every month. Anonymous researchers visit our stations. We act on what is found. We aim to improve continuously the service we provide to our customers and to London. By fulfilling our purpose we enable others to fulfil theirs.

This, our third Charter, sets out what we have done over the past year to improve services, and what we plan to do in the coming year. We met 10 of our 12 targets last year. This Charter shows how this year's targets compare with last year's performance. We shall, of course, try to beat them. A better system of measurement is used this year, so the figures are not directly comparable to those in last year's document.

This Charter is our commitment to live up to the high standards people expect from us.

Dennis Tunnicliffe
Managing Director

Fig. 3.9 London Underground Ltd: Welcome

Our customers tell us they want a reliable and quick train service, bright, welcoming and efficient stations, a safe environment and helpful staff, at a value-for-money price. We aim to deliver these by investing in stations and trains and in ageing, largely unseen but vital areas like track and signalling. We are also investing in our own people through training and development so that they can do a better job for our customers.

Train service regularity: achieved when an interval between trains is less than twice the planned interval

Achieved 1994/95	95.5%
Target 1994/95	95.5%

Fig. 3.10 London Underground Ltd: Improving the underground

Train cleanliness – Average satisfaction rating by customers	
Achieved 1994/95 Target 1994/95	64% 65%
Station cleanliness – Average satisfaction rating by customers	
Achieved 1994/95 Target 1994/95	68% 70%
Ticket office queueing – Customers waiting more than three minutes to buy a ticket	
Achieved 1994/95 Target 1994/95	2.5% 2.5%
Escalators in customer service – Hours in service as % of possible hours	
Achieved 1994/95 Target 1994/95	90.5% 90%
Lifts in customer service – Hours in service as % of possible hours	
Achieved 1994/95 Target 1994/95	93.5% 93.5%
Feelings of safety and security – Average satisfaction rating of customers	
Achieved 1994/95 Target 1994/95	83% 83%

Fig. 3.11 London Underground Ltd: Bright, welcoming and efficient . . . a safe environment

- 'Helpful staff' – on information, staff availability and helpfulness (Fig 3.12)
- 'Value for money' – on financial issues such as investment in renewal and improvement of facilities and services, fares and refunds (Fig 3.13)

Information on trains – Average satisfaction rating by customers	
Achieved 1994/95	73%
Target 1994/95	75%
Information on stations – Average satisfaction rating by customers	
Achieved 1994/95	64%
Target 1994/95	65%
Staff available and helpfulness – Average satisfaction rating by customers	
Achieved 1994/95	63%
Target 1994/95	64%

We welcome comments on our service and suggestions for improvement. Please speak to any member of staff or drop a line to the Customer Services Centre, 55 Broadway, London SW1H 0BD. If you have a problem and station staff cannot resolve it, there is a Customer Contact Board at each of our stations with details of other people who will be able to help you. Please do give praise when it is merited so we can identify and thank those who serve you well.

If you contact us we will:
- give our name
- respond within seven working days
- keep you informed if we have to conduct an investigation
- tell you what we have done and why.

We hope to satisfy you with our answers, but if we do not you can contact London Regional Passengers Committee, which has been set up by Parliament to represent your interests.

Fig. 3.12 London Underground Ltd: Helpful staff

'. . . value for money . . .'

Paying for improvements

Running the underground, maintaining its equipment and improving the condition of its track, trains and structures is an expensive task. Last year, £560 million was invested in the renewal and improvement of the existing underground system. This is in addition to the £600 million it cost to operate the service – a cost wholly covered through fares revenue. We are constantly seeking ways to reduce costs while maintaining safety and quality, to release more money for improvements. Only a small part of the money invested in the underground – about 15 per cent – comes from fares and other income. The remainder comes from government grant. We are increasingly seeking alternative sources of finance.

Fares

It remains our policy that our customers should contribute towards the cost of improvements. Fares fell behind London earnings in the 1980s but are now in line with them again. We plan to make modest real fare increases in future years as our investment programme delivers further benefits.

Penalty Fares

To protect the honest fare-payer from fare-dodgers we have introduced a Penalty Fare system. Anyone on the system without a valid ticket or permit will be liable to pay £10 on the spot. Purchasing a ticket before travelling will ensure that we can identify the real fare-dodgers and make sure they are not subsidised by honest customers.

Our refund pledge

It is a cornerstone of the Charter that, in return for the fares you pay, we provide a refund if we delay you seriously. During 1993 we raised our standard. If, because of our failure, you wait on a platform for more than 15 minutes longer than advertised, or the underground train you are on is delayed by 15 minutes, we will refund you with a voucher to the value of the delayed single journey. Previously the threshold for refunds was 20 minutes.

Fig. 3.13 London Underground Ltd: Value for money

- 'How to claim' – on refunds for delays in train services (and note 'the small print') (Fig 3.14)
- 'Performance check' – charts of train service reliability (Fig 3.15).

Claim forms for refunds are available from stations or from our Customer Services Centre. If you have a single or return ticket or a One or Seven Day Travelcard you will need to attach it to the form. Holders of single or return tickets should not pass through the automatic gates – please ask a member of staff to allow you through the side gate and retain your ticket. You should send your form 'freepost' to the Customer Services Centre within 14 days of the delay. To help us to process your claim quickly please complete a separate form for each delay. We aim to reply to your claim within seven working days. We are sorry that we have failed to achieve this recently because of the volume of claims arising from the serious power failures of November 1993. We intend to return to the standard by the autumn.

> The small print
>
> You will understand that we cannot give refunds in circumstances preventing us from safely running trains such as security alert, freak weather or because of action by a third party; nor when we have publicised in advance an alternative route, for example, because of engineering works. Special conditions will apply if we have an industrial dispute.

Investment in the Underground 1993/94

Central Line renewal	£145 million
Infrastructure	£128 million
Trains	£52 million
Stations	£105 million
Other	£130 million
Total	£560 million

Fig. 3.14 London Underground Ltd: How to claim

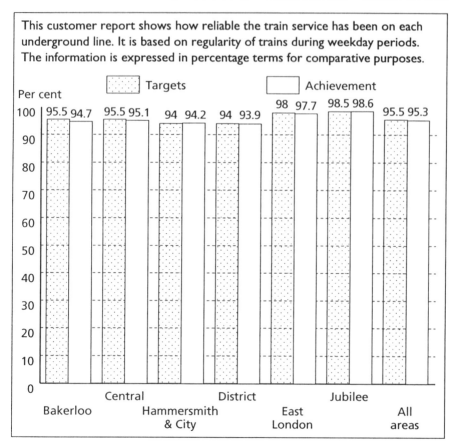

This customer report shows how reliable the train service has been on each underground line. It is based on regularity of trains during weekday periods. The information is expressed in percentage terms for comparative purposes.

Fig. 3.15 **London Underground Ltd: Performance check**

Marketing research programmes and methods

London Underground carries out a wide range of market research programmes. The programmes are collated by the Market Research Department to provide a wide range of data for management. Three key pieces of research are used company wide to help inform business decisions and whether goals are being met. These are:

- customer satisfaction survey – this survey randomly samples 1800 people on 23 aspects of service every month. The results are fed back to both the front-line management and senior management to ensure they are constantly kept aware of how they are doing, and how they can improve.
- marketplace performance survey – this comprises 21 visits to all stations per year by mystery shoppers who score every aspect of both staff and infrastructure performance. This report is fed back to line management in the same way as the customer satisfaction survey and the two can be used in conjunction to pin-point particular areas that need improvement.

- passenger preference report – this report shows the key concerns of customers and allows LUL to identify and prioritise efforts.

There are also a large number of other pieces of market research that are carried out on an ad hoc basis for a particular business unit which enables their management to identify and work on specific local issues.

London Underground publishes many leaflets covering how to use the system, special help available for the visually and physically impaired, and those using the system with aids such as pushchairs. Communication campaigns include details of how to use ticket machines, tourist attractions and their most appropriate station for these, and also advice on helping LUL to address the problems of security alerts and litter. Many posters are also multilingual to help the foreign customer.

The Underground has a large Communications Department which incorporates the Press and PR function. This actively promotes the company and encourages LUL managers to meet the public at the stations, as well as playing a part in their local station community.

Adopting quality frameworks – The EFQM model

From the launch of the Total Quality Leadership Programme in 1990 until 1994 LUL managers and quality advisers found it difficult to develop a coherent and corporate quality programme. In 1994 it was agreed that the European Foundation for Quality Management (EFQM) Model and Framework for self-assessment be adopted, and LUL duly joined the EFQM (*see* Fig 3.16).

The EFQM Model allows managers and staff to see the 'big picture' of a quality programme, and it identifies the key areas and elements for action and success:

- **Enablers – what an organisation does, and how it does things**
  - leadership
  - policy and strategy
  - people management
  - resource management
  - processes

- **Results – the impacts of what the organisation does**
  - customer satisfaction
  - people satisfaction
  - impact on society
  - business results.

Enablers Criteria

Leadership – the behaviour of all managers in driving the organisation towards total quality.

Policy and Strategy – the organisation's mission, values, vision and strategic direction and the ways in which the organisation achieves them.

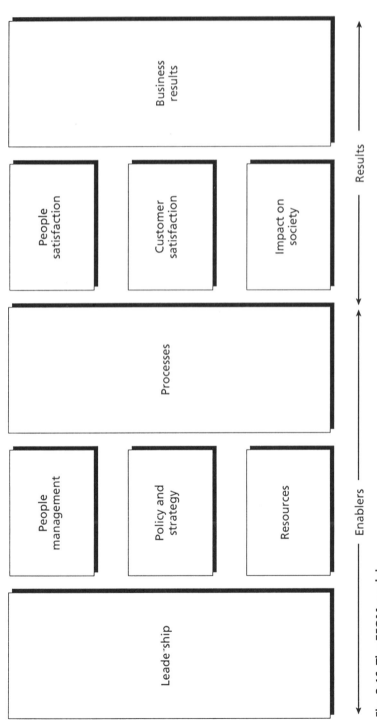

Fig. 3.16 The EFQM model

People management – how the organisation releases the full potential of its people to improve its business continuously.

Resources – how the organisation's resources are effectively deployed in support of policy and strategy.

Processes – The management of all the value-adding activities within the organisation.

Results Criteria

Customer satisfaction – what the perception of external customers is of the organisation and of its products and services.
People satisfaction – what the people's feelings are about their organisation.
Impact on society – what perception of the organisation is among society at large.
Business results – what the organisation is achieving in relation to its planned business performance.

MARKETING MANAGEMENT ISSUES FOR LUL

Despite the volume of work and effort at LUL to promote a market-orientated approach and a quality programme in the last five years, to an outside observer LUL still appears to be essentially service led.

Marketing research is being undertaken on a greater scale, and is reported to managers locally and at the centre of the organisation. The EFQM Model provides both a general framework for understanding what needs to be done and specific areas to focus on for improvement. The opportunities for change and threats can be perhaps be summed up as in Table 3.23.

The London Underground 'brand'

The diverse origin of many of the lines forming the underground has left a variety of station designs and sites needed ranging from deep-level tube lines in the centre of the city to stations serving small country towns in the outer suburbs.

The street access to every station is marked by the world-famous underground logo. Before this logo came into use stations had used the traditional British form of displaying the name of the company and station on the exterior of the street-level building and the name of the station at each ends of the platforms. The tube line incorporated the station name in the tiling of platform walls together with 'way out' signs. The bar and disc signs appeared on platform walls from 1913, together with a frieze repeating the name of the station along its length.

The London Underground world-famous map was designed and first used in 1933 and it has served as a model for tube maps all over the world.

Table 3.23 London Underground Ltd: opportunities and threats

Key activity	Opportunity	Threat
Understand customer requirements through market research	Conduct appropriate research on the key issues	Undertake the same
Being prepared to act on the data	Top management need to believe what the data is telling them and act	The data is reported and the report is ignored
Using customer data to devise specifications for services (standards)	Standards are related to what customers are looking for, on the issues they identify	The data is only collected for 'safe' issues, or relates to what managers look for
Delivering services to the specification agreed (standard)	Continuous tracking of performance via market research to monitor performance	Ad hoc or no tracking of performance
Communicating the specification (standard) to customers	Promising only what can be delivered, and communicating via appropriate media	The Charter bears no relation to customer needs, and is ignored

London Underground operates two different types of rolling stock tube and surface stock. The surface stock is similar to full-size British Rail mainline stock but the tube stock is considerably smaller in order to fit in the single track circular tube tunnels. Another reason for the different types of stock is that replacement has to be spread over many years. Trains are therefore replaced in batches, usually on a line by line basis, taking into account traffic requirements, technical improvements and modern design expectations. Currently the London Underground has ten main types of passenger stock: three surface stocks and seven tube stocks.

New rolling stock, signalling and power supplies are currently being installed on the Central Line. One of the most distinctive features of the new trains is in the use of colour. The new corporate livery of red doors and cabs with white body supported by a blue panel along the lower sides has replaced the unpainted finish familiar to underground users over the last 20 years. Customer facilities include 'talk-back' facilities for customers to communicate with the driver in an emergency and digitised speech announcements at station. The needs of the disabled have been taken into consideration by using contrasting colours and door chimes.

Table 3.24 London Underground Limited: the lines

Line	Description	Length M	Stations	passen-ger trips %
Bakerloo	Elephant and Castle to Harrow and Wealdstone	14	25	7
Central	Ealing Broadway and West Ruislip to Hainault and Epping	52	51	17
Hammersmith and Circle	A circle combining central points of the Metropolitan and District Lines, Hammersmith to Whitechapel	13 9	27 19 (28 rush hour	16.5
District	Upminster to Ealing, Richmond and Wimbledon (branches to Edgware Road and Olympia)	40	50	16.6
Jubilee and East London	Charing Cross to Stanmore, Whitechapel to New Cross and New Cross Gate	14 4	17 7 (8)	2
Metropolitan	Baker Street to Amersham (branches to Chesham, Watford, Uxbridge)	41.5	34	11
Northern	Morden to Edgware, Mill Hill East and High Barnet via Bank or Charing Cross	36	49	17
Piccadilly	Cockfosters to Heathrow Airport and Uxbridge	43.5	52	12
Victoria	Walthamstow Central to Brixton	14	16	8

SECTION 4

Cases in business goods marketing

Ethical issues in marketing research

Ross Brennan

KEY THEMES

- researching industrial markets
- ethical and unethical research methods

BRIEFING NOTES (Chapter 1)

- The marketing concept (pages 4–6)
- Managing marketing research (pages 17–21)

Plastique Ltd is a medium-sized company in the plastic mouldings business. They compete for a well-defined market segment, within which they have a 20 per cent market share, making them number two in the market after Alpha Plastics plc which is believed to have a share of 45 per cent. Plastique Ltd relies heavily on this segment, from which they derive 75 per cent of their revenue and around 90 per cent of their profits.

Recent attempts to identify profitable opportunities for product or market development have been unsuccessful, leading the Managing Director to conclude that the company will have to rely on this market for survival and growth for the foreseeable future. In view of this, the MD was very concerned to hear a rumour that Alpha Plastics plc might have developed a new plastic moulding process which would enable it to improve quality while reducing prices by as much as 15 per cent. She is determined to find out as much as possible about the Alpha Plastics plc development as possible, as quickly as possible, in order to develop a counter-strategy. In her view, the survival of Plastique Ltd probably depends on her ability to obtain and exploit meaningful information quickly. Her job, and the jobs of the 50 other people working for the company, could be at stake.

She is considering a number of possibilities to obtain the market intelligence that she requires.

1 Carry out a detailed search of the plastic mouldings trade press to see whether any information has leaked out of Alpha Plastics plc.
2 Ask a good friend to get in touch with Alpha Plastics, posing as a potential

customer, and to gather as much information either over the phone, or by visiting the Alpha Plastics plant.

3 Invite the Sales Director of Alpha Plastics (an old friend) out to an expensive and alcoholic lunch, and pump him for as much information as possible.

4 Persuade her production supervisor to apply for the job of production manager at Alpha Plastics (currently vacant) and to use the interview and plant visit as an intelligence-gathering opportunity.

5 At the next plastic mouldings trade fair, to visit openly the Alpha Plastics stand and collect every piece of product and promotional literature that they offer.

6 Ask her niece, who is studying production engineering at Middlesex University, to ring up Alpha Plastics and ask for an interview and visit to help with a (fictitious) project on 'advanced manufacturing techniques in the plastics industry'.

7 Speak informally to known customers of Alpha Plastics, and ask them what they know about the new production technique.

8 Engage a private detective to gather information on the Production Director at Alpha Plastics, who is suspected of highly embarrassing (but legal) sexual impropriety, with the intention of obtaining the information by blackmail.

Question
Please make a judgement on the ethics of each of the above possibilities using the following scale:

1 Wholly ethical behaviour.
2 Acceptable behaviour, minor ethical misgivings.
3 Barely acceptable behaviour, considerable ethical misgivings.
4 Unethical, but I would still give it serious consideration.
5 Wholly unethical. Behaviour entirely unacceptable.

Use Table 4.1 as a structure for your answers.

Table 4.1 Ethical issues in market research

Statement	Your response
1 Consult trade press	
2 Friend poses at customer	
3 Take Sales Director out for lunch	
4 Instruct employee to apply for job	
5 Visit stand at trade fair	
6 Niece pretends to do student project	
7 Speak informally to known customers	
8 Obtain information for blackmail	

Distribution in Hungary

James Patterson

KEY THEMES

- market segmentation and targeting
- political change and the marketing environment
- market development strategy
- distribution channels

BRIEFING NOTES (Chapter 1)

- The marketing mix and the marketing environment (pages 6–7)
- Buyer behaviour and market segmentation (pages 13–15)
- Setting objectives and devising strategies (pages 45–46)

THE STATE MONOPOLY

Prior to the collapse of Communism in Hungary and the subsequent rise of the new political and economic order, the supply of stationery was run as a state monopoly. In this instance, stationery includes paper, writing material, exercise books, pre-printed invoices, envelopes and statements; in effect, materials designed to fulfil needs for both the commercial and educational sectors of the Hungarian economy. Despite this objective, the centralised, bureaucratic organisation was essentially inefficient.

Although the business was centralised, that is with goods being manufactured, purchased and supplied centrally, the distribution arrangements were organised on a regional basis. The country was divided into six regions including Budapest, the criterion used for this division being purely based on historical boundaries. A regional manager was appointed for each region, with the responsibility for running the region and reporting directly to the general manager in the capital (a political appointee in Budapest). Each region was autonomous, in so far as it only serviced its own geographical territory as defined, and all staff came under the control of the regional manager. All regional managers received a civil service remuneration based on the status of their appointment.

Warehousing was established in each region and serviced from central stores in Budapest. These regional warehouses supplied the needs of retail outlets as well as supplying larger customers direct, such as schools and local government offices. The retail shops, also state owned and regionally controlled were supplied with what was considered the correct mix of stock. This was dictated by both political needs and what was available. The retail shops were supposed to supply the stationery needs of the local community both educationally and commercially.

THE PRIVATISATION

In the reconstruction of the Hungarian economy following the fall of the communist regime, it was decided to privatise many industries. One of these was the former state-controlled distribution of stationery.

As the business was already organised on a regional basis, it was decided that the privatisation should follow a similar pattern. The six businesses were to become fully autonomous, with their own boards of directors, able to buy and sell where they wished, and competing with each other where feasible. The new independence would permit the companies to modernise and invest in new technology where appropriate (provided of course that they made good profits) and would enable them to compete with the new entry competition.

A consequence of the political and economic changes was the entrance of other competitors into the market. A number of German and Austrian companies took advantage of the new liberal Hungarian attitude towards inward investment and the relatively stable economy, particularly when compared with other former Eastern Bloc states. It is no surprise that Hungary has attracted over 50 per cent of all inward investment into former Eastern Bloc states, totalling $5.3 billion.

THE SOUTH TRANSDANUBIAN REGION

The city of Pecs, fifth largest city in Hungary, is in the centre of the South Transdanubian region, which comprises the counties of Baranya, Somogy, Tolna and Zala. The city has a population of 172 000, with a regional population of 1.3 million. This comprises 12.7 per cent of the total Hungarian population. Pecs has a long and often violent history of invasion, capture and liberation. In consequence it is a melting pot of people of different ethnic origins and diverse cultures. The city boasts a rich cultural variety in particular its theatres and its world-famous university.

Much of the city's historic economic importance was based on its geographic location, at the base of the Mecsek mountain serving as a gateway to other Balkan regions, and the rich agricultural land upon which it is situated. From the 17th century onwards, tanning became a major industry. There is still some of that skill remaining, although sadly it is neither as extensive nor as recognised as it once was, when gloves for the Pope and other well-known personages, were supplied from Pecs. Coal mining and latterly uranium mining have been the major local industries, but both have now lost their markets, the former because of the changing energy needs and growing international competition and the latter because the former sole customer, Russia, no longer requires the output. As a result the area suffers from structural unemployment and is urgently seeking new employment opportunities.

THE REGIONAL COMPANY

Pecs, as the regional capital, is the site of the new regional stationery company headquarters. It is situated in Perezulu Utca just off Szechanyi Square in the city centre. There is also a warehouse and various shops in the region. This building also houses the retail shop and showroom and it is possible for anyone to walk in off the street and purchase even small items such as a pencil or notebook.

This state of affairs may have been satisfactory when it was a nationalised monopolistic industry, but it is becoming increasingly apparent that as an individual commercial enterprise it is difficult to conduct business with wholesale and retail customers and service them both effectively. For example, the following require different approaches to business:

- to consult with the directors of the Zsolnay Ceramics factory, potentially a very large user
- to sell wholesale
- to provide the appropriate retail shop service.

The different market segments exhibit different price elasticities, require different product ranges, and have quite different purchasing criteria. By trying to address all these segments simultaneously with, essentially, a single marketing mix, the company is undermining its own competitive position.

The cash sales made in the shops throughout the region are valuable to the company, since they contribute to the cash-flow, particularly when compared with the credit facilities that have to be offered to non-retail customers. They also provide a better gross profit than the return earned on bulk orders. On the other hand, commercial contracts with large regional firms offer substantial levels of turnover, the potential for long-term business, and concentrating here could eliminate the need to maintain retail premises at all.

In its conversion to a commercial, market-driven enterprise, the company initially inherited South Transdanubia as its territory, just like the other six regions; however, the management have now realised that:

(a) the geographical organisation is very restrictive
(b) certain areas cannot be serviced economically within the region and would be better serviced by local enterprises, although the company would hope to continue supplying the intermediary
(c) there are areas in neighbouring regions of urban population with schools, colleges and commercial/industrial activity that could be serviced by them, as well as if not better than by the local company

(d) the environment is changing rapidly and competition is increasing almost daily.

This has led the new Managing Director, an ambitious entrepreneur, not only to look covetously at the other regions, particularly those bordering South Transdanubia, but to actively consider competing with his old partner organisations, in an area of business that both he and his staff know as well as they do.

Authors note:
This case is largely based on the author's own observations whilst on a visit to Pecs, Hungary in November 1993, as well as on secondary material.

Svenska Ackumulator AB Jungner: marketing planning in a multinational company

Frederick E. Webster Jr

KEY THEMES

- industrial goods marketing
- marketing strategy and planning
- business market segmentation
- competitive pricing strategy
- marketing research and sales forecasting

BRIEFING NOTES (Chapter 1)

- Buyer behaviour and market segmentation (pages 13–15)
- Segmentation of organisational markets (pages 15–17)
- A marketing model for pricing decisions (pages 40–42)
- Marketing planning and strategy (pages 43–52)

Mr Arne Nilsson, Deputy Managing Director of Svenska Ackumulator AB Jungner, liked to describe his company as 'Sweden's smallest multinational corporation'. In 1971, total sales had reached 132 598 000 Swedish crowns (krona), a growth of 16 per cent over 1970 (in 1972, 1 krona = 0.193 US$; after devaluation in 1973, 1 krona = 0.223 US$). The principal product of the Jungner Group of companies was the NIFE line of nickel cadmium alkaline storage batteries and power supply systems which accounted for about 85 per cent of total sales. From company headquarters in Oskarshamn, Sweden, Mr Nilsson was responsible for all NIFE products and for co-ordinating the marketing activities of subsidiary companies in Argentina, Austria, Belgium, Brazil, Germany, Italy, Mexico, the Netherlands, Spain, Switzerland and the USA, as well as in Sweden. Sales in Scandinavia, as well as most export volume, were managed by the parent company, again under Mr Nilsson's direction.

All of the subsidiary companies, with the exception of the Belgian, Dutch and Swiss companies manufactured nickel cadmium batteries (with material or semifinished products supplied from Sweden and some parts bought locally) as well as marketing them. In addition, the Brazilian and Spanish companies also manufactured lead acid batteries (sold under the brand names Lorica for Brazil and Pebe for Spain), which accounted for only 10 per cent of total Jungner Group battery sales. Many of these subsidiaries also exported into other countries, with sales representatives operating in an additional 70 countries. Normally, export orders were handled by the parent company in Sweden, but when transportation, production or tariff considerations favoured it, products might be shipped from a subsidiary. The parent company made the decision whether to quote from a subsidiary or from the parent company.

Oskarshamn was a port and industrial town with a population of 25 000 located on the eastern (Baltic) coast of Sweden about 65 kilometres north of the port city of Kalmar and about 230 kilometres south of Stockholm. A small airline provided two flights daily, each way, between Oskarshamn and Stockholm with an intermediate stop in Västervik.

In addition to batteries, the company marketed a line of power supply equipment, some of which was manufactured by the Elektro-Herman AB subsidiary of the Jungner Group. In other cases, subsidiaries either had power supply equipment manufactured locally by subcontractors or manufactured it themselves, always selling it under the NIFE brand name. The NIFE product line also included a line of emergency lighting equipment.

Among the other activities of the Jungner Group were AB Ruda Glasbruk, a glass-manufacturing business which was closed down in 1972; AB Riddarkontor which leased office premises in Stockholm on a service basis; and a line of mechanical products including signalling equipment (for ships, aircraft and railways), the Thermotron liquid petroleum gas driven heater for heating vehicles, workmen's huts and small boats, and a vertical milling machine line. In addition, Jungner held minority interest in Nordiska Ackumulator-fabriker NOACK AB (with Varta AG as the majority shareholder) and in Jungner Instrument AB (with the Incentive Group, which was part of the Wallenburg Group). NOACK was a manufacturer of lead acid batteries and controlled about 40–50 per cent of the market in Finland, Norway and Sweden. The company had been formed by merging the Jungner lead acid batteries activities with those of Boliden Batteri AB, a company formerly owned by Varta. Jungner Instrument had at one time been wholly owned by Jungner but was sold as management developed a feeling in the mid-1960s that the Jungner Group was too diversified for its size. Jungner had at one time also owned a shipyard and a nautical instruments company.

As the company's sales volume increased, the range of potential applications became broader and more complex, Arne Nilsson increasingly felt the need for a formal marketing planning system. Once again, in early 1973, he was trying to design such a system; three earlier attempts to develop a planning system had failed to get off the ground, the most recent in 1971 and 1972. Mr Nilsson reviewed the causes of these earlier disappointments in the hope of discovering a better way to begin the planning task. He believed that the subsidiaries' competitive effectiveness would decrease without such a system and he was concerned that many of them, especially those in the largest and most industrially developed markets, were actually losing market share. There was serious competition from other manufacturers of nickel cadmium batteries and other types of alkaline batteries, as well as from the lower priced lead acid batteries. Mr Nilsson explained:

The problem is not only marketing planning but more generally one of co-ordination as we move away from complete autonomy for the subsidiaries toward a more consistent marketing strategy for NIFE products worldwide. Our central marketing organisation can be an important sales tool but we are not using it properly now.

The marketing organisation for NIFE products is shown in Figure 4.1. In each subsidiary there was a chief executive officer who had a three-way reporting relationship:

(a)   to Arne Nilsson for marketing matters on NIFE products
(b)   to Karl Robert Ameln, Managing Director of the Jungner group, for overall subsidiary policy and administrative matters
(c)   to Carl-Olof Steen, Mr Nilsson's peer as Deputy Managing Director, for financial matters. Four Regional Marketing Directors, located in Sweden, handled problems of co-ordination of export sales from Sweden with subsidiary marketing activities and the direction of the sales efforts of agents in countries with no subsidiary company.

THE PRODUCT LINE AND APPLICATIONS

The company's basic product was a pocket-type nickel cadmium alkaline storage battery (or 'accumulator'). In a pocket-type battery, the active materials are enclosed in pockets fabricated from perforated steel strips. The founder of the original company, Waldemar Jungner, was a Swedish inventor who had patented the original battery system in 1899. The brand name NIFE came from the original system which had used nickel (Ni) and iron (Fe), although cadmium was later substituted for the iron.

The basic function of an electric storage battery is to receive electric power from some external source and then to store it in chemical form for release upon demand. A typical battery installation consists of from 20 to 1000 cells. Nickel cadmium batteries typically cost somewhat more than lead acid batteries, but the extra cost was often justified by greater reliability and other advantages which gave the nickel cadmium battery an economic advantage in the long run, especially in more demanding performance applications. Among the many advantages claimed for NIFE batteries were immunity to electrical abuses such as overcharging and momentary shorting, ability to withstand low temperatures and rough handling, low weight and compact size, simple maintenance, long life, stable capacity, negligible self-discharge, faster charging and no corrosive fumes. Not only did nickel cadmium batteries have long life but they gave relatively constant power output over the life of the battery, whereas lead acid batteries deteriorated more steadily. NIFE nickel cadmium batteries were made in three different lines allowing differ-

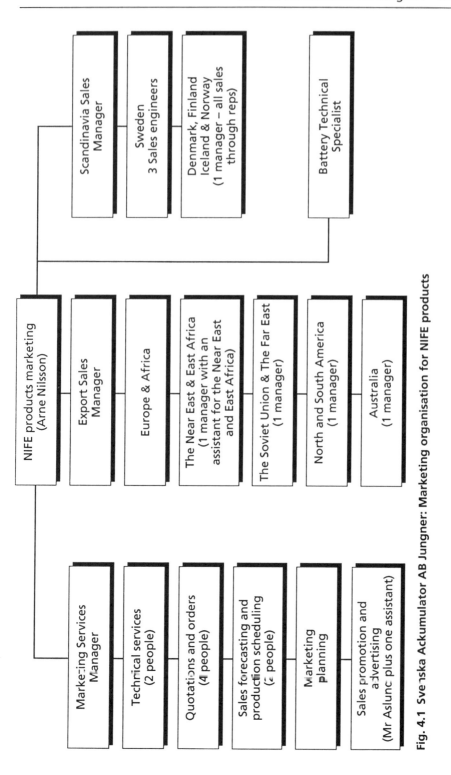

Fig. 4.1 Svenska Ackumulator AB Jungner: Marketing organisation for NIFE products

NIFE products marketing
(Arne Nilsson)

Scandinavia Sales Manager

Sweden
3 Sales engineers

Denmark, Finland
Iceland & Norway
(1 manager – all sales
through reps)

Battery Technical
Specialist

Export Sales Manager

Europe & Africa

The Near East & East Africa
(1 manager with an
assistant for the Near East
and East Africa)

The Soviet Union & The Far East
(1 manager)

North and South America
(1 manager)

Australia
(1 manager)

Marketing Services Manager

Technical services
(2 people)

Quotations and orders
(4 people)

Sales forecasting and
production scheduling
(2 people)

Marketing
planning

Sales promotion and
advertising
(Mr Aslund plus one assistant)

ent trade-offs between capacity, performance (rate of output), and weight and size. This made it easier to select the optimum battery for any particular application.

A major application of nickel cadmium batteries was in railroad operations where they were used for train lighting and air-conditioning, diesel engine cranking, and in signalling equipment for railroad crossings. Other important applications included standby emergency power for computer installations, power plants, hospitals and airport runway lighting. Nickel cadmium batteries were also used in ships (for emergency lighting and motors for closing hatches), in telecommunications systems, in process control systems in processing industries such as petroleum refining and chemicals, and in a wide variety of other uses. In general terms, battery power was important in mobile applications (trains, ships, aircraft and missiles) where a main-line supply was unavailable and in emergency applications such as standby power for lighting, for diesel engine cranking, in emergency power supply systems for hospitals, airports, computer systems, public utilities, etc. Mr Nilsson grouped customers into six categories: computer users, government, communication and transportation systems, public utilities, institutions and industrial users. Traditionally, railroads had been the single most important users. The importance of particular applications varied widely among the subsidiary companies' markets (*see* Table 4.2), which Mr Nilsson believed to be further evidence of the need for more co-ordination of sales activities.

In recent years, the product line had grown to include other components of a total supply system. These included inverters, rectifiers, frequency converters, battery chargers, alarms, filters, output voltage regulators, automatic charge controllers, emergency power controls, and systems products (other than batteries) had grown 35 per cent in sales over the previous year (*see* Table 4.3). Future growth in total NIFE product sales was expected to come mainly from power supply systems. As noted earlier, some of these items were manufactured by the Elektro-Hermas subsidiary (including all of these components sold in Scandinavia or exported from Sweden). Briefly, the functions performed by these various products can be described as follows:

- rectifiers – convert alternating current (AC) to direct current (DC)
- frequency converters – convert d.c. at one frequency to another frequency
- inverters – convert DC to AC, as would be required when an emergency power supply from nickel cadmium batteries (DC) was used to feed loads normally supplied by line supply (AC)
- battery chargers – provide constant voltage electrical power to the batteries from an outside source
- automatic charge controllers – permit automatic change-over of battery chargers from floating (float voltage) to high-rate charging (increased voltage)
- alarms – can be attached to charger to indicate over-and/or under-voltage operation, set to any voltage level desired
- voltage regulator – regulates voltage output from the battery, compensating for normal variations in output

Table 4.2 Svenska Ackumulator AB Jungner: market applications for NIFE nickel cadmium batteries; importance of subsidiaries, percentage of 1971 total

	Lighting[1]	Stationary cranking	Mobile cranking	Mobile operation	Signal and alarm	Telecom-munications	Standby power[2]	Auxiliary power[3]	Inverter supply	Total
Sweden	26.1	1.5	9.5	0.8	31.3	14.1	14.7	0.6	1.4	100.0
Germany	62.5	7.9	8.7	5.1	0.9	1.2	0.6	0.4	12.7	100.0
Austria	41.7	1.4	14.9	5.1	3.2	31.0	1.3	0.7	0.7	100.0
Italy	36.4	4.9	26.2	13.1	6.0	5.3	7.1	0.9	0.1	100.0
Spain	35.7	8.1	23.2	5.6	12.3	5.3	8.2	0.6	0.5	100.0
USA	28.9	1.6	20.4	0.5	2.3	13.7	13.7	0.0	13.9	100.0
Brazil	4.8	0.9	35.1	0.4	13.2	0.1	44.1	0.2	1.2	100.0
Argentina	9.2	1.9	8.7	14.4	33.5	1.6	27.1	0.3	3.3	100.0
Switzerland	60.2	9.4	19.1	0.2	0.0	4.2	0.1	1.9	4.9	100.0
Netherlands	49.8	3.9	26.8	2.3	0.2	8.3	4.8	0.0	3.9	100.0
Belgium	18.8	3.2	19.9	2.7	8.5	32.0	12.3	2.6	–	100.0
Export	36.9	0.0	9.2	2.3	1.3	4.7	43.1	1.8	0.7	100.0
Total	33.0	3.0	17.9	3.7	9.0	7.2	20.4	0.6	5.2	100.0

1 Including stationary, emergency lighting and lighting for railroads, ships and aircraft, runway lighting, portable hand lanterns and navigation aid (buoys).
2 'Standby' power applications usually involve a battery working in parallel over a rectifier connected to the mains, as in switchgear tripping and control, magnetic cranes and vehic e braking systems.
3 'Auxiliary' power systems do not have batteries working in parallel with the mains supply and usually involve 'emergency' inverter supply for AC-operated equipment.

Table 4.3 Svenska Ackumulator AB Jungner: sales results and growth by product

	Total sales batteries and power supply systems		Annual sales growth NIFE batteries		Annual sales growth power supply systems*	
	1970 Kr 000	1971 Kr 000	1969/70 %	1970/71 %	1969/70 %	1970/71 %
Argentina			2.3	13.6	1200.0	-7.7
Austria			3.3	6.5	–	–
Belgium			0.0	25.0	–	–
Brazil			3.5	43.9	3.0	23.5
Hollsand			33.3	15.6	80.0	-11.1
Italy			10.3	39.5	-25.0	133.3
Mexico			–	–	–	–
Spain			3.1	21.2	25.0	40.0
Switzerland			100.0	25.0	–	-33.3
USA			9.5	-17.3	-13.3	7.7
West Germany			45.6	59.7	60.0	70.8
Export from Sweden			54.2	36.5	–	500.5
Scandinavia			10.6	1.0	60.0	62.5
Total Group	80 500	96 400	14.8	17.2	31.4	35.4

* Excluding Elektro-Hermas sales to outside customer.
Note: The ratio of power supply systems sales to battery sales varied widely among subsidiaries

- filter – filters out so-called 'ripple voltage', short jumps in voltage, to below 0.15 per cent;
- emergency power control – connects a battery to a 'load', normally emergency lighting, in the event of a failure of line supply.

Jungner had produced or purchased for resale several smaller items on a limited scale including wall lamps and hand lamps with built-in NIFE batteries, battery-powered hospital lamps, and produced small sealed cells for use in portable TV sets, movie and photographic equipment, cordless household appliances, control and alarm systems and so on. There were a number of possible combinations of the components between a battery charger and a load giving numerous applications for various combinations. Batteries could account for from 20 to 90 per cent of total power supply system value.

RELATIONSHIPS WITH SUBSIDIARIES

The Managing Directors and Presidents (the title depended on the country) of the foreign subsidiaries were generally free to conduct their business as independent profit centres, subject to certain policies. Such decisions as hiring personnel or increasing the size of the salesforce or production workforce were made locally, although any major changes were usually discussed with Oskarshamn.

Most subsidiaries employed their own salespeople although some, such as NIFE USA, sold through independent agents such as manufacturers' representatives. In the US, several major original equipment manufacturer (OEM) accounts were handled as 'house accounts', by the Sales Manager. (The Sales Manager's duties were then being handled by the President of the American company, Mr Ted Ulrich, as the company had been without a Sales Manager for several months.) The house accounts in the US included the Electromotive Division (i.e. locomotives) of General Motors, the General Electric Co., and so on. In late 1971, Mr Per Georg Sjöström, Managing Director of NIFE Italy, had spent some time in the US analysing the 'rep' organisation to determine if a direct selling operation might not be preferable. When he had been Managing Director of NIFE Germany several years before, Mr Sjöström had made such a change. From his study of the US situation, he concluded that direct coverage was not feasible at this time because of Jungner's relatively low sales volume and the large area of the US. He did, however, recommend that the company should experiment with direct sales coverage in such relatively concentrated market areas as Detroit, New York and Los Angeles.

The nature of the sales organisation in other countries varied widely. As noted before, the Dutch, Belgian and Swiss subsidiaries were strictly sales companies, whereas the others also had manufacturing operations. The type of sales organisation also varied. For example, the German company had salespeople assigned to geographic territories and responsible for the entire product line, whereas the Dutch company had product specialists who were responsible for the entire country. In some countries there was a sales manager and in others this remained the general manager's responsibility. Sales compensation practices also varied although most company-employed salespeople were paid primarily on a salary basis with some variable compensation added through commissions or bonuses.

Pricing practices were complicated by the multiplicity of factors that had to be considered in each situation, including local tariff regulations and duties, the cost of labour in each country, other operating expenses, the need to maintain economical production volumes in Sweden and the requirements for competing effectively with both alkaline and lead acid batteries. The company generally tried to follow a conservative pricing strategy, emphasising product quality and rendering service and technical advice specific to each application. None the less, it was often necessary to vary from list prices in order to meet specific competitive situations.

Subsidiary general managers often complained about pricing conditions. For example, one manager made the following observations:

> There is disagreement as to whether demand is price sensitive. I say it is and they say it isn't. The only thing I know is that we keep raising our prices and my share of the nickel cadmium market has gone from 70 per cent to 50 per cent in three years. The lead acid manufacturers haven't changed their prices since 1968; the alkaline manufacturers generally follow our price increases although often by somewhat smaller increments.

Another manager reported:

> We have a good situation because we are the market leader. When I raise my prices my competitors are happy because they can raise their prices as well.

The major controls on the subsidiary companies were financial in nature. Financial goals, in terms of net profit on sales and return on capital invested, were developed at Oskarshamn in consultation with the local general managers. The schedule to which this was done is shown in Table 4.4. Major investment decisions, such as changes in plant capacity, were made in Sweden. There was wide variation in the financial performance of the subsidiaries, as shown in Table 4.5.

Labour negotiations were conducted locally but the advice of Oskarshamn was usually solicited concerning bargaining strategy and Sweden was kept informed of major changes in labour conditions.

PREVIOUS ATTEMPTS AT MARKETING PLANNING

The first attempt at marketing planning was made in 1964, as new professional management came into the company to supplement traditional family management and new expansion plans were developed. The 1964 planning attempt failed, Mr Nilsson said, 'because it was too ambitious'. A second attempt was made in the late 1960's and it also failed, apparently for similar reasons – it tried to do too much. When he launched the third attempt at

Table 4.4 Svenska Ackumulator AB Jungner: annual schedule for group budgeting and planning

1 Dec	Approval of plans from group management to the subsidiaries
26 Oct 6 Nov	Definite follow-up of budget and plans at certain subsidiaries
30 Sept	Budget and three-year plans arrive at the head office
1–11 Sept	Budget control and check up of the plans at certain subsidiaries
27 Aug	Distribution of comments to the plans and forms to the subsidiaries
1 May	Material for the plan revision of the subsidiaries is distributed from the head office

Note: The three-year plan for subsidiaries was introduced late in 1972. The rest of the budgeting and planning sysem had been in effect for many years.

Table 4.5 Svenska Ackumulator AB Jungner: selected financial and performance data on foreign subsidiaries, 1971

	Profit contribution % of sales*	Return on capital %	Total employees
Argentina	34.6	10	66
Brazil	47.8	21	367
Belgium	25.1	26	4
Netherlands	25.9	21	19
Italy	33.9	12	70
Switzerland	22.2	21	4
Spain	30.5	9	130
West Germany	30.8	10	96
USA	21.7	–	70
Austria	32.9	10	35
Mexico	23.5	–	**
Total foreign	33.1	–	–

* After variable costs but before indirect costs including allocated charges and capacity costs.
** There were no employees other than the General Manager in 1971. Plans for 1972 called for adding six staff employees and five workmen.

marketing planning, in 1971 (he had not been responsible for the first two), Mr Nilsson had tried to avoid being too ambitious and had focused on an objective of trying to gather data as the basis for future planning. Not only was there a lack of data within the company, both centrally and at the subsidiary level, but there was also a lack of understanding of what a marketing plan was and how to make one among the subsidiaries general managers.

In a memo dated 15 January 1971 to all subsidiary companies, Mr Nilsson had announced his intention to develop a marketing plan. Using a PERT schedule for the development of the plan, Mr Nilsson had specified the major activities that were to be completed in developing the plan, who was to complete them, and when they should be completed. Excerpts from the memo follow:

> The activities on the Marketing Plan will start on 15 January, and on the PERT-Plan you will find the time limits for the different activities. The Activity Specification is rather brief, but the intention is just to give an indication of the data we want to collect.
>
> As you will see, this Marketing Plan is not only intended to be a tool for the activities from Sweden but also for the whole Group. You will be approached by people from Oskarshamn – acting on the different activities – and asked to assist them in their work.
>
> It is also important that the time limits specified for the different activities be kept. We want to have the Marketing Plan worked out as soon as possible and therefore we must ask you to give the data you are asked for within the period specified.
>
> The Marketing Plan is to be based on team work within the group and we hope that you will give us all possible assistance.

Attached to the cover letter was a six-page document specifying major activities to be completed as part of the planning process. These included both gathering information and developing a marketing plan. The major activities involved are outlined and summarised below, as indicated in that document.

Position analysis

This involved analysis of existing products including the manufacturing programme of the parent company and of subsidiaries, analysis of competitors' market shares, a technical and economic evaluation of all products in comparison with competitors' products, assessment of manufacturing capacity, sales capacity, in the field and in the home organisation, appraisal of product knowledge within the Group, analysis of customs duties and tariffs, and some study of innovations to be expected in the future.

Objective

Based upon information developed in the position analysis, decisions were to be made in several areas including desired product policy, both short term and long term, and desired market shares by geographic area.

Market strategy – long term

Several areas were defined here including improved product knowledge to be developed in the organisation, the selection of specific markets for expansion, the development of a competitive profile (that is, the Jungner Group's competitive posture in terms of technical advice, product characteristics, delivery, guarantee, pricing and discount policies, and sales financing), and a so-called 'general market strategy' which would specify the contractual terms with representatives and agents and draw them closer to the Group, and which would develop guiding principles for national and international sales promotion and public relations activities.

Activity programme– rolling one year plan

Group management was to establish the 'guiding principles' for the next 12 months, including particular markets and application fields, based upon the long-term market strategy, and to define the responsibilities and authority of various marketing staff members (most of whom had yet to be employed). Within these guidelines, the various marketing managers were to be responsible for developing detailed operational plans for the year, these plans to be revised every four months, and to include an analysis of factors influencing the development of the market, analysis of customer preferences and investment plans, a sales forecast and specific plans for sales activity, advertising, trade fair activities, public relations and sales promotion, training, staff recruiting and sales conferences.

For a variety of reasons, including generally weak economic conditions which forced management and staff attention onto current details of business operations, the position analysis that was to be conducted during 1971 did not proceed very far. When six weeks had gone by with little progress, Mr Nilsson attempted to revive interest in the marketing planning activity. Recognising that his own time availability would be a significant constraint, he asked Jungner's Manager of Advertising and Sales Promotion, Mr Gunnar Aslund, to assist him in gathering the necessary information and analysing it. On 16 February 1971, Mr Aslund sent a letter to the subsidiary managers asking them to provide information on an attached form (*see* Table 4.6) and explaining this request as follows:

> We attach two data sheets forming an integral part of the data plan, which we need for the position analysis. We are fully aware that we could pick up some of the figures asked for by using official statistics, but we would like to base this plan mostly on figures that can be obtained by you on your own home market. We trust you can give us better information than we can get from different institutes, and besides it is always interesting to compare statistics from different sources.
>
> Some items can however be answered only by you, for instance how our competitors are represented on your market. In this connection, we want to know not only what type of representation they have and their market shares, but also for instance how their sales are organised, price situation, standard and special discounts, new items, and so on.
>
> Of course, we are also interested in other information you can give us which may be of interest for our analysis of the market situation in your country. We need the information asked for within four weeks, i.e. 16 March at the latest.

It was a couple of months before Mr Aslund began to receive the information

Table 4.6 Svenska Ackumulator AB Jungner: information request form

Country .... Currency					
Basic data					
Year					
Electric power production per inhabitant (kWh)					
Telephone – number in use (head lines per 100 inhabitants)					
Diesel locomotives/electric locomotives					
Steam locomotives					
Railway wagons					
Domestic manufacture, lead acid excl. motor vehicle starting					
Domestic manufacture, alkaline					
Total import, lead acid excl. motor vehicle starting					
Total import, alkaline					
NIFE import					
Forecast					
Year					
Total import lead acid plus alkaline					
NIFE sales					

Price situation:

....

Customs and custom duties:

....

Other facts influencing the import and other comments:

....

(*Case Note:* A second sheet had space for describing the competitive situation in terms of (a) local manufacture; (b) import; and (c) competitors' representatives.)

he had requested. Some of the subsidiaries were able to supply reasonably complete information on competitors' sales and marketing activities. The Italian company responded on 9 April, for example, with information about the product lines of ten battery manufacturers and 42 major manufacturers of inverters, rectifiers, chargers and emergency lighting sets, although in the latter case the volume of the market was unknown to the manager. A week later, the Italian company sent detailed information on the market including population figures, electric power production, number of telephones, railway coaches, etc., and a detailed analysis of competitors. The Argentine company responded on 16 April with somewhat less detailed information but covered number of telephones, etc., as well as offering a forecast of sales and review of the price situation.

Information continued to arrive in June and July not only on market data but also including information about tariffs and duties, and some information about the number and qualifications of various staff employees, as had originally been requested in the January 1971 letter from Mr Nilsson and again asked for at a later date. However, some subsidiaries provided only minimal information and others found it difficult or impossible to respond at all.

Using the information collected during this period, Mr Aslund tried to find some economic or other factors which were related to demand for nickel cadmium batteries and which correlated with NIFE sales. There were no particularly strong relationships to be found. He realised that the forecasting methods used in the various countries varied tremendously and that some subsidiaries made no forecast at all.

In another letter dated 22 December 1971, Mr Nilsson wrote to the subsidiary companies' general managers explaining these results and why a decision was made to base the forecast of future sales on a projection of the trend in energy production in each country. It had been found that the countries fell roughly into three groups when analysing NIFE sales in Swedish crowns per million kilowatt hours of energy production. In Italy, Germany, Switzerland, Belgium and the United States, this figure was roughly 10–30, although all had shown some growth in this ratio over the period 1966 to 1971 except for the US, which has shown a slight decline. Spain and the Netherlands formed a second clustering where the ratio was roughly 50–60, with Spain showing a slight decrease over the period and the Netherlands a slight increase. Finally, the third group comprised Brazil, Argentina, Sweden and Austria. These had all begun in the 110 range in 1966 but Brazil and Argentina had grown dramatically in the five-year period, reaching over 200, whereas Sweden had grown only slightly and Austria had shown a slight decrease to around 95.

Using these three groups, Mr Nilsson (with Ms Aslund's help) had developed a tentative five-year forecast for each subsidiary, to 1976. As he explained in his letter:

We had judged it realistic that the countries of Group 1 (Italy, Germany, Switzerland, Belgium, and the US) could increase their sales by 20 per cent per year during the period 1972–76, in addition to the market share required to keep step with the growth of power production. In order to place the USA in a position that is close to that of the other countries, we have calculated that the countries of Group 2 (Spain and the Netherlands) should be able to increase their sales by 10 per cent per year and for Group 3 (Brazil, Argentina, Austria and Sweden) we calculate a 5 per cent annual increase.

The remainder of the letter explained that the projections had been based on straight-line extrapolation of energy production figures of the past ten years as reported in the *UN Statistical Yearbook* and that these had been compared with the estimates of various institutes, which tended to be somewhat more optimistic. He then concluded:

The present curves and figures are as realistic as practically possible and will be the preliminary base of the planning of our production and sales during the next five years. As mentioned before, we know that there are special national character- istics that can affect the final result, but we cannot and should not take this into account when making an estimate of the total. Instead, we ask each of you to make an estimate for your own market using our basis of calculation and to give us your viewpoints not later than 31 January 1972.

We want to point out that this is a rolling forecast and it will be revised every year, with check points every six months.

Initial reactions were not long in coming. On 16 January the Argentine General Manager wrote that the results developed for his country seemed to be con- siderably in excess of the stated 5 per cent per year annual growth – 'It appears that energy production will double in five years, which seems an exaggera- tion for this country.' The Dutch manager, in a letter dated 24 January, com- mented likewise that the projected energy production for Holland seemed a bit high (approximately doubling in ten years) but added:

We are however gladly prepared to accept the figure given for our sales increase since our sales in Dutch florins have increased faster than 10 per cent as an annu- al average over the past five years. As a result of the unfavourable economic cli- mate existing in the country at the moment, however, it is hard to guarantee a continuation to the same extent.

On 9 February Ted Ulrich, the American subsidiary President, wrote a long letter questioning the basis of the estimates. Some excerpts follow:

. . . you have selected power generation as the basis for your market survey where- as my preference would be for industrial production. This differs somewhat from Gross National Product as GNP also includes services as well.

The nature of power generation as an index may change from country to coun- try. For example, about 60 per cent of the 1.4 billion kilowatt hours used in the US in 1970 went for residential and commercial uses. Only 40 per cent went for indus- trial consumption. I suspect that in other countries, we might find a greater por- tion of generating capacity going to industrial utilisation. And the industrial field is where more battery applications are found than in other groups.

However, none of these indicators is capable of accurately predicting our sales in the future. In making any market prediction for an industrial product, a personal analysis must be made of that market, of that product, of the competitive situation, of current penetration of the product in the market and that item's potential.

Mr Ulrich concluded his letter by saying that he felt that a 20 per cent annual growth rate would be more realistic for the US than the 30 per cent rate used, and pointed out that the devaluation of the dollar in late 1971 would further reduce the expected dollar sales of the US company.

The Brazilian Managing Director wrote on 2 March and said he didn't understand the figures that had been sent but presented an alternative set of data and calculations which came to very much the same conclusion.

As seemed to be true with the letter from the Argentine Managing Director, there was confusion between the rate of growth of energy production and the projected rate of growth in sales, a misunderstanding that the 5–10–20–30 per cent growth figures were increments on top of growth rates in energy production, as explained in Mr Nilsson's letter. In other words, sales were expected to grow faster in all markets than the growth in energy production and this implied an increase in market share.

The strongest objections came from the Belgian company. Some excerpts from that letter will give the flavour of the remarks:

Your theoretic sales estimate survey has definite qualities but in my opinion it lacks a certain realism, even though you agree that it should have a personal touch to it.

It is interesting that most of the Group 1 countries are subject to strong competition from lead acid batteries, especially from local manufacturers.

The graphs you have drawn up are interesting with regard to the past but hardly mean anything with respect to the future.

The only reasonable way to form an estimate of future sales is to study the possibilities for maximum growth in each of your subsidiaries and to eliminate as far as possible the obstacles to that full growth.

The author next pointed to what he considered to be errors in the calculation of the ratio of Jungner sales to power production in Belgium in which the revised figures showed a higher ratio (mid- 30s instead of mid-20s) and concluded:

In summary I cannot give a favourable opinion on your estimates. I even fear that the NIFE sales situation will deteriorate in the years ahead for the following reasons which I have discussed with you before and to which I asked you to find a solution:

(a) The lead acid battery is increasingly being favoured because of its low price and because of its improved performance as the result of the new Planté type plates. We no longer have a technical argument to justify the higher price of the nickel cadmium battery.

(b) Price competition is so strong that we are unable to be competitive for pocket-plate cells of over 50AH. The situation is the same for sealed cells.

Based upon these reactions, Mr Nilsson had decided not to push the development of the marketing planning system further at the moment. In reviewing these previous attempts at planning, he felt that a great deal remained to be done. He wondered at times if it were possible to develop an effective marketing planning system in a company as small as the Jungner Group with operations so diverse , and yet he remained convinced that a marketing plan was needed if Jungner was to continue its growth in an orderly and profitable fashion. New programmes, such as the development of a specific power supply system product concept to be introduced shortly, would require co-ordinated and detailed market development activities if they were to succeed.

Several obstacles had been encountered in previous attempts to develop a marketing planning system, including a basic lack of market intelligence, and Mr Nilsson doubted that there was any easy solution to these basic problems. They reflected the stage of market development in many different countries as well as differences in the skills and knowledge of local management. As he thought about these problems, Mr Nilsson came to believe more and more that the question was not whether to develop a marketing plan but how to go about that complex task in this particular organisation.

APPENDIX A: COMMENTS BY MANAGERS ABOUT THE DEVELOPMENT OF A MARKETING PLANNING SYSTEM

'I don't think we have been on the line of information for the marketing plan that was made. Information was collected from us but later on not disclosed.'

'I don't think that they had enough information to go about developing a marketing plan or enough experience to go ahead without our help, without asking more questions of the field.'

'We badly need some kind of planning system. The way we have been working until now is all right, but in middle Europe, with every country working independently, where we no longer have national markets, it is not right to have everybody doing what he thinks is best.'

'It depends very much on the country. There are some countries where we are not as much interested in batteries alone as in systems. One important consideration is the degree of industrialisation of the country.'

'In my country, a developing country, I cannot imagine the potential of the country. It is impossible for us to determine this. We need some centralised research from here in Oskarshamn, some basic information is essential for us.

'A marketing planning system would force the collection of information and would improve our understanding of our markets.'

'Why don't we have the information now? Because we don't have the organisation to do this and besides, in our country, such information does not exist. It is much better here in Sweden.'

'In the Soviet Union, the information is generally available but there are a lot of other factors to consider including trade barriers and the availability of hard currency. But whether our sales could be increased there if we had better market knowledge, I am not very sure.'

'I'll tell you what a good marketing planning system would be: one that would help me sell more batteries. Period.'

'Things change so fast, new applications come up every day, that it is almost impossible to plan. For example, they had to use nickel cadmium batteries in magnetic cranes, in Italy, where nobody had thought of it before . . . to hold the load up there for a certain time after the current goes off. This was 15 per cent of our sales last year and it came out of nowhere. But you can create these windfalls as well.'

'Perhaps there would be better transfer of such ideas if we had a marketing planning system. But I don't see why you need a marketing planning system to get this kind of information exchange. It is fundamentally a communication problem.'

'The fact that the market is changing so fast is an argument for having a plan, not against it.'

'No, there is no forcing of a plan on us. Nobody tells us "You will devote X per cent of your marketing effort next year to this product or to this market." It would be valuable, I think, if somebody would tell us "there is a market, and here is a market, and there is another market." '

'We have lots of data but nobody has been able to put it together into a marketing plan.'

'I see very little evidence of a clearly stated marketing strategy and of clearly stated marketing objectives.'

'That is true from here in Sweden but I am sure that each of the subsidiaries has its own marketing plan.'

'With the present organisation here in Oskarshamn, it is impossible to do it. We don't need somebody asking 'Why don't you sell any batteries to railroads in Venezuela?' There are no railroads in Venezuela.'

'Oskarshamn management tried to set specific objectives, but they were unsuccessful. Should market data come from Oskarshamn? That would be ideal.'

'Communication with Oskarshamn is improving. We used to come back here every three years, now we come back annually.'

'There is very little opportunity to do central research. Sweden can't generate information for the rest of the world. Many of my colleagues here have been arguing for figures, for data to be provided by a central staff, but those sitting here around the table should be the experts on their markets and if they can't find the figures themselves, how can they expect that somebody sitting here in this place on the back side of the world can do it? I think it's impossible.'

Data are relatively easy to come by in the US for example and relatively difficult in Mexico. The trick would be to develop a marketing planning system that was flexible enough to cope with the tremendous variability in data availability and reliability.'

'As I understand it, the company is going to have an IBM system next year that will analyse all shipments with respect to application, and information will be more rapid than it is today. We get information now, but not fast enough. The computer will help this.'

'Everybody is not unhappy about the fact that there is no guidance, but they all seem to miss it . . . the lack of direction, planning, marketing, etc. Being part of a large international firm, you would expect more guidance than you get.'

'When you have an excellent profit contribution, nobody questions your judgement.'

'I am new to the company, having been here only a year, so I view it as an outsider, and I am a little surprised to learn that there is little systematic planning. There are goals, definitely, mostly profit contribution and return on investment goals, but most people working outside of Oskarshamn have a very strong feeling that their voices are

hardly heard in any discussion. When you hear people asking for marketing information, they are really asking for guidance and help.'

'I am running one of the larger companies but I have very little staff capacity for doing
such marketing studies. I am getting sick from not even knowing what the total market volume is. We make a lot of rough guesses but they can't be too good.'

'I have detailed information about sales for each salesperson and district so I know
what we are calling on. But I don't know what the total market is and I have no idea
what prospects we are missing.'

'This is a purely technical company. You can wake them up in the middle of the night
and ask them about the application and they can draw a precise curve for you. If I
could get in marketing information 10 per cent of what I get in technical information,
that would be fantastic! They are product oriented, not sales oriented. We spend all
our time in meetings like this talking about the product and whether it should have
this or that, a 1-inch drain plug threading or ¾ inch, and I could not care less!'

'I don't know how they could keep in touch with so many markets because the markets differ so widely, even within the Single Market, for example. But basic systems
and techniques could be developed that would also give the marketing department
some feeling that they were at least getting comparable information.'

I wonder if Jungner should take one of their subsidiaries and develop a marketing
plan there. That should be simple. Make it successful somewhere, then you can easily sell the idea to other companies and develop the necessary management confidence
and enthusiasm for it.'

'I have never seen in writing a definition of the goals of the parent company.'

SECTION 5

Cases in business services marketing

Innovative Cleaning Solutions: The industrial cleaning winning formula?

Derek Thurley

KEY THEMES

- marketing industrial services
- new product development
- researching industrial markets

BRIEFING NOTES (Chapter 1)

- Segmentation of organisational markets (pages 15–17)
- Managing market research (pages 17–21)
- New product development (pages 23–25)
- Marketing services (pages 25–29)

Industrial cleaning is one of the most significant service industries in any country – it is also one of the most fragmented. There are cleaning firms employing part-time labour throughout the United Kingdom. The market is vast. It is also increasingly ecologically monitored. Growing demand for cleanliness at the workplace requires increased standards of efficiency whilst the labour carrying out the tasks can be part-time, sometimes inadequately trained and poorly motivated. Unsocial hours, cleaning when the area is not operational, sometimes at night or early morning, can also contribute to this malaise.

Innovate Cleaning Solutions is a supplier of cleaning products to the industrial cleaning industry. Surveys undertaken by Innovative Cleaning Solutions reveal that there is no standard cleaning philosophy. Most companies take their current supplier's advice, and as long as the work is completed satisfactorily then all is well. Investigations into the operator's store reveal a mixture of products and cleaning materials. Systematic stock control as a rule is not very apparent. There would seem to be scope for a more efficient cleaning material system.

Stephen Smith, Marketing and Business Development Manager, discovered the Airkem system in Canada and recognised its potential. He is considering its application to European markets. Figure 5.1 indicates the way the correct

But only *Airkem*

Quik Fill® dispensing system sets the standards for accuracy, safety, and economy.

Modular 3-gallon buddy jugs conveniently transport ready-to-use chemical. Just fill and take to the work site.

Bilingual wall chart shows exactly how to use Quik Fill in easy-to-understand visual instruction.

Durable, high impact plastic won't rust or break.

Built-in drip tray eliminates spills when filling spray bottles.

Quick connect and friction-fit connectors allow fast, easy, and safe mixing and filling.

Quik Fill's sturdy Central Supply is neat in appearance, easy-to-move with optional wheels, and takes up minimal floor space (approximately 32 inches wide by 14 inches deep). Its portability provides greater convenience than stationary floor or wall-mount supply systems.

Unique filler gun with barrel extension fits securely in built-in "holster" on Central Supply.

Quik Fill's easily disposable space-saving super concentrate rectangular containers fit securely on the bottom shelf.

Removable drip tray keeps storage area neat and clean.

Fig. 5.1 Innovative Cleaning Solutions: Industrial cleaning system

Can Fill Your Needs.

A complete range of versatile systems that...

Give you the right tools for the job... to lower labor and training costs.

Select the most convenient dispensing unit from the Quik Fill range to accommodate your choice of buddy jugs and super concentrate packaging. Everything is color coded to facilitate training and ensure safety and cleaning effectiveness.

Modular Unit includes Quik Fill gun assembly, two pick up assemblies, drip tray and shelf

Mobile Unit includes an interlocking Modular Unit plus heavy duty 8" wheels and properly balanced 4-foot handle

Go to where they're needed... to save you time.

The Mobile Unit's heavy duty wheels and handle provide portability, allowing you to transport the unit up and down stairs and over carpet. It moves to the cleaning chore quickly and conveniently, and reduces lifting stress.

Fit your storage requirements... to save on inventory space.

The Quik Fill Satellite Station fits into tight spaces, accommodating two concentrate chemical packages and two buddy jugs. The Mini Satellite Station holds one of each. 2½ gallon super concentrates replace cumbersome 5 gallon pails and 55 gallon drums.

Satellite Stations are constructed of durable, vinyl-coated wire and include Quik Fill gun assembly and pick up assembly(s)

Mobile Work Station includes wheels, handle, triple valve option for two different product applications plus water rinse, 25-foot hose, two pick up assemblies, shelf, modular mold, foam and spray wands

And cut cleaning and labor costs by up to 50%!

Mobile Work Station™ proportions and applies chemical directly onto surfaces to be cleaned, cutting cleaning time and labor costs in half. The Work Station features fingertip on/off control, and foam and spray wands which can be used for cleaning, sanitizing, and deodorizing, as well as fresh water rinsing. Ideal for any area where drains are available.

combination of chemicals and cleaning aids can be transported by trolley to become a mobile workstation. Finger-tip control sprays and spinbuffing enable hard surfaces and carpeting to be tackled easily. Freshening the air in these situations is a bonus. Trials of this approach have proved satisfactory. From a company viewpoint it means an initial large expense to switch over to this concept, but the results are in most cases excellent. It is no surprise that some industrial cleaners have expressed concern about having to buy the system, since they would then have to rationalise their supply arrangements and move to exclusive contracts with Innovative Cleaning Solutions.

Research indicates this scheme to be a winner, yet Innovative Cleaning Solutions are approaching the market cautiously.

The 19th Hole Conference Rooms

Stephen Hearnden and Paola Bradley

KEY THEMES

- marketing of business services
- marketing research
- segmentation of organisational markets

BRIEFING NOTES (Chapter 1)

- The marketing concept (pages 4–6)
- The marketing mix and the marketing environment (pages 6–9)
- Marketing services (pages 25–29)

The Evergreens is a 250-acre luxury leisure complex situated in a picturesque part of the Cotswolds, accessible by car (with a motorway exit three miles away) and with a main intercity rail service station a ten-minute taxi ride away. Some 20 miles distant, there is a small airport which can accommodate executive jets and which is also used as a base for a flying club.

The complex comprises a 50-room hotel, furnished to a very high standard, with a newly modernised leisure club, including a gym and indoor swimming pool. The restaurant has been awarded two stars by a leading food guide for the past seven years. It is the only establishment within an 80-mile radius to have achieved this, consequently it is very busy, particularly at weekends, when bookings must be made at least three weeks in advance. The complex is most noted for its championship grade 18-hole golf course, which operates on a membership-only basis; hotel guests are allowed access on payment of a modest green fee.

Until five years ago, the banqueting room at the hotel was constantly in demand for conferences. The management were approached on several occasions by large organisations wishing to book facilities for seminars and were unable to accept reservations due to the lack of smaller, syndicate-style rooms. This and the available space to build adjacent to the hotel, led the management to invest in building a purpose-built four roomed conference and seminar suite.

The 19th Hole Conference Rooms were completed four years ago. They were decorated to a very high standard in a contemporary interpretation of traditional style with carved limed oak panelling and furniture and elaborate soft furnishings. This style is very much in keeping with the rest of the complex. The fully airconditioned facilities provide:

- slide projectors, video recording and playback, and overhead projectors are available in every room
- telephone lines and facsimile machines are also available on request
- photocopier is situated in a small room adjacent to the lobby, operated by a card purchased from the reception desk.

The 19th Hole was set up as an autonomous unit. The unit has to purchase delegates' rooms and food from the hotel, likewise green fees from the golf club, albeit at preferential rates. Alf Gerrard, a 56-year-old ex-Hospitality Manager with a large London conference arena, was appointed as Marketing Manager. Two assistants were also appointed, both to act as administrators and liaison officers/conference facilitators.

The high standard and reputation of the Evergreens has ensured a steady flow of business for the Conference Rooms. The facilities have been fully booked for 10 months of the past year, generating considerable income (in the region of £400 000 annually) for itself and the hotel. This has entailed turning some potential customers away. The majority of business has come from three large multinational companies who use the venue for 'in-house' training programmes. A number of professional firms also use the facilities for regular meeting/recreation breaks at the weekends. The growth in training programmes in the past two years has, in part, been responsible for the recent increase in enquiries, particularly from firms specialising in delivering courses designed for senior management.

The volume of recent interest has meant that there has been no promotion expenditure for the past nine months. Previously, advertisements were placed in professional publications. Specific firms were also targeted directly by mail, a personal letter and attached colour brochure. Personal visits were also made to these firms by Alf Gerrard. However, Mr Gerrard's recent serious illness has curtailed this activity. His two assistants have been running the 19th Hole in his absence.

The informal feedback from conference organisers and delegates on the conference facilities and the liaison staff is generally positive. However, some have commented on the need to update some of the conference equipment. The most highly praised aspect is the food – which reflects the calibre of the hotel catering staff. The recent bedroom refurbishment has also been well received by clients.

A large international hotel chain has started discussions with the local authority to build a 200-bedroom hotel next to the airport. It expects the hotel to be awarded a three-star rating. The owners of the Evergreens have heard that this complex could include a large banqueting complex. This unconfirmed information is causing some concern.

The price of keeping in touch – BT's international phone service

Ross Brennan

KEY THEMES

- price elasticity of demand
- competition in a slowly growing market
- price strategy

BRIEFING NOTES (Chapter 1)

- Managing market research (pages 17–21)
- A marketing model for pricing decisions (pages 40–42)
- A note on price elasticity of demand (pages 42–43)

> *BT's mission, our central purpose, is to provide world-class telecommunications and information products and services, and to develop and exploit our networks, at home and overseas, so that we can:*
>
> - *meet the requirements of our customers,*
> - *sustain growth in the earnings of the group on behalf of our shareholders, and*
> - *make a fitting contribution to the community in which we conduct our business.*
>
> Source: *BT Annual Review 1993*

British Telecommunications plc (BT) is a gigantic company (1994 turnover was more than £13 billion, with around 160 000 employees) which dominates the UK telecommunications market. From the resounding mission statement, quoted above, it is clear that BT wants to do more than dominate the UK market, it wants to be a serious player in the worldwide telecommunications business. For a long time, the only substantial international business that BT has had is sending international telephone calls from the UK to and from other countries. However, international calls are of enormous importance to BT. If it is to achieve its ambitions as a world player, BT will first have to protect this mundane but gold-plated business from the ravages of competition.

The market for international telephone calls to and from the UK was valued at around £2 200 million in 1993; BT had a share of about 76 per cent of this market. Most of the remainder of the business is with the second largest telecommunications operator in the UK, Mercury Communications Ltd, a subsidiary of the UK-based multinational Cable & Wireless plc. It is likely that these two companies will face new entry competition in the international telephony business in the late 1990s. While some of the new competitors may be small companies aiming for niche markets, a serious threat will be posed if (as seems likely) some of the major American telecommunications companies decide to enter the market. In particular American Telephone & Telegraph (AT&T), the largest American telephone company, has been increasing its stake in the UK telecommunications market in the latter part of the 1980s and early 1990s. The line taken by the UK government, advised by Oftel – the industry regulatory body for telecommunications – has been to continue to liberalise the UK telephony market, so it is likely that new entrants would face few legal hurdles.

International telephone calls have long been the most profitable line of business for BT. Profit margins are difficult to measure in this kind of business (since many of the costs are for the basic telephone network which also carries domestic telephone calls) but have been estimated to be in excess of 60 per cent. Concrete information is hard to come by, since BT guards service profitability data jealously, but in 1990 the *Financial Times* published some estimates of the profitability of telephone calls on BT's most important international routes. (*see* Table 5.1).

Clearly, the information in Table 5.1 is dated, and it is to be expected that profit margins will have shrunk somewhat as competition has become more intense. However, in 1991 it was estimated that BT was earning 81.9 per cent return on capital employed (ROCE) in providing international calls, compared to 74.3 per cent ROCE on national calls, 43.4 per cent ROCE on local calls, and an overall ROCE of 22.6 per cent for the business as a whole.

Table 5.1 BT's top international money-spinners

	Revenue £m 1987–88	Profits £m 1987–88	Profit Margin %
USA	192	121	63
West Germany	56	27	48
France	39	17	43
Australia	35	25	70
Japan	29	22	75
Canada	29	20	68
Netherlands	26	14	52
Italy	21	8	36
Switzerland	21	9	44
Spain	20	11	55
South Africa	17	13	76
India	15	11	75
Sweden	15	8	52
Hong Kong	14	9	62
Norway	14	8	59

Source: *Financial Times*, 3 October 1990, p11

BT continues to make impressive profits from international telephone calls despite the fact that British international telephone calls are the cheapest in Europe. A three-minute cheap rate call to New York would cost £1.50 from London (via BT), £2.58 from Amsterdam, £3.21 from Frankfurt and £3.49 from Brussels. The major UK competitor, Mercury, aims to price its international telephone calls at a discount to the BT price of between 10 and 15 per cent. In the mid-1980s, when Mercury entered the market, its main target market was the City of London financial institutions which make very heavy use of international telecommunications services. Mercury's marketing strategy was not just to offer low prices, it also emphasised the benefits of 'dual-sourcing' telecommunications services (which are critically important to the business success of many City firms) and the high quality provided by its state-of-the-art digital network. New entrants to the market in the 1990s may be expected to set their prices according to their target markets and chosen market positions – which could range from 'superb quality at a premium price' to 'basic service at rock bottom prices'.

Because BT still controls a very large share of the UK telecommunications market, the Government (via Oftel) has chosen to restrict its freedom in price setting. Since 1985 BT has been subject to the 'RPI minus X' formula. This formula applies to a basket of BT services which includes all the major services. 'RPI minus X' means that the weighted average annual price increase for the basket of services must be at least 'X' points below the general rate of inflation (measured by the general index of retail prices – the RPI). In 1991, for example, the RPI figure was 5.84 per cent, and the value of 'X' was 6.25 per cent, so that BT had actually to reduce the average price of its services. In fact, 1991 was the first year in which international telephone calls were included in the basket of services to which the price formula applied, and an average cut of 9.6 per cent in the price of international calls was implemented in September 1991. Prices on the competitive North American routes were further reduced in January 1993.

Strangely, despite benefiting from lower charges and greater choice, British telephone users make far fewer international calls than their fellow Europeans. The Germans make on average twice as many international calls per telephone line, the Belgians three times, and the Swiss ten times as many as the British. More curious still, this pattern is particularly evident for *business* telephone calls – where one might expect there to be little or no difference in the behaviour of managers in different countries. There is no technical reason for the variations in calling rates. International telephone calls can be dialled directly (without operator assistance) from any UK telephone. It is as convenient for a UK resident to call internationally as it is for any other European. Furthermore, while the demand for local and national calls is inelastic with respect to price, the demand for international telephone calls is known to be relatively elastic, suggesting that lower prices should call forth a substantially greater volume of calls.

Up to 1990 the volume of demand for international telephone calls seemed to be a never ending path of buoyant growth, but the international telephone call market is now growing relatively slowly. (*See* Table 5.2.)

With slower market growth, a declining market share, and the prospect of aggressive new entry competition, the Product Manager in BT responsible for international telephone calls faces a tricky marketing problem.

Table 5.2 Growth in telephone call volume (1987–93)

	1987 %	1988 %	1989 %	1990 %	1991 %	1992 %	1993 %
Inland call volume	7	8	11	10	4	1	0
International call volume	11	14	13	13	6	4	6

Source: BT Director's report and financial statement.

Elite Technology Services

Ross Brennan

KEY THEMES

- marketing in small and medium-sized enterprises
- relationship (interactive) marketing
- marketing communications

BRIEFING NOTES (Chapter 1)

- Doubts about the notion of the marketing mix (pages 7–9)
- Marketing services (pages 25–29)

Nick Hall has a very good grasp of interactive marketing. His qualifications are in information technology, and he has never read a marketing book in his life, but he understands interactive marketing because his living depends on it.

It was Christian Grönroos (1980) who drew attention to the fact that, in service industries, much of the marketing activity takes place in direct interaction with the customer. Conventional marketing, essentially the process of getting customers interested, was in his opinion a relatively small part of the job of marketing services firms. Interactive marketing, the process of achieving such high levels of customer satisfaction that customers want to use your service again (and again), is a more substantial task. In large firms, the problem is often that the 'marketing' function is separated from the 'operational' function which is actually responsible for delivering the service. Since interactive marketing is the most important part of the marketing process, and since under those circumstances it is managed by people other than marketers, this can lead to problems. First, marketers may make the mistake of thinking that, like in consumer goods companies where the marketing of the product can be detached from the manufacturing process, it is not their job to worry about service delivery. Second, and the problem which Grönroos considers even worse, the operational staff who deliver the service may think that it is the marketing department's job – not theirs – to worry about customer satisfaction and service quality. So both Grönroos and Ewert Gummesson (1987) emphasise the crucial role of the *part-time marketer* in service industries. Most marketing in these organisations is done by people who are, at least on paper, paid to do something else, like mend washing machines, or wait at table. In such organisations the job of the professional full-time marketer becomes as much to train, inform and motivate the part-time marketers, as to 'do marketing' in the conventional sense.

Still, the problems of training, informing and motivating part-time marketers are not ones that Nick Hall has to confront, because his is a sole trader company and he rarely employs anyone to help. Sometimes, Nick will admit, he has problems training, informing and motivating himself, but generally that's when he has made enough money to live on for a few months and decides to take things easy for a while.

Nick Hall started up Elite Technology Services (ETS) in Welwyn Garden City, Hertfordshire, in 1991. Like many business decisions, this one was based on chance and instinct rather more than on cold, analytical judgement. Having been made redundant four times in his short career as a software developer – by no means unusual in this highly volatile industry – and having learned a lot about sales, marketing and enterprise from his most recent employer, Nick decided to go it alone. One thing was certain, the chances of being made redundant a fifth time were now pretty low.

ETS is in the business of developing relational database systems for clients. Relational database systems are implementations of relational database software packages (Borland's Paradox is an example) which meet the needs of a client to store, sort, collate and retrieve information. The applications are widespread. Marketing and sales information systems, personnel records and customer records are some of the kinds of information which might be managed using a relational database. Order-processing systems, where the client needs a system into which order data are put, and out of which all of the various reports and forms associated with an order come, is an area in which ETS has had particular success. ETS has developed such systems for firms as diverse as an engineering company, a firm making fine chocolates and a condom manufacturer.

There are two key sources of business for ETS, subcontracting work and direct contracts.

Subcontracting work

Subcontracting was how Nick got started in the business. His approach to marketing was direct and reasonably effective. He identified members of the Paradox Users' Club as a likely target market, got hold of an address list, and started ringing people up. The direct sales approach won him a certain amount of subcontracting business, either taking over a complete job from a contractor who had taken on too much work, or taking over a component of a job where his skills were particularly valuable. The software development business tends to run with very 'lean' organisations. There are a great many small firms with few full-time employees, who rely on finding reliable subcontractors to help out when they get busy.

Direct contracts

Direct contracts with clients are a more profitable line of business, since the profit on the contract does not have to be divided between multiple businesses. But identifying customers for direct contract work has not been easy. In fact, it is generating good quality new sales leads that is Nick's biggest headache. As a one-man business, he simply cannot afford much time off from actually doing the work to investigate new marketing ideas. Although direct contracts generally arise as a result of a tendering process, with at least two and perhaps more firms bidding, many of these contracts are not well publicised. As in so many areas of business, it depends on 'who you know' and 'having an ear to the ground'. Nick says:

> I tried employing a telesales company based in Barnet to drum up some business, but it was pretty much a waste of money. I got one or two promising leads, that's all. Nothing concrete came of it, no new business. To be honest, the best source of new business I have is recommendations from my existing customers. But that is a bit haphazard, you know – unpredictable. I did think of asking some computer stores if they would give away some of my promotional literature when they sold relational database packages. But it turns out that Borland already thought of that! So in many places, when you buy Paradox, you are given a list of Borland-approved software developers. And guess what! To get on the Borland approved list, you have to pay them a large sum of money!
>
> Recently, with all the publicity about BS5750, I've also found myself handicapped compared to BS5750 accredited competitors. There's really no way I can go for BS5750 accreditation, though – it's just too expensive and too time consuming for a business as small as mine.
>
> Time really can be a problem. Software suppliers know a thing or two about marketing, and they regularly bring out updated versions of their products. Every time they do that, I either have to take time out to learn the new version, or I can carry on doing business with customers who use the old versions. Ultimately, if you stick with the old versions, you are in a declining market. But, if you take, for example, the new version of Paradox – Paradox for Windows – it's like learning a whole new software package from scratch!

ETS manages to get by reasonably successfully with its existing base of customers. They come from a variety of industry sectors, and from a wide geographical area. There are no obvious parameters to use to segment this highly fragmented market. And Nick Hall carries on with his unconscious but so far effective strategy of interactive marketing. Nick's keys to success?

> First, I'm one of the best at what I do in the country. I usually get it right first time, and if I don't I put it right very quickly. Second, I make sure that I really get to know my contacts in the client firms. So, while I could do a lot my business over the phone, by fax, or by e-mail, I like to actually go and talk to people. I think I'm pretty good at handling people, and that makes a real difference in this business. Of course, I can run into problems when my contact leaves the firm – that often means the end of my business relationship with them. But I am proud of the fact

that 80 per cent of my customers come back for repeat business. Out of the remaining 20 per cent, some of them have gone bust – no, definitely not because their database systems let them down!

References

Grönroos, C. (1980), Developing a Long Range Marketing Strategy for Services, *Long Range Planning*, *13*, April, 36–42.

Gummesson, E. (1987), The New Marketing – Developing Long-term Interactive Relationships, *Long Range Planning*, *20*(4), 10–20.

British Telecommunications plc: Facing up to the 1990s

Ross Brennan

KEY THEMES

- response to changes in the marketing environment
- market development through acquisition
- new product development
- marketing, corporate and human resource strategies
- marketing high technology services

BRIEFING NOTES (Chapter 1)

- The marketing mix and the marketing environment (pages 6–7)
- The marketing planning process (page 44)
- Setting objectives and devising strategies (pages 45–46)
- Identifying strategic options using SWOT (pages 46–50)

THE TELECOMMUNICATIONS BUSINESS ENVIRONMENT

Remarkable changes took place in the UK telecommunications industry in only ten years from 1981 to 1991. Prior to 1981 the monopoly supplier of all telephone services was the Post Office (Telecommunications Division). British Telecom was created in 1981 as a nationalised enterprise separate from the Post Office and, subsequently, in 1984, the first tranche of shares was sold to the public. Competition was introduced to the industry at about the same time. Although BT retains much the largest share of the overall market, competitors have made serious inroads in such areas as the sale of terminal apparatus (such as phones), the supply of value-added services (such as electronic mail), and the provision of in-company telephone networks for major corporate users. Even in the ordinary telephone call business, Mercury Communications Ltd (a subsidiary of Cable & Wireless) is beginning to represent a real threat.

In the 1980s, BT could live fairly comfortably with its new competitors because the economy as a whole was growing rapidly. Even though BT's share of the market declined steadily, the business grew at an impressive rate because the total market expanded even more rapidly than the economy at large.

Accustomed to almost effortless growth in turnover and profits, BT has suffered a rude awakening with the recession of the early 1990s. Just as competition was beginning to bite harder, so the rate of total market growth slowed down. Turnover and profits have been hit (*see* Table 5.3).

Throughout the 1980s, BT and Mercury enjoyed a virtually undisturbed duopoly in the supply of basic telecommunications services, since the political decision was made not to grant any more licences for public telecommunications operation. And throughout the 1980s BT was required to reduce the 'real' price of many of its services by a specified amount – first it had to reduce 'real' prices by 3.0 per cent per year, then by 4.5 per cent per year then, from 1991, by 6.25 per cent per year. Impressive as these figures sound, many critics argued that they are not very stringent in an industry where improvements in technology are bringing about substantial reductions in cost.

Technological change has had a dramatic impact on the telecommunications industry. An increasing proportion of telephone calls are carried on optical fibre cables and are switched through computerised telephone exchanges. This has increased quality substantially. A feature of the 1980s was the introduction of cellular radio systems, operated by Cellnet (60 per cent owned by BT) and Vodafone. While these systems revolutionised mobile telephony in the 1980s, new developments will lead to an even greater expansion in the 1990s. By the end of the 1990s it may be that even ordinary residential telephone users have the choice between the traditional fixed wire telephone system, and a 'wireless' alternative offered by one of a number of competing carriers.

STRATEGIC DEVELOPMENT AS A PLC

Business portfolio

As a public enterprise BT's main international interests lay in the exchange of telephone and telex calls between the UK and foreign countries. A range of other international services was provided, such as international private circuits (telephone lines rented from telephone operators for the use of a single organisation), international data services and videoconferencing, but none of these generated anything like the revenue of international telephony. In virtually all cases international services were provided under a 'correspondent agreement' with BT's overseas partners. BT concentrated its marketing efforts on the UK, leaving the management of demand in other countries to the local national or international telecommunications carrier (described as 'cartel practices' by the *Financial Times*).

Although very large, BT was narrowly based in terms of the range of services it offered and its geographical markets. The first reflex of the company when freed from public ownership was to reduce the vulnerability which this seemed to entail. So it was that BT went in search of new business opportunities, extending the portfolio of services it offered to the UK market, and looking for opportunities in overseas markets. An early development was the

Table 5.3 British Telecommunications: financial position, 1991

Summary group profit and loss account
For the financial year ending 31 March

	1991 £m	1990 £m
Turnover	13 154	12 315
Operating costs	9 623	9 105
Operating profit	3 531	3 210
Employee profit sharing	39	34
Net interest payable	417	484
Profit before exceptional charge and taxation	3 075	2 692
Exceptional charge	–	390
Profit on ordinary activities before taxation	3 075	2 302
Tax on profit and ordinary activities	995	767
Profit on ordinary activities after taxation	2 080	1 535
Minority interests	–	26
Profit attributable to shareholders	2 080	1 509
Dividends	818	720
Retained profit for the financial year	1 262	789

Exceptional charge: a provision of £390 million was made in the year ended 31 March 1990 to cover the costs of restructuring the group and refocusing its operations.

Summary group balance sheet
at 31 March

	1991 £m	1990 £m
Assets employed:		
Fixed assets	16 119	15 503
Current assets	4 412	3 644
Creditors: amounts falling due within one year	(4 797)	(4 896)
Net current liabilities	(385)	(1 252)
Total assets less current liabilities	15 734	14 251
Financed by:		
Creditors: amounts falling due after more than one year	4 468	4 320
Provisions for liabilities and charges	602	595
Minority interests	92	112
Capital and reserves	10 572	9 224

agreement of a joint venture with Du Pont of the USA for the development and manufacture of optoelectronic components. Amongst the other ventures entered into by BT were:

- acquisition in 1986 for C$322 million of a 51 per cent interest in Mitel Corporation of Canada, a manufacturer of telecommunications equipment;
- the acquisition in 1989 for US$355 million of Tymnet Inc., an American-based organisation operating an international data communications network
- acquisition in 1989 for US$1.48 billion of a 20 per cent stake in McCaw Cellular Communications Inc., an American cellular telephone company.

In the UK BT's activities now extend beyond the traditional telephony business to such activities as a share-dealing service (Sharelink Limited, 65 per cent owned by BT) and alarm services (Telecom Security Ltd, 90 per cent equity stake). An early attempt to dominate the UK value-added services market through a joint venture with IBM was shelved when it met resistance from the regulatory authorities concerned that these two giants would wield too much monopoly power.

This initial enthusiasm for business development outside of the UK and in diverse business areas waned in the late 1980s as it became clear that not all these ventures had proved successful. In 1990 BT decided to divest itself of the 51 per cent stake in Mitel, at which point the original investment of C$322 million was worth C$109 million. According to the *Financial Times* (23 January 1990), 'buying control of Mitel was a costly mistake'. On its stake in McCaw, bought as a strategic investment in the largest mobile communications market in the world, BT had suffered a paper loss of US$560 million by the middle of 1990. McCaw's 1989 financial results showed a loss of US$289 million on revenue of $504 million. Many analysts doubted the wisdom of BT's investment, estimating that it would be the mid-1990s before McCaw began to make a profit in such a highly competitive market.

There was clearly a risk that too much management attention was being spent on diverse overseas activities while the core business came under increasing pressure. In addition to home-grown competitors, there was a growing domestic threat from major international companies such as America's AT&T and MCI. The UK telecommunications market is one of the most open in the world. To ambitious overseas companies, the UK market itself is attractive, but there is the added attraction that the UK forms a bridgehead in Europe. Continental European markets will become more open to competition as the Single European Act takes effect. The strategic focus of attention within BT shifted back to the company's core business of operating telecommunications services.

Price rebalancing

Like the majority of public telecommunications operators worldwide in the 1970s, the British Post Office cross-subsidised services to residential customers

Table 5.4 British Telecommunications plc: return on capital employed by service, 1989–91

Year	Sales £bn	Profit/loss £m	Capital employed £bn	Return on capital %
Rental etc., domestic				
1991	1.37	−528	4.47	−11.8
1990	1.21	−581	4.06	−14.3
1989	1.14	−489	3.35	−14.6
Local calls				
1991	2.06	1 069	2.46	43.4
1990	1.99	995	2.48	40.2
1989	1.88	931	2.68	34.7
National calls				
1991	2.84	1 843	2.48	74.3
1990	2.60	1 656	2.21	75.0
1989	2.25	1 440	2.50	57.6
International calls				
1991	1.72	802	0.98	81.9
1990	1.69	785	0.93	84.9
1989	1.48	693	0.82	84.1

Table 5.5 British Telecommunications plc: pricing policy and regulation, 1985–91

	Year commencing 1 August						
	1985	1986	1987	1988	1989	1990	1991
% RPI movement for the relevant period	7.00	2.50	4.20	4.60	8.30	9.80	5.80
RPI formula in effect	−3.00	−3.00	−3.00	−3.00	−4.50	−4.50	−6.25
% permitted increase in prices	4.10	−0.10	1.30	2.80	3.80	5.50	−0.20
% actual increase (reduction) in prices	3.70	−0.30	—	—	3.50	5.30	−1.00

BT is permitted to raise the price of a 'basket' of services by the general rate of inflation (measured by the increase in the retail price index) less a factor X. The 'basket' includes all BT's major services

from those to business customers. In practice this meant that the charges for telephone system rental and for connection were below the fully allocated costs of provision, while very large profits were made on long-distance and (in particular) international calls. This was a form of social policy, which encouraged wider ownership of the telephone even amongst fundamentally unprofitable customer segments, and was only economically viable as long as there was a monopoly provider. Entrants to the market in the 1980s found a soft target in the large business customer segment, where customers were paying prices far in excess of the costs of provision. Mercury and other competitors could undercut BT's prices and still make a substantial profit on their own costs.

The obvious response from BT was to 'rebalance' its prices. This would have meant large rises (above general inflation) in rental and connection charges and in local calls, and actual price cuts for long-distance and international calls. However, any ambitions BT had to rebalance prices rapidly were held in check by Oftel, the regulatory authority for the telecommunications industry. Table 5.4 shows how, even in 1991, the rate of return on capital employed in the local telephone network was much lower than that on capital employed in the national and international networks. Although some price rebalancing had taken place, it was fairly limited. The tool employed by Oftel to control pricing was the 'RPI minus X' rule. The prices of main services as a 'basket' were constrained by this rule. The effects of the rule are demonstrated in Table 5.5. The 'RPI minus X' rule had the effect of requiring BT's prices to decline in real terms (i.e. after taking account of inflation) so that customers benefited from the improvements in technology and lower costs of providing telephone service.

Human resources policy

The ancestry of BT can be traced back to the civil service, and many of the manpower practices in the organisation had clear roots in the 1970s civil service. The company is heavily unionised in both manual and managerial grades. Over 80 per cent of employees belong to four main unions recognised by the company. There has been little overt industrial conflict in recent years. In the 1980s a sequence of changes was implemented to transform people management within the organisation. A long-standing system of management appraisal was augmented by the introduction of 'management by objectives'. The focus of formal management appraisal became performance against agreed objectives. In a later logical progression, performance related pay was introduced for management grades, so that outstanding (or appalling) performance against objectives could be suitably rewarded through the annual pay review. A management bonus scheme was also introduced, to reward people who performed well in a one-off project. As part of the same process to increase the flexibility of managerial pay, 'personal contracts' were introduced progressively from senior management grades down to middle management. BT's position as a monopolistic provider generating large profits enabled it to make the offers to staff 'too good to refuse', so avoiding any real risk of industrial action. By 1992 it was estimated that, of 4000 middle managers who had been offered personal contracts, fewer than 200 remained on terms and conditions negotiated by the managers' union, the Society of Telecommunications Executives.

Managers who had, until the late 1980s, received only a salary, now found themselves with a remuneration package which might include a bonus, a car, a share option scheme, private health insurance and a free telephone call allowance. Many of them were in the same place doing the same job but with a much-enhanced package. If they questioned how BT could afford to do this without demanding some *quid pro quo*, the answer was to be found in Project Sovereign.

PROJECT SOVEREIGN

BT has often been accused of being insufficiently responsive to customers and over-staffed. A response to these twin criticisms was precipitated by the environmental pressure of growing competition in a stagnating market. In order to sustain profits growth, and to satisfy shareholders, BT devised a strategy which combined restructuring with manpower reductions. This was launched in 1990 as 'Project Sovereign'. Sovereign was about cultural change, reorganisation and human resources reductions. The cultural change built further on a total quality management (TQM) programme which BT had initiated in the mid-1980s. TQM in BT could be summarised in the phrase 'meeting the customer's agreed requirements, first time, every time'. The idea of internal customers was introduced, and departments were encouraged to draw up 'supplier/customer agreements' with those departments which they directly served or which served them. These agreements would contain the performance standards expected by the customer of the supplier, and the corresponding responsibilities of the supplier to the customer (for example, in providing a clear and realistic statement of requirements).

By 1990 it had become clear that, despite an extensive programme of training, TQM had only had partial success in transforming the culture of the organisation. Sovereign aimed to reinforce the cultural change by giving those jobs which directly affected customers greater prestige. As part of the Sovereign process, all management jobs were subject to job evaluation and, if necessary, regraded. Within this process, greater weight was placed on contact with the customer than had hitherto been the case. A completely new organisation was devised which placed the customer, quite explicitly, at the apex (*See* Fig. 5.2).

Three marketing and sales divisions formed the interface between the business and the customer – Business Communications for the business customer, Personal Communications for the domestic customer, and Special Businesses for a range of specialised services such as maritime radio and videoconferencing. The customer-facing divisions are supported by Products and Services Management – responsible for interpreting customer requirements specified by the marketing units and transforming them into practical products and services. Worldwide Networks is the division responsible for managing the existing networks (the 'factory floor' of a telecommunications provider) and for developing technical solutions to satisfy evolving customer needs.

Finally, in 1991, after years of failing to bite the bullet of staff reductions, the number of employees in BT declined substantially (by 19 000 or 7.7 per

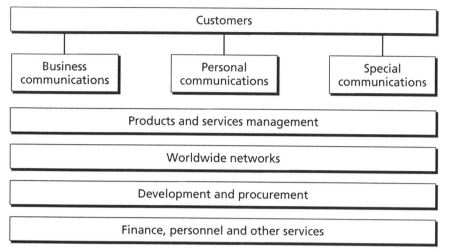

Source: *BT Annual Review,* 1991.

Fig. 5.2 Putting customers first: BT organisation from April 1991

Table 5.6 British Telecommunications plc: selected operating statistics, 1987–91

	1987	*1988*	*1989*	*1990*	*1991*
Business growth					
% growth in telephone call volume					
inland	7.0	8.0	11.0	10.0	4.0
international	11.0	14.0	13.0	13.0	6.0
% growth in exchange line connections					
business	5.3	8.1	10.5	10.2	4.4
residential	2.5	3.4	3.3	2.9	1.7
total	3.0	4.3	4.7	4.5	2.3
People employed					
Total employees (000)	234	237	244	246	227
Quality of service					
% faults cleared within two working days	74.3	90.2	94.6	90.1	97.1
% operator (100) calls answered in 15 seconds	83.5	86.7	86.1	87.7	89.2
% local calls failed	2.2	1.9	1.4	1.0	0.4
% national calls failed	5.4	3.6	2.4	1.2	0.5
% public payphones serviceable	95.6	77.0	92.0	96.5	95.0

cent between March 1990 and March 1991 – *see* Table 5.6). Part of this was achieved through management redundancies (all voluntary) directly attributable to Sovereign. Additional staff reductions were achieved through a reduction in directory enquiry work (charging for enquiries was introduced during this period), by contracting-out certain services, and through business disposals. All indications are that BT will continue to reduce its staffing levels in years to come.

LOOKING TO THE FUTURE

Casual observation suggests that BT has had some success in improving its public image. Apart from the ritual baying of the tabloid newspapers whenever a further set of financial results is reported – since BT's profits are enormous in absolute terms – media coverage of the company has become more sympathetic. This is perhaps not surprising considering the tangible improvements which have been made in services. Table 5.6 shows consistent improvement in a number of quality of service parameters. More faults are cleared up within two working days, fewer calls fail and, the biggest PR coup of all, over 95 per cent of public payphones are serviceable at any one time. Contrast that with the scandal of 1987 when public phones were regarded as a national disgrace! Even the introduction of charging for the Directory Enquiries service was accomplished with little negative PR.

Indeed, as it looks towards the year 2000, BT can look back with some satisfaction on the previous decade. In the face of growing competition it has retained a large majority share of the UK telecommunications market. It has weathered a crisis of public confidence in the mid-1980s and is no longer high in the list of most disliked national institutions. A start has been made on the process of transforming the organisational culture and slimming down staff numbers at very little cost so far in terms of industrial conflict.

However, the telecommunications market in the UK becomes ever more competitive. While local cable television companies (often part-owned and supported by major American telecommunications operators) are allowed to carry telephone calls over their cables, BT has been prohibited by the Government from competing in the huge market for home entertainment. BT is not permitted to take part in franchises to provide cable television service.

In addition, BT remains, arguably, a one product, one market company. Admittedly this is taking a broad definition of product (telecommunications services) and of market (the UK). However, within those definitions of product and market BT seems likely to face competition which will simply continue to increase in intensity, and a core market which is likely to grow more slowly in the 1990s than in the 1980s. As a public limited company BT has delivered an almost exemplary record of growth in operating profits, dividends and earnings per share. It remains to be seen whether this record can be maintained into the late 1990s.

SECTION 6

Questions relating to the cases

QUESTIONS RELATING TO THE CASES

Case 1 market research brief – London Electricity plc: appliance retailing business

Questions

Imagine that you are a market research consultant responding to this Brief.

1 Provide an outline of the research process which you would propose for this project.

2 What question areas would you expect to cover at the primary stage of the research?

Case 2 Advertising the Autostore

Questions

1 Explain why the advertising manager made different assumptions made about the 'conversion rate' for Capital FM as compared to *What Car?*.

2 The *London Evening Standard* might be a reasonable alternative to either *What Car?* or Capital FM for advertising this new product to the specified target group. Carry out the analysis to establish the estimated cost per aware prospect and cost per buyer for a campaign in the *Evening Standard*. (You will need to find out a little about the readership of the *Evening Standard* and its advertising rates. Consult *British Rate and Data* or some other media directory.) Assume that:
   (a) you will use a quarter-page monochrome advertisement;
   (b) preparation costs are the same as for What Car?;
   (c) the objective is to make 80 per cent of Evening Standard readers who are in the target group 'aware'.
   Make your own assumptions where necessary to complete the calculation.

3 What recommendation would you make to the advertiser, considering the three media analysed?

Case 3 Castlemaine XXXX

Questions

You are a marketing consultant who has been asked to suggest how the Castlemaine XXXX brand could win extra market share.

1 Prepare an analysis of the product marketing strategy for Castlemaine XXXX, identifying the ways in which the different components of the marketing mix have been integrated to create a coherent plan.

2 What alternative courses of action can you suggest to increase market share? What are the pros and cons of the various alternative strategies?

Case 4 Ice-cream wars: The UK ice-cream-market in 1990

Questions

Adopt the role of a marketing manager responsible for developing a strategy for Wall's Ice Cream to respond to the threat from Mars.

1 Summarise the opportunities and threats facing Wall's Ice Cream.

2 Make proposals for amendments to Wall's marketing strategy to respond to these threats and opportunities.

Case 5 A case of too many cooks? The UK electrical goods retailing sector

Questions

1 Identify the strategic marketing alternatives open to Norweb in the electrical retailing market.

2 Evaluate the alternatives open to Norweb, and recommend a strategy for implementation.

Case 6 The 'quality' newspaper price war of 1994

Questions

1 You have been miraculously transported back in time to June 1993, but are fortunately still in possession of this case study. Mr Rupert Murdoch has asked for your opinion on his proposals to cut the price of the *Sun* in July and, subsequently, to cut the price of *The Times* in September. What advice would you give Mr Murdoch?

2 Now, suppose that you are not giving advice to Mr Murdoch, but to Mr Max Hastings, then editor of the *Daily Telegraph*. Given your insight into the future, what action would you propose Mr Hastings should take?

Case 7 Taiwai SA

Question

You are Fred Uppers. Bearing in mind the board strategy and the set of memos from Fiona to you, prepare your report making recommendations to the board. This may be in the form of a distribution analysis and five-year plan.

Case 8 Famagusta Bakery Ltd

Questions

1 What marketing objectives would you specify for Famagusta Bakery Ltd?

2 Identify and evaluate the strategic options available to the company.

3 Propose a marketing action plan for the company for the 12 months following the case date. Specify marketing actions, timescales, and an outline budget.

Case 9 Sketchley and Supasnaps: under the same roof!

Question

You as the Marketing Manager of the two merged businesses have the task of promoting the strong brand images referred to in the text. What would be your promotional plan for this project?

Case 10 Rationing or demarketing? That is the question

Question

Antibiotics and tranquilisers are two categories of drugs which, it has been suggested, are heavily over-prescribed in the National Health Service. Antibiotics, which are used to fight bacterial infections, are often prescribed for minor conditions which would clear up on their own. Tranquilisers, which are used to control anxiety conditions, are often prescribed where some kind of behavioural therapy might be more effective. But general practitioners (family doctors) come under pressure from patients to prescribe such drugs. It has been suggested that many patients will only be happy if they leave the doctor's surgery with a prescription. How could you use marketing, or demarketing, techniques to address this problem?

Case 11 The Beaufort Hotel

Questions

You are Andrew Davis. Under the guidance of Rupert McIntyre you have been asked as part of your next task to prepare a strategic marketing plan and a supporting promotions option report for the hotel.

1 Using the Boston Consulting Group matrix, try to map the positions of the Beaufort's SBUs: the hotel accommodation, the bar and the restaurant .

2 Based on your matrix and other information in the text, outline and support broad marketing strategy for the hotel and each of the SBUs.

3 Write a report specifying promotion alternatives open to the Beaufort to support this strategy.

Case 12 The Niger Restaurant

Questions

1 Carry out a SWOT analysis of the Niger business.
2 Identify the pros and cons of opening a new outlet in the West End.
3 Specify primary and secondary target markets for the West End restaurant, and outline the promotional activities which you would undertake to support the launch.

Case 13 Freddy Slinger's bed and breakfast

Questions

You are an independent marketing consultant engaged by Stuart Slinger. Prepare a report providing:

(a) your views on the new product components Stuart intends to develop and their match with the target market;
(b) your proposals for promoting the relaunch of the business.

Case 14 London Underground Ltd: Customer Charter

Questions

You are a marketing consultant engaged by London Underground Ltd to investigate the effectiveness of their Customer charter.

1 What research objectives would you specify for the research project?

2 Suggest an outline methodology to achieve your research objectives.

Case 15 Ethical issues in marketing research

Question

Working in a small group, compare your answers concerning the ethics of the eight possible actions. For each statement find out the highest and lowest response recorded by an individual within the group. Identify those statements upon which there was the greatest degree of disagreement in the group. Discuss the actions described by those statements, and establish why some members of the group thought this action was far less ethically acceptable than other members of the group.

Case 16 Distribution in Hungary

Questions

1 How should the managing director decide which market segments to target?

2 What are the pros and cons of pursuing a market development strategy, and looking for business in new geographical territories?

Case 17 Svenska Ackumulator AB Jungner: Marketing planning in a multinational company

Questions

1 How would you account for the difficulties encountered by Svenska Ackumulator AB Jungner in the introduction of a marketing planning system?

2 If you were Arne Nilsson, what steps would you take to design and implement a workable marketing plan?

Case 18 Innovative Cleaning Solutions: The industrial cleaning winning formula?

Questions

1 If you were Stephen Smith, would you continue researching this concept? If so, what criteria would you use to decide whether or not to proceed?

2 How would you launch this product? Would you test launch it? If so where and why?

Case 19 The 19th Hole Conference Rooms

Questions

Adopt the role of Kate Parkinson, the recently appointed Manager of the 19th Hole Conference Rooms.

The Evergreens General Manager has indicated that the present demand levels at the conference rooms may warrant significant expenditure to improve and expand the present facilities, particularly as increasing the number of attendees would increase the hotel occupancy rate. What market research would you have to carry out in order to prepare a comprehensive report on this matter, bearing in mind the cost implications of each proposed method?

Case 20 The price of keeping in touch – BT's international phone service

Questions

You are a marketing consultant engaged to advise the Product Manager. Prepare an initial report in which you:

(a) summarise the key factors likely to affect BT's pricing of international telephone calls in the late 1990s;

(b) outline what market research (if any) you would propose in order to make more informed pricing decisions;

(c) identify the options open to BT in pricing international calls.

Case 21 Elite Technology Services

Question

How would you advise ETS to go about increasing the volume of new business?

Case 22 British Telecommunications plc – facing up to the 1990s

Questions

1 Summarise the competitive and macro-environmental factors influencing BT's marketing strategy.

2 Considering the various strengths and weaknesses identified in the case study, suggest how BT should respond to the opportunities and threats which you have identified.

INDEX

Also available from Pitman Publishing

MARKETING
PRINCIPLES AND PRACTICE

The second edition of this best-selling text has been revised and up-dated to provide an even more student-friendly guide to the whole of the marketing process. Now printed in two colours and with a greater number of illustrations and diagrams. *Marketing Principles and Practice* is the perfect text for use on introductory and modular marketing courses.

The new edition contains additional material on:

- advertising

- direct marketing

- public relations

and includes questions, exercises and European mini-cases throughout.

Dennis Adcock is at Coventry Business School, **Ray Bradfield** is at Southampton Institute of HE, **Al Halborg** is at Coventry Business School and **Caroline Ross** is at Coventry Business School.

0 273 60734 0

MARKETING
A RESOURCE BOOK

This text provides a wide range of thought provoking and flexible material ideal for use in group work, seminars, exam preparation and as a study aid for any marketing student. It includes extracts from the press and from journals and aims to present a European and international perspective. It is completely up-to-date and takes a fresh and original approach to the role of marketing.

Key features

- each chapter clearly focuses on a principal marketing area

- will complement any undergraduate marketing text

- is completely versatile and flexible in use

- ideal for use in self-assessment and class work

- each chapter contains key definitions, concepts, questions, projects, references and articles

Andy Hutchings is Senior Lecturer in Business and Management Studies, Faculty of Teaching, Professional and Management Studies, The University College of Ripon and York St John.

0 273 60735 9

MARKETING
A MULTIPLE CHOICE STUDY GUIDE

Multiple choice questions are used on an increasingly wide range of courses, by students as a revision aid and by lecturers as a supplementary test bank to the recommended text. This new book of self-testing, multiple choice questions is conveniently arranged under the principal marketing subject headings and graded in order of difficulty. Complete with answers and an introduction on the best use of the book, it will be invaluable to students in their preparations for an increasing number of examinations, which make use of multiple choice questions.

For use in seminars or course preparation, every fifth question is left unanswered.

Key features

- covers a broad range of marketing subjects

- questions of varying difficulty

- multiple choice questions are distinctly arranged under key marketing headings

- ideal study guide and revision aid

Dr Everett Jacobs is Senior Lecturer in Business Studies & Chairman, Business Studies Board of Study, Sheffield University Management School